Academic Nations in China and Japan

The descriptions Chinese and Japanese people attribute to themselves and to each other differ vastly and stand in stark contrast to Western perceptions that usually identify a 'similar disposition' between the two nations. *Academic Nations in China and Japan* explores human categories, how academics classify themselves and how they divide the world into groups of people.

Margaret Sleeboom carefully analyses the role the nation state plays in Chinese and Japanese academic theory, demonstrating how nation-centric blinkers often force academics to define social, cultural and economic issues as unique to a certain regional grouping. The book shows how this in turn contributes to the consolidating of national identity while identifying the complex and unintended effects of historical processes and the role played by other local, personal and universal identities which are usually discarded. While this book primarily reveals how academic nations are conceptualized through views of nature, culture and science, the author simultaneously identifies comparable problems concerning the relation between social science research and the development of the nation state. This book will appeal to not only Asianists but also those with research interests in cultural studies, Japanology and Sinology.

Margaret Sleeboom teaches anthropology at Amsterdam University and is a Research Fellow at the International Institute for Asian Studies.

The Nissan Institute/RoutledgeCurzon Japanese Studies Series

Editorial Board
J.A.A. Stockwin, Nissan Professor of Modern Japanese Studies, University of Oxford and Director, Nissan Institute of Japanese Studies; Teigo Yoshida, formerly Professor of the University of Tokyo; Frank Langdon, Professor, Institute of International Relations, University of British Columbia; Alan Rix, Executive Dean, Faculty of Arts, The University of Queensland; Junji Banno, formerly Professor of the University of Tokyo, now Professor, Chiba University; Leonard Schoppa, Associate Professor, Department of Government and Foreign Affairs, and Director of the East Asia Center, University of Virginia

Other titles in the series:

The Myth of Japanese Uniqueness
Peter Dale

The Emperor's Adviser
Saionji Kinmochi and pre-war Japanese politics
Lesley Connors

A History of Japanese Economic Thought
Tessa Morris-Suzuki

The Establishment of the Japanese Constitutional System
Junji Banno, translated by J.A.A. Stockwin

Industrial Relations in Japan
The peripheral workforce
Norma Chalmers

Banking Policy in Japan
American efforts at reform during the occupation
William M. Tsutsui

Educational Reform in Japan
Leonard Schoppa

How the Japanese Learn to Work
Second edition
Ronald P. Dore and Mari Sako

Japanese Economic Development
Theory and Practice:
second edition
Penelope Francks

Japan and Protection
The growth of protectionist sentiment and the Japanese response
Syed Javed Maswood

The Soil, by Nagatsuka Takashi
A portrait of rural life in Meiji Japan
Translated and with an introduction by Ann Waswo

Biotechnology in Japan
Malcolm Brock

Britain's Educational Reform
A comparison with Japan
Michael Howarth

Language and the Modern State
The reform of written Japanese
Nanette Twine

Industrial Harmony in Modern Japan
The intervention of a tradition
W. Dean Kinzley

Japanese Science Fiction
A view of a changing society
Robert Matthew

The Japanese Numbers Game
The use and understanding of numbers
in modern Japan
Thomas Crump

Ideology and Practice in Modern Japan
Edited by Roger Goodman and Kirsten Refsing

Technology and Industrial
Development in Pre-war Japan
Mitsubishi Nagasaki shipyard,
1884–1934
Yukiko Fukasaku

Japan's Early Parliaments, 1890–1905
Structure, issues and trends
*Andrew Fraser, R.H.P. Mason and
Philip Mitchell*

Japan's Foreign Aid Challenge
Policy reform and aid leadership
Alan Rix

Emperor Hirohito and Shōwa Japan
A political biography
Stephen S. Large

Japan
Beyond the end of history
David Williams

Ceremony and Ritual in Japan
Religious practices in an industrialized
society
*Edited by Jan van Bremen and
D.P. Martinez*

Understanding Japanese Society
Second edition
Joy Hendry

The Fantastic in Modern Japanese
Literature
The subversion of modernity
Susan J. Napier

Militarization and Demilitarization in
Contemporary Japan
Glenn D. Hook

Growing a Japanese Science City
Communication in scientific research
James W. Dearing

Architecture and Authority in Japan
William H. Coaldrake

Women's Gidayū and the Japanese
Theatre Tradition
A. Kimi Coaldrake

Democracy in Post-war Japan
Maruyama Masao and the search for
autonomy
Rikki Kersten

Treacherous Women of Imperial Japan
Patriarchal fictions, patricidal fantasies
Hélène Bowen Raddeker

Japanese–German Business Relations
Competition and rivalry in the
inter-war period
Akira Kudō

Japan, Race and Equality
The racial equality proposal of 1919
Naoko Shimazu

Japan, Internationalism and the UN
Ronald Dore

Life in a Japanese Women's College
Learning to be ladylike
Brian J. McVeigh

On the Margins of Japanese Society
Volunteers and the welfare of the urban
underclass
Carolyn S. Stevens

The Dynamics of Japan's Relations
with Africa
South Africa, Tanzania and Nigeria
Kweku Ampiah

The Right to Life in Japan
Noel Williams

The Nature of the Japanese State
Rationality and rituality
Brian J. McVeigh

Society and the State in Inter-war Japan
Edited by Elise K. Tipton

Japanese–Soviet/Russian Relations since 1945
A difficult peace
Kimie Hara

Interpreting History in Sino-Japanese Relations
A case study in political decision making
Caroline Rose

Endō Shūsaku
A literature of reconciliation
Mark B. Williams

Green Politics in Japan
Lam Peng-Er

The Japanese High School
Silence and resistance
Shoko Yoneyama

Engineers in Japan and Britain
Education, training and employment
Kevin McCormick

The Politics of Agriculture in Japan
Aurelia George Mulgan

Opposition Politics in Japan
Strategies under a one-party dominant regime
Stephen Johnson

The Changing Face of Japanese Retail
Working in a chain store
Louella Matsunaga

Japan and East Asian Regionalism
Edited by S. Javen Maswood

Globalizing Japan
Ethnography of the Japanese presence in America, Asia and Europe
Edited by Harumi Befu and Sylvie Guichard-Anguis

Japan at Play
The ludic and logic of power
Edited by Joy Hendry and Massimo Raveri

The Making of Urban Japan
Cities and planning from Edo to the twenty-first century
André Sorensen

Public Policy and Economic Competition in Japan
Change and continuity in antimonopoly policy, 1973–1995
Michael L. Beeman

Modern Japan
A social and political history
Elise K. Tipton

Men and Masculinities in Contemporary Japan
Dislocating the salaryman doxa
Edited by James E. Roberson and Nobue Suzuki

The Voluntary and Non-profit Sector in Japan
The challenge of change
Edited by Stephen P. Osborne

Japan's Security Relations with China
From balancing to bandwagoning
Reinhard Drifte

Understanding Japanese Society
Third edition
Joy Hendry

Japanese Electoral Politics
Creating a new party system
Edited by Steven R. Reed

The Japanese–Soviet Neutrality Pact
A diplomatic history, 1941–1945
Boris Slavinsky translated by Geoffrey Juke

Academic Nations in China and Japan
Framed in concepts of nature, culture and the universal
Margaret Sleeboom

Academic Nations in China and Japan
Framed in concepts of nature, culture and the universal

Margaret Sleeboom

LONDON AND NEW YORK

First published 2004 by RoutledgeCurzon
Published 2014 by Routledge
2 Park Square, Milton Park, Abingdon, Oxfordshire OX14 4RN

Simultaneously published in the USA and Canada
by Routledge
711 Third Avenue, New York, NY 10017

First issued in paperback 2014

*Routledge is an imprint of the Taylor and Francis Group,
an informa business*

© 2004 Margaret Sleeboom

Typeset in Sabon by
Keystroke, Jacaranda Lodge, Wolverhampton

All rights reserved. No part of this book may be reprinted or
reproduced or utilized in any form or by any electronic, mechanical,
or other means, now known or hereafter invented, including
photocopying and recording, or in any information storage or
retrieval system, without permission in writing from the publishers.

British Library Cataloguing in Publication Data
A catalogue record for this book is available from the British Library

Library of Congress Cataloging in Publication Data
A catalog record for this book has been requested

ISBN 978-0-415-31545-6 (hbk)
ISBN 978-0-415-86449-7 (pbk)

To my mother and the memory of my father

Contents

Series editor's preface	xiii
Acknowledgements	xv
Notes on the text	xvii
Abbreviations	xix

PART I
Framing the nation 1

1 **Introduction: Framing the nation in China and Japan** 3
   Group classifications and distinctions 3
   The problem of framing the nation 4
   Framing the nation and Orientalist categories 5
   Framing the nation and reducing 'Them' and 'the Other' 7
   Trends in categorizing groups 9
   Three forms of grouping 10

2 **The power of national symbols: The might of a Chinese dragon** 17
   Feeding (on) symbolic power 17
   The might of a multiple interpretable dragon 20
   Symbols as effective triggers of associated sentiments in
   *   linked contexts 26*

3 **The coherent force of struggle and diversity in Chinese**
   nationalism 30
   Natural group markers 30
   Origins, coherent force and consanguinity 31
   Coherent force: The dialectical unity of merger through
   *   struggle 35*

x *Contents*

PART II
Group categorization 39

4 Natural categorization 41
Chosen peoples and codified brains 41
The evolution of Us cultural brains and Them civilized
brains 43
Instinctive distancing: Are we closest to macaques
or Ōbei-ans? 47
A Japanese solution to climatic deterioration: Animism
renaissance 49
The king's fall from the forest and Western Cartesian thought 52
Digging up genetic roots: The reappropriation of the past 54
Natural group categories in short 56

5 Culturalist categorization 59
The universality of primitive forest culture: Umehara
Takeshi's Jōmon 60
Yin–yang regulation of the two hemispheres: Ye Qiaojian 63
Hu Fuchen: Taoist universality and Chinese scientific
wisdom 65
Universal markers of betrayal and linguistic supremacy:
Tsuda Yukio 68
Cultural categories 72

6 Global categorization 75
Borderless values 77
Balancing scientistic arguments against Japanese uniqueness 80
Aidagara, kanjinshugi *and autopoiesis 82*
Key persons and national systems strategies: Mutual trust
and uncertainty 85
Rigid analogous processors and adaptive parallel processors 89
Scientism and the unit of the nation 90

PART III
Group-framing habits and strategies 95

7 Grouping 97
Group architecture 99
Framing group differences 101
Grouping in short 106

Contents xi

8 Framing the nation in the short history of the International
Research Centre for Japanese Studies (Nichibunken, 1987–)   108
*Institutionalized nation-framing and its failure as social
science 108*
Nichibunken 110
Structural aspects of knowledge production 120
The unit of the nation 124

9 Nation-centred political strategies in academic thought:
Examples from China and Japan   126
A neglect of the local and the specific 127
Subordination of the universal to the national 131
The nation and its various interest groups 133
Controlling the 'national organism' and the 'system' 134
Habitual nation-framing and its consequences 140

10 Nation-framing as an academic strategy in the PRC   142
Social science and state building in the PRC 142
Appraising national policies 144
National prescription and conservatism 147
The failure to imagine other views of the nation 148
The political predictability of framing the nation 150
Framing the nation in the PRC: Some features 151

11 Core themes and an outlook on future research   153
The universal and particular in framing the nation 156
Framing the nation and spatial and temporal order 158
Examples from China and Japan 160
Features of nation-framing 162

Appendix I: Joint research, Nichibunken (1988–96)	165
Appendix II: General research meetings, Nichibunken	169
Appendix III: Fields of basic research	171
Glossary	173
Notes	175
References	203
Index	214

Series editor's preface

World news in the early months of 2003 was dominated by the war in Iraq, which caused serious rifts in the existing structures of international co-operation. Public opinion in Japan, with its pacifist tradition under the 1946 Constitution, was on balance opposed to military action against the regime in Iraq. The Government, however, of Mr Koizumi gave verbal and some material support to the American-led campaign.

At the time of the Gulf crisis and war of 1990–1 Japanese leaders and articulate opinion agonized about whether to participate or not. The decision to provide a total of $US13 billion to the cost of ending the Iraqi occupation of Kuwait, but no troops on the ground, caused much international criticism. This criticism set in train a shift in Japanese opinion that was to lead to rather more participatory security policies 10 years later. What is striking, however, about international reactions to Japanese support for the Iraqi war of 2003 is that it hardly raised a ripple of interest in the world's media. The centres of decision and action were a very long way from Tokyo.

Japan, of course, had its own pressing concerns much closer to home, in the shape of North Korea. For Japan, the Korean situation represents a crucial test of foreign policy, and for a while in the later months of 2002 it seemed possible that a breakthrough in relations between Japan and North Korea might be possible. Mr Koizumi visited Pyongyang on 17 September 2002 and signed a joint statement with the Korean leadership, envisaging normalization of the two countries' relations. But further progress was frustrated by the issue of Japanese citizens spirited away to North Korea several years before. The news conveyed by the North Koreans to the Japanese side on 17 September that eight of the thirteen abductees had died affected Japanese public opinion far more than the Korean leader's unprecedented apology. Later, the North Koreans admitted defiantly to an American government delegation, that they were engaged in nuclear development in breach of a 1994 agreement. This has been followed by further increases in tension over North Korea. Even though the prospect of war in the peninsula does not strike most Japanese as likely, many see the Korean situation as deeply troubling.

This is also at a time when the Japanese economy is suffering from deflation, bank indebtedness and lack of growth, with the problems of an xiv *Series editor's preface*

ageing population already beginning to bite. Japan remains a huge economic power with a far higher standard of living than China, but by contrast the Chinese economy is moving dynamically.

Japan thus has a raft of problems to confront. But social change is also important. Younger Japanese are paradoxically becoming both more nationalistic and more internationalist. They are less inhibited about championing the symbols of nationhood and thinking about Japan as a major power, but also happy to interact more freely and naturally than their elders with people from other parts of the world. To adapt a phrase of Ronald Dore, the Japanese are still Japanese, but their Japaneseness is steadily evolving.

The Nissan Institute/RoutledgeCurzon Japanese Studies Series seeks to foster an informed and balanced, but not uncritical, understanding of Japan. One aim of the series is to show the depth and variety of Japanese institutions, practices and ideas. Another is, by using comparisons, to see what lessons, positive or negative, can be drawn for other countries. The tendency in commentary to resort to out-dated, ill-informed or sensational stereotypes still remains, and needs to be combated.

Dr Margaret Sleeboom in this volume investigates efforts in both Japan and China to understand or 'frame' the nation. 'Nation' in any case is now a complex idea, having become nearly universal over the past two centuries or so. There are 'old' nations and 'new' nations, nations to which their populations are deeply attached and nations attracting a more fragile and qualified set of loyalties. But attachment to nation is not necessarily something that just happens as part of a natural process. It can be created, reinforced, cemented on the active initiative of governments and intellectuals usually having overt or tacit endorsement from governments. Symbols, past heroes, past history, versions of 'national' character, features distinguishing the nation from those of past and present adversaries – all these are the stock-in-trade of the intellectual myth-makers about nation. The use of the word 'myth' does not entail that all their history is wrong, but that it is deliberately tailored to creating a comprehensible story focused on the concept of nation.

For her case studies, Dr Sleeboom takes the International Research Centre for Japanese Studies (more usually known as *Nichibunken*) in Japan and the Chinese Association of Social Sciences in China. She makes intriguing comparisons between the two, and using insights from the discipline of social anthropology, shows the character and importance of academic nationalism in two major east Asian countries.

J.A.A. Stockwin

Acknowledgements

First of all, I am very grateful to Prof. Arthur Stockwin and Dr Roger Goodman for encouraging me in my research and to make possible the publication of this book.

I take this opportunity also to express my gratitude to academic institutes in Beijing and Kyoto. In particular, I would like to thank the Institute of Philosophy of the Chinese Academy of Social Sciences (where I stayed from September 1997 to June 1998) for its open and friendly welcome, and the International Research Centre for Japanese Studies (where I stayed from September 1996 to June 1997) for its hospitality. I am especially indebted to the Amsterdam School for Social Science Research (ASSR), whose generous support made possible this study, the Netherlands Organization for Scientific Research (NWO) for its financial assistance, and the International Institute for Asian Studies for giving me the opportunity to work on it. I also would like to thank *Nations and Nationalism*, *Studies in Ethnicity and Nationalism* and *Japan Forum* for kindly permitting the re-publication of the three articles that have been transformed into Chapters Two, Three and Eight, respectively, of this book.

I am very happy to express my special thanks to Peter van der Veer, my Ph.D. supervisor, whose support and trust were crucial to my development and the completion of this book; Gerd Baumann, who gave me inspiration, encouragement and advice; and, Matthijs van den Bos, who never ceased to be a supportive critic and friend.

I also wish to thank others who facilitated my research and work: Johannes Fabian, my MA supervisor, who encouraged and helped me to find my way back to the academic world; Jan van Bremen and Frank Pieke who encouraged my research and helped me by their critical reviews of my research applications; Sytse Strijbos, Min Jiayin, Hamagauchi Eshun, Zhang Nan, Tony Saich and Hans Sonneveld, who facilitated my fieldwork and shared their knowledge with me; Anton Blok, Rogier Busser, Frank Dikötter, Harry Harootunian, Peter Pels, Kurt Radtke, Leo Douw and Woei Lien van Woerkom-Chong whose advice and feedback have been of great support; and, Anne Kennelly who weeded out a forest of errors in the manuscript. And of course there are Dynke de Boer, André Celtel, Fang Yuji, Bart Gaens,

xvi *Acknowledgements*

Robin Laurance, Sun Cuihua, Takeuchi Akiko and Toru, Marja Witte and Vivian Philippus who have played a special role during my fieldwork in east Asia. Finally, I am thankful for the support and love I received from family, friends and tutors.

Notes on the text

Chinese terms and names are written in *Hanyu pinyin*, with the exception of a few names that are better known in the Wade–Giles transcription, such as Sun Yat-sen (Sun Zhongshan) and Chiang Kai-shek (Jiang Jieshi). If my sources use the Wade–Giles system, I add the *pinyin* transcription in square brackets when possible.

In my Roman transcription of Japanese terms I use *Romaji*.

As for the word order of surnames and given names, I stick to the conventions used in the languages of origin. For instance, in the personal name 'Kawai Hayao', 'Kawai' is a Japanese surname and 'Hayao' a given name. Similarly, in 'Deng Xiaoping', 'Deng' is a Chinese surname and 'Xiaoping' a given name.

Abbreviations

BP	before the present
CAS	Chinese Academy of Science
CASS	Chinese Academy of Social Sciences
CC	Central Committee
CCP	Chinese Communist Party
E	English
FLP	Foreign Language Press
IIAS	International Institute for Advanced Studies (Keihanna)
J	Japanese
JT	*Japan Times*
NBK	*see* Nichibunken
Nichibunken	Kokusai Nihon Bunka Kenkyū Sentā (International Research Centre for Japanese Studies)
NN	Nichibunken Newsletter
NPC	National Party Conference
PHP	Peace Happiness and Prosperity (Research Institute of)
PRC	Peoples' Republic of China
SSTC	State Science and Technology Commission
YB	yearbook

Part I
Framing the nation

1 Introduction
Framing the nation in China and Japan

This book, based on extensive periods of fieldwork in academic circles, inquires into the roles researchers assign to their part of the world on the platform of international relations. It explores the ways in which researchers 'frame the nation', which is partly a result of them being framed by the nation. By this I mean that researchers partly define their research in terms of the nation by virtue of a historical environment that defines the world in terms of nationhood, also when such a frame may not be of relevance to the research problematic at hand. The former meaning is explored in the first two parts of the book on classification methods, while the latter takes the form of case-studies in Part III.

Group classifications and distinctions

This book is about classification, more specifically, about approaching academic issues by classifying nations and world regions. Thinking about human categories involves making distinctions between them, and distributing them over various categories. Although we use human categories all the time, we are hardly aware of the large variety of categories we use and the ways in which they change and overlap. Intellectuals tend to be aware of the categories used in their own research area rather than in others. For instance, the psychologist, apart from looking at the constants and variables linked to, say personality structure, may treat culture as a relatively unproblematic constant; the cultural anthropologist, on the other hand, may well regard culture as a variable and treat biological factors as constants. Interdisciplinary research, on the other hand, may prompt us to use different categories and different classificatory methods to understand and define problems.

We make distinctions between societies and cultures and label them. For instance, we distinguish between patrilineal and matrilineal societies, ones that are wealthy and poor, developed and undeveloped, civilized and primitive and so on. Depending on the way we are used to analyse problems and what in life we find problematic, we categorize things differently, that is, we use different criteria to mark groups. These markers delineate the borders

4 Framing the nation

between groups in a variety of ways. Some markers are used to emphasize only the differences between two extremes (bipolar opposites). Others mark both similarities and differences between groups (patterns of contrast), or show the gradually changing shades of differences between groups (bipolar continuum). I also make a distinction between different kinds of markers: those that use culture, nature and universals to delineate the differences and similarities between national and regional groups.

The ways of marking and the kinds of markers used in academic research are usually related to the disciplinary and socio-political background of the author and the time spirit. In this book I look at the ways in which marking styles are related to the kinds of markers used for making national and regional group distinctions in a selection of case-studies from the Chinese and Japanese academic worlds. In other words, I look at how the nation is framed in two countries that may be thought to be very different. The examples from China and Japan to throw light on the similarities in which we frame groups despite the great differences we perceive.

Why do I use examples from China and Japan? Is it because I believe that the nation in these countries in some way is different from the nation elsewhere? Definitely *no*, although of course each nation has its own 'unique' history. The choice of examples from these two countries only has illustrative value in the light of my aim to understand various forms of categorizing groups. The examples have no representative value of academic research in these two countries. As shown below, one cannot only find parallels in modes of categorization between Orientalism and so-called 'reversed Orientalism', but also between the ways in which Chinese and Japanese scholars classify nations. The examples used, therefore, merely contribute to an understanding of taxonomies of classifications, and I am convinced that a similar study can be conducted in other parts of the world. In other words, elsewhere, too, it is possible to study the ways in which nations are classified, form the framework through which scholars understand their research problems, and the ways in which researchers themselves give meaning to the nation by the ways the 'nation' functions as a unit of research. In this sense, the concept of 'framing the nation' has a double meaning, indicating a process of interaction between a conditional framework of research and a practice in which the nation obtains its meaning.

The problem of framing the nation

This study focuses on the bias resulting from using the nation as a framework of research to the exclusion of other units of analysis and comparison. Some conceptions of the nation are premised on the notion of cultural uniqueness, others on that of biological uniqueness. Racial discourse may elucidate the general problem of framing the nation. Racial explanations of human behaviour refer to physiological features, even though other factors may be more plausible. Racism selectively blinds the racist academic and excludes other explanations. Racial categories, then, prejudice the mind of the racist researcher. In nation-centric research based on the notion of race, race may be defined through the political borders of the nation-state or the bio-cultural notion of homeland. Thus, some Chinese equate Chineseness with the possession of certain bodily features; others equate it with the 'Chinese family'. In a similar way, nation-centric blinkers affect academic definitions of 'unique' national characteristics, while common factors such as the influence of nation-state politics, the outcome of unintentional processes, and the role played by other local, personal and universal identities are discarded or expanded into essentializing and sweeping generalizations. This is what makes nation-centric approaches relatively biased in a way hard to detect. For, in some cases the bias is stronger than in others, and the bias is hidden in the research framework.

Framing the nation and Orientalist categories

This book targets those academic works that dogmatically, systematically or thoughtlessly use the nation-state as their framework of analysis. Historically, it grew from the national and regional functions specific regions had in both policy-making and academic thought, often referred to as Orientalism. This kind of regionalism and nation-centric thought is not only evident in Orientalism but also in other forms of academic thought that habitually, mechanically or strategically centre on the national and regional unit.

In his *Orientalism*, Said described the Orient as a product of the Occident, as an idea that corresponds to unequal military, economic and political relations between imperialists and colonialists and the dominated. The ideology that defined the Orient, Orientalism, functioned in academic life through doctrines and theses on the Orient; through styles of thought, by making an ontological and epistemological distinction between the Orient and the Occident; and as a corporate institution, an authority involved in describing, teaching, and controlling the Orient. In this view, the authority of Orientalism made it impossible to think, write and behave without taking into account the constraints imposed by Orientalism.

Said also referred to Gramsci's distinction between civil society and political society in explaining the pervasive influence of Orientalism. The former constitutes voluntary affiliations of indirect domination, such as schools, the family, and unions; the latter concerns direct domination by means of the army, police, and the central bureaucracy. In Western civil society ideas influence institutions and people by creating consent, and when certain cultural ideas dominate, he speaks of hegemony. Hegemony instils Orientalism with power and influence, providing Europe with a collective notion of Us and Other, corresponding to the Orientalist categories of a superior Us and a backward Other. To Europeans, the familiar European was classified as rational, virtuous, mature, and normal, while the exotic Oriental was set apart as irrational, depraved, childlike and different. In such classification

6 Framing the nation

schemes, temporal categories projected the Oriental into the past of modern Europe as primitive, backward, undeveloped, and uncivilized, thereby justifying Occidental paternalistic and condescending attitudes toward its Oriental object. Thus, the power to define and classify the Other as very different from Us became an indispensable tool for backing up military domination.

Said's work poses important questions about the role of the expert in defining his object of study, the generation of knowledge and, consequently, the power of applying knowledge. But Orientalism, in the first instance, was meant to deal with the orientalization of the Middle East. A comparison of the West's relationship with China and Japan indicates the existence of multiple forms of dominance and hegemony. China was never colonized in the sense that India was; and, Japan was never colonized (parts of it were, by the Japanese themselves) or militarily dominated by 'the West', apart from by the allied forces (SCAP) after the Pacific War. Neither was Japan essential to the self-definition of a historically rootless Occident. And yet, Japan has been defined in the same condescending and detemporalizing manner by experts of Japanese studies such as Chamberlain, Sansom and Reischauer (Minear 1980). Japan posed no particular religious threat, nor was it regarded as a possible source for the philological roots of European languages. Japan's élite had built a tradition of defining itself by reference to its own historical schools of which some were oriented on China. Only later, in the latter half of the nineteenth century, the West became Japan's main reference group, with which it was soon in competition for its own hegemonic sphere. Although scholars, missionaries and travellers wrote works on Japan that fit in with the Orientalist tradition as described by Said, they were not just an extension of a relationship of domination by Europe of Japan. In fact, the reverse thesis is just as plausible. Writings on the West and the experience of Japanese travellers, bureaucrats, samurai and scholars in the West were important factors in Japan's effort of building a strong nation-state, and subsequently, the hegemonic expansion of Japan in Asia.

The treatment of China by sinologists and China experts raises further issues against the (localized version of the) thesis of Orientalism, as Occidentals were led into adapting classifications of Us versus Them by the Chinese and vice versa. Chinese literati has provided an enormous corpus of scholarly contributions to the study of its own civilization, based on empirical, historical and philological research. Western knowledge of China was at least partially dependent on Chinese images of China, not in the least for reasons of a linguistic nature. The time and energy needed for mastering the Chinese language, especially ancient, classical and literary Chinese, left little scope for generating Orientalist definitions greatly diverging from those offered by Chinese traditional scholarship itself. Therefore, the affinity between Sinology and Chinese self-images may well explain so-called Orientalist notions of China as a static and exotic society. Moreover, the foreign scholar's high regard for ancient Chinese tradition did not necessarily reflect a duty to rescue some portion of a lost, past classical oriental grandeur in order to

Introduction 7

facilitate amelioration in the present Orient. It may well result from an adoption of Chinese élite reverence for antiquity.[1]

Although both China and Japan have been construed in the image of what was seen as a progressive development to modernity, debate always concerned the tensions between universalistic aspects of this modernity and the extent to which it represented a particular 'Western' mode of development. Similarly, Marxist theory posed the problem for Chinese and Japanese Marxists of turning localized historical movements into 'inevitable' revolutions that were to observe universal laws, that is, applicable to all societies. It is therefore incorrect to presume that Chinese and Japanese self-images were a direct result of imperialist domination. It would assume Chinese and Japanese populations to be orientalized, passive objects, utterly incapable of giving direction to history and unfit to deal with relations of power and domination. For instance, the Japanese nineteenth century policy of 'Using the barbarian to control the barbarian', signifying the importation of military equipment and knowledge for warding off the Western barbarians, does not testify to the predicament of a corner-driven helpless victim. Rather, it bares witness to a mutual relation, albeit a lop-sided one, of threat and resistance, and creation and destruction. Japan's way of dealing with foreign threat had a parallel in Nara and Heian Japan, when it imported legal institutions, religious and political ideas, and science and technology from China. This time, however, the West took the place of China as perceived teacher and dangerous bully, and even before the rise of its own imperialism and military expansion, Japan developed its own intellectual tradition, reminiscent of what Said has coined Orientalism (cf. Tanaka 1993).

Framing the nation and reducing 'Them' and 'the Other'

Orientalism has played a role in the rise and expansion of modern nation-states. This realization, however, should not divert our attention from the fact that many modes of 'Orientalism' have existed long before it was written about. Nor should we forget that Orientalism is akin to many genres of ethnocentrism, expressed in the discriminatory notions and generalizations we make about units of comparison, such as culture, society, race, region, country, and species. Thus Asian nationalism and debates on national identity can not be explained as a mere reaction to so-called Western imperialism in the form of 'reversed Orientalism' (Al-Faruqi 1988). For, it is not a mirror image of something else, nor is it mere reactive resistance to imperialist action or modernity, not even when it defines itself as such. Although Said's *Orientalism* has provided an insight into the ways in which culture is intertwined with relations of dominance, it also tended to reduce cultural tradition to a function of an abstract notion of power, in which the historical nature of dependence is not specified sufficiently. Orientalism, in the first instance, was meant to deal with the orientalization of the Middle East. Orientalism

8 Framing the nation

in China and Japan, countries never colonized in the sense that was India, took on a different shape.

In this book, I intend to deal with examples of both Orientalism and 'reversed Orientalism.' Just as Orientalism has as its main referent 'the Other' (Fabian 1983), reversed Orientalism has a They in the form of a powerful bully. 'They' also plays an indispensable role in domestic politics as a negative example. For instance, notions of collective self-victimization and national persecution are easily spotted by their use of set performative expressions. For example, 'They imperialists' exploited 'Us poor but brave victims'; and, 'We' cannot overcome Our national trauma's if 'We' follow 'Their' rules and ways of thinking.

Critics of this kind of self-victimizing discourse in Japan, such as Peter Dale, Ivan Hall and Karel van Wolferen, in turn, seem to ascribe to the Japanese nation-state a strong but mysterious sense of agency. Although Peter Dale in his *The Myth of Japanese Uniqueness* (Dale 1995) rightly criticizes theories of Japanese uniqueness (*nihonjin-ron*), he explains their production by referring to certain totalitarian notions peculiar to Japanese history. This history, paradoxically, can only be understood by 'deepening our familiarity with the trajectory of German nationalism from 1808 to 1945' (Dale 1995: 215). But, such historical reductionism cannot explain why in China (and other countries) very similar theories of uniqueness have flourished and still do. Similarly, in *The Enigma of Japanese Power* (1989), Karel van Wolferen characterizes the Japanese political system as lacking in principle and accountability, implying that other political systems are not. This Japanese system fosters certain forms of cultural and historical constructions, subtle forms of censorship, and indoctrinates the peoples, in a way reminiscent of pre-war Japan. Again, the concentration on identifying the 'character' of the nation leads to gross generalizations and tends to lack a comparative perspective (cf. Van Wolferen 1989: 405–50).

Similar forms of essentialization can be found in Ivan Hall's *Cartels of the Mind* (1998), in which 'Japanese intellectuals and cultural spokesmen manipulate their dialogue with the outside world to deflect scrutiny, put down criticism, and raise false hopes of intellectual decartelisation' (Hall 1998: 181). No doubt xenophobic practices take place, but acclaiming them to be uniquely Japanese, protectionist anachronisms (Hall 1998: 18), concluding that Japan is 'hopelessly secluded', contributes to the erection of cartels all the same. A comparative perspective may reveal that besides national political culture there are other structural factors involved that are important in understanding the dynamics of such nation-centred intellectual discourse.

The same applies, of course, to approaches that idealize Japaneseness, such as in the case of David Williams' *Japan and the Enemies of Open Political Science* (1996). His reduction of Japanese national culture (and even Asia) to the classics of the Kyoto school and its polarization against an essentialized West (represented by positivism) lacks a comparative perspective, is ana-

Introduction 9

chronistic. Moreover, it focuses mainly on high culture and canonical texts, which would require social science to undergo a paradigmatic revolution in order to benefit from it, and before it could solve the (by Williams perceived) crisis in Western thought. Issues at stake in such highbrow approaches are likely to be matters of national politics and intellectual heritage rather than societal issues.

Trends in categorizing groups

In the 1970s, an increasing number of social scientists pointed out that Euro-centric theories of modernization deployed by intellectuals in nation-states both in- and outside Europe placed too little value on the particular cultural and historical circumstances of developing nations. In the 1980s, even before Edward Said published his famous critique of *Orientalism*, this situation started to change. In the latter half of the 1980s, a strong emphasis on the cultural aspects of societies in social science research became quite common, in particular after the end of the Cold War and the collapse of the Berlin Wall. Greater emphasis was placed on the cultural aspects of development, and in the social sciences in particular, the cultural and national aspects of various forms of organization, behaviour and thought became a main concern. This culturalist trend was partly set off by publications, such as Francis Fukuyama's *End of History* (1992) and Huntington's *The Clash of Civilizations* (1993). It was accompanied by an equally strong reaction of re-emphasizing the uniqueness of Eastern cultures, a reassertion of Asian values, and a denial of the existence of Asia (Miyazaki Masakatsu 1992; Saeki Keishi 1998: 21–41).

For several reasons such developments may have influenced academic research adversely, especially in cases in which academic debate is deployed in official developmental policies, leading to various political versions of nationalist modernization. By stressing the importance of the criteria that support ideologies of national uniqueness, the universal aspects of strategies of development may be neglected. In education, attention is paid only to the historical reading of national tradition by just a few powerful interest groups. Defining national identity usually means favouring the representation of one group above that of others. Different interest groups create different iden-tities. Although the various groups partly share a range of tools of identity creation and images, they are used and manipulated in a variety of ways.

Indeed, different national circumstances in nation-states undoubtedly call for different measures and approaches to the development of indigenous resources. But an (possibly unintentional) overemphasis on cultural values may tempt decision-makers to apply easy solutions to difficult problems, especially, if the concept of cultural values is taken to refer to simplistic notions of national identity. National identity is a complex theme, hotly disputed by different interest groups and at the same time incapable of repre-senting the voiceless. No one has come up yet with a definition of the term

10 *Framing the nation*

'national identity' that is acceptable to all subjects of a nation-state, and includes all people living in it.

Three forms of grouping

There is only a limited number of ways of constructing an identity for groups although the number of existing identities, of course, is countless. Here, I briefly explore how various forms of identity are constructed within a limited range of parameters such as culture and race. I focus on how conceptions of the nation-state, ethnic groups, races, classes, regions, East and West are constructed in Chinese academic theory and in meetings of scholars of various political and academic background. I also want to know how and why particular theoretical constructions of the nation-state change over time. To simplify my vocabulary, I speak of 'groups' and not of, for instance, China, the East, the West or the capitalists. The distinctions made between the ways in which group identity is created are of analytical value. In reality, various combinations of categories combine into an infinite number of group identities.

A general analysis of the basic sources and categories used for delineating groups makes for a broad distinction between groups and regions classified by means of natural markers, cultural markers and universal markers. This distinction between markers is heuristic and is used to acquire an idea of the flexibility with which academics construct notions of group identity. In this case the distinction between markers serves to examine academic delineation of national and regional identities in China. It also serves as a tool for exploring the ways in which approaches make allowances for national change, development and exchange and how rigid definitions of national identity function in academic and political contexts.

A main aim of this book is to classify and analyse three forms of academic nation-framing to show how by framing research problems in terms of the nation-states and world regions various kinds of boundaries are created that are linked political ideologies. The examples from China and Japan, I must repeat, have *illustrative value, and in no way are representative for academic life in these countries.* Instead, they are meant to yield insights into how the use of regional units of analysis influences research results and the ways in which we perceive the world.

Among the sources and categories used for delineating groups I make a distinction between natural, cultural and globalist categories, which in practice, however, combine into an infinite number of possible group identities. The distinction between natural, culturalist and globalist ways of categorizing groups is of *heuristic* value and serves to estimate, for instance, the flexibility of notions of group identity. It gives us an idea of which academic approaches make allowances for, for instance, national change and exchange, and which employ rigid definitions of national identity.

Introduction 11

Naturalist grouping

Distinctions between groups based on, what are perceived as, natural markers are rigid in the sense that boundaries are erected between units of comparison that are hard to traverse. After all, as sources for creating absolute difference, natural categories of distinction, such as genetic make-up, climatic change and environment, the brain and blood, are chosen for their overpowering influence over the human capacity to change. Natural markers facilitate symbolic manipulation on the basis of meanings extracted from what is perceived as natural. They provide crude means of discrimination, legitimizing and consolidating rigid forms of social division and power distribution in society. Defining these categories as natural has to do with the way these classifications are thought of as being natural and, by implication, considered to be unalterable, traditional and inclined to natural balance.

The academics that habitually apply such categories in the analysis of social behaviour are bound to have rigid and static notions about the potential of human development. They may regard cultural and political characteristics of society as secondary, as the indirect consequences of a 'natural' process of the development of human society. Although such 'natural' processes are derived from various sources in nature, they are not usually brought into direct relation with (scientific) laws of nature. Rather, they are associated with intriguing powers that are ascribed to, for instance, the 'holistic system' of society, the 'Japanese brain' or 'evolution of the Chinese people' (see Part II). Additionally, such naturalist approaches tend to apply the method of long-term history on to millennia of civilizational development. The aim is to yield evidence for advice on short-term actions to take in solving long-term world problems. As a result such an approach resembles a mode of large-scale fortune-telling rather than serious empirical research.

Nations and civilizations seem to be internally 'unified' when concepts of 'nature' such as 'milieu', 'race', 'genetic make-up' and 'natural dialectics' are applied to the we-group as an integral unit, and foretell its collective prospects. One example, is Umehara Takeshi's idea that to Japan 'indigenous' Ainu are the carriers of the original essence of the Mongolian race and that they can show the way back to living in the natural harmony of their native forest life (Umehara Takeshi and Hanihara Kazurō 1982).[2] Another example is the quasi-Marxist point of view of Li Shaolian. Li regards the evolutionary laws of the dialectical unity between the differentiation and merger of races in China's civilizational history as responsible for the 'national coherent forces' (*ningjuli*) at work in China, thereby explaining its unity dialectically and predicting its unified future scientifically.[3]

Culturalist grouping

Theories built by means of cultural grouping assign a shared identity to the inhabitants of nations (or world parts) on the basis of spiritual and cognitive

12   *Framing the nation*

factors, using cultural markers, such as shared history, customs, language, cultural knowledge, group-psyche and family organization. These features are believed to originate in an ancient cultural source, to have emerged a very long time ago, or to be embodied in the national language, mind, cultural genes and national un/subconscious. Some culturalist classifications exclude groups of people on the basis of 'natural criteria', such as possessing a particular kind of brain or instinct. Such brain or instinct, then, is thought to be a result of the long-term development of the cultural traits of the group they characterize. Thus some academics use the 'cultural gene' argument and support it by claiming that the brain has been altered and shaped by certain linguistic habits, or, attribute certain kinds of behaviour to language acquisition, creating differences between social groups that are hard to overcome. Liu Changlin, for example, summarized the Chinese mode of traditional thought as the ten aspects of the 'cultural gene' (*wenhua jiyin*), roughly corresponding to the psychological features of female thought (Liu Changlin 1990: 578–81).

Cultural classifications generally presume that designated groups are capable of crossing natural boundaries, such as those created by racial markers. Although cultural attributes are employed to draw a clear distinction between cultural zones, in most academic theory of this kind the possibility of learning from other cultures and the exchange of at least practical skills and knowledge are not denied in principle. In terms of academic method this means that the newcomer has obtained the required hermeneutic tools for understanding his or her new in-group. When conflict occurs, however, the possibility and the sense of adoption of foreign knowledge and skills are easily questioned as some form of moral betrayal. The temporal dimension of cultural tradition then may be compressed and moulded into static shapes, such as the cultural gene, the national unconscious and the character-forming sediments disposed of by ancient national tradition. Such static shapes become weapons employable in cultural classification for reversing the global tides of the rise and fall of civilizations, and an instrument for isolating outsiders, dissenters and powers that are believed to intrude into the time-honoured tradition of insiders.

Despite the relative flexibility of cultural boundaries, in cultural regions seemingly small differences, too, can escalate into major conflicts, fuelled by disputes over language, socio-cultural belonging, sacred symbols, territorial rights and the infringement of sovereign rights. The use of abstract notions such as the family metaphor, historical roots and the collective mind contributes to the perception of cultural symbols as stable and everlasting. Quasi-kinship ties easily link the cultural with the natural, and therefore are perceived as symbols of stability. Such stability is expressed in great intimacy, spontaneity and mutual understanding, and a special knowledge of linguistic and behavioural codes attributed to those symbolic ties.

The creator of cultural zones excludes people on the basis of notions of infidelity and a betrayal of accepted notions of linguistic and cultural behaviour. But when 'outsiders' adopt the 'correct' codes (linguistic, social, customary) of behaviour, compared with crossing 'natural' boundaries, their assimilation may take place with relative ease. Nevertheless, the presentation of cross-cultural differences as being etched into the brain, sunk into the unconscious, or intrinsic to humans through notions of birth, home or the 'cultural gene' expresses an unwillingness to accept external cultural influences and a distaste for universal ideals of scientific objectivity and independence of thought.

Globalist grouping

Globalist values in academic nation-framing are ambiguous as they are presented as the outcome of universally applicable criteria for the delineation of groups, but at the same time, perhaps unintentionally, maintain a hidden agenda of group bias. An insistence by the academic on the absolutely objective nature of his/her universalism makes it hard to question or discuss the deployment of criteria of distinction in relation to local circumstances. Thus globalists insist on the universal applicability of concepts such as civilization, modernization, struggle, class, field, universal religion, science, universal wisdom and art, and advertise the universality of their globalist principles, but ultimately base those theories on sources from their *own* national tradition. For instance, Ohmae Kenichi in his *The Borderless World* (1990), adopts a view of self-organization and network relations, which has become quite widespread among sociologists and economically oriented academics who attribute to Japanese society a holistic tendency for spontaneous self-organization. Such view does not take into account the political and ideological factors affecting the modes of organization of companies and other institutions, and takes for granted or ignores relations between management and labour. Underlying these globalist notions of progress, development and modernization hides the presumption that all sources needed for attaining happiness and prosperity are potentially available to all peoples under the right conditions and by applying the right methods. In globalist theories that centre on the nation, which could be said to engage in globalist nation-framing, the right conditions for universal progress are found especially in *our* nation or part of the world, and the right methods have been developed or passed on by *our* tradition.

The problem with such theories is that, despite their centrality of the nation, pretence of universal applicability is kept up. Thus while property and happiness are advertised as attainable for everyone, essential resources may be monopolized by some groups, or their access may be limited to only a few privileged or qualified groups. In itself, this can be explained by other principles from economics, biology and psychology, and so on. But globalists 'objectively' explain the success of prospering groups in making use of universal principles of, for instance, management, by referring to scare resources, which are not accessible to everyone. Academic globalists only

14 *Framing the nation*

need to indicate the criteria for one field of 'global' excellence such as success in world trade, define its criteria as 'universally' valid and argue that the superiority of *our* nation in that field is due to its inherent quality.

Academic globalists, who try to distil a universal concept of civilization from the objective study of local cultures, find it hard to accept that any theoretical criterion used for defining civilization is bound to be influenced by the local, including the one in which the globalist has been groomed. Even harder to accept is the fact that once the *analytical* concept of 'civilization' enters the *political* arena, the concept becomes tainted by motives that are not related to any scientific criteria but to subjective labels stuck on to friend and foe, insider and outsider, the familiar and unfamiliar. It is therefore especially important for anyone who wants to create a theory of civilizations to explicate the criteria for selecting boundary markers and specify the consequences of their selection in both space and time.

In summary, the depiction of relations between groups in nation-centric and regionalist thought by means of the three modes of group categorization as discussed above yields the following tentative overview (Table 1).

In this introductory chapter I discussed categorizations and functions of the nation and the region in academic thought. I especially pay attention to approaches that habitually and categorically examine research problems in the light of principles in terms of the unit of the nation. In such approaches the nation's particular culture, psychology, customs, language and history are used as a matter of course in explanations that reduce or expand research problematic to the dimension and scale of the nation. I delineated nation-centric and regionalist ideologies from Said's concept of Orientalism, and refer to them as variants of groupism and group categorization, while making a distinction between natural, cultural and globalist forms. Finally, I placed the discussion on the Asian region and nationalism in the context of East Asia in the 1980s and the 1990s.

In short, this book identifies and compares theories that make a dogmatic and systematic use of the nation as a framework of analysis in academic research and to the unreflective application of dualistic notions of Eastern and Western identities. I refer to such practices of biased identity construction as framing the nation. The way academic theory categorizes and delineates identities I call academic grouping. Examples of academic grouping from east Asia illustrate that the bias of framing research problems around the unit

Table 1 Group categories in nation-centred thought

	Naturist	*Culturist*	*Globalist*
Markers	Rigid	Flexible	Ambiguous
Boundaries	High	Perforated	Hidden
Social division	Absolute	Conditional	Functional
Approach	Synthetic	Hermeneutic	Objectivist

Introduction 15

of the nation is not confined to 'the West', though the examples in no way can be regarded as representative for social science research in east Asia.

In Chapters Two and Three, I discuss the role of national symbolism and national histories in nation-centric research. In Chapter Two, I discuss the power of the nation's symbolic dimension over the creation of knowledge and the ways in which the two are linked together through the state. The example of the Chinese dragon as interpreted in Chinese academic debates in the final decades of the twentieth century illustrates this. In Chapter Three, I discuss the role of the notions of national homogeneity and national diversity in discussions of Chineseness. I show that both notions are employed equally in discourses of Chinese uniqueness, and show how cultural and racial conceptions of human groupings are deployed alongside one another in its defence.

In Part II (Chapters Four, Five and Six), I use a heuristic distinction between natural, cultural and globalist ways of grouping nations and world regions (such as East and West) to gain insight into the consequences of the academic framing of the nation. The nature of boundary markers used in identity construction, together with the ways nations and regions are staged internationally, and the role of natural, cultural and/or universal categories in academic theory provide a clue to the politics of identity creation.

In Chapter Seven of Part III, I make a distinction between the various methods by which alterity is envisaged (horizontal polarization (lateral juxtaposition), vertical stratification, and temporalization), making a distinction between Other and They. These strategies of contrast are usually applied together, although often only one prevails, depending on the politico-institutional context. The way in which these three methods occur in patterns, together with certain modes of identity construction and boundary markers tells us about the political biases of academic nation-framing. The case-study of the International Research Centre for Japanese Studies (Nichibunken, 1987–present), in Chapter Eight, shows the role of framing the nation in its short history. I show how initial conditions of the establishment of Nichibunken set the stage for an altered, nation-centric development of its curriculum and research agenda. Although the specific institutional structure and localized forms of nation-centric discourse are products of a history that in various senses can be called Japanese, the practice of framing the nation and the way it influences nationalist discourse are not unique to either Nichibunken or Japan.

In Chapter Nine, I argue that nation-centric research affects the social sciences by neglecting the local and the specific and by subordinating the universal to the national. Furthermore, it privileges the views of the nation of some interest groups over those of others, and renders itself ineffective by focusing on the control of national metaphors instead of national institutions. National efforts of deploying development and modernization strategies in China and Japan have been based on the presumption that certain formulas and models exist that can be applied not only in national policy-making but

16   *Framing the nation*

also in social-science research. In Chapter Ten, I illustrate this with regards to the use of political guidelines in academic research. I argue that instead of aiding national policy-making, nation-centred approaches in the social sciences diminish the capacity of checking its effectiveness and evaluating its results, thereby diminishing the possibility of reliable knowledge of the workings of nation-state policies. Observations of research in the Chinese Academy of Social Sciences (CASS) illustrate the inherent handicap of nation-centric social science in attaining national self-knowledge, its tendency to conservatism, its failure to imagine alternative views of the nation and its political predictability.

2 The power of national symbols

The might of a Chinese dragon[1]

National symbols, such as the national flower and the crown may seem fairly innocuous. It is only when symbols gain meaning as effective triggers of associated sentiments in many linked contexts, including that of daily life, that they become powerful. The way they affect society and state organization, however, is largely unpredictable. In order for state symbols to become effective, however, it needs to command loyalty to its rule. And it is what is perceived as the proven ability of the state to correct disobedience to its rule and violation to its sovereignty that commands commitment and loyalty. As long as the link between symbol and effect can be made credible as a natural connection of cause and effect, by rational or irrational means, by folk narrative or academic theory, triggering the national symbol works in the mind of its believers. In this chapter, I discuss the role of academics in the creation of national symbolism. Using some examples of historical and anthropological interpretations of the notion of the dragon, I argue that the cognitive aspect of nationalism is of crucial importance to the efficacy of national symbols.

Feeding (on) symbolic power

Neither instrumentalist nor functionalist approaches can adequately explain the history of nationhood. On the one hand, the instrumentalist approach cannot account for the force with which nationalism is pursued and ignores the subjective functions of nationalist expression. The functionalist approach, on the other hand, occupies itself with the location and characterization of quintessences, the functional continuities along the historical path, which the nation is believed to have followed. This approach crystallizes history around contemporary views of national essences that are projected back into the past.

A comparison of competing views of the nation in their historical contexts facilitates a better understanding of the circumstances through which the nation is remembered, envisaged, measured and recreated in time. The conceptualization of nations as homogeneous or unified wholes ignores the fundamental contentious nature of definitions of the nations and nation-states

18   *Framing the nation*

and the multiple interpretations given to their symbolism. The concept of homogeneous nation-states is a construct used for expressing highly subjective and changing notions of group identity. In academic debates, then, various theories strategically link the nation and the state together by conflicting versions of their historical, racial, linguistic and political connection. Some academics look for analytical criteria to justify the correlation between characteristics of the dominant nation in a nation-state and the territory that rulers claim to be theirs.

Nationalists believe it natural that only native intellectuals can perform this task. Widely accepted images of, for example, China as a proletarian state and Japan as a 'middle-mass society' are thought by some to defy the intellectual faculties of sceptical outsiders, who are believed incapable of understanding the true spirit of the nation as experienced by its true subjects. In political debates the nation-state is a construct used for expressing subjective and changing notions of group identity. Yet, academic definitions of national identity tend to link the concepts of nation and state together by discussing the nation-state in terms of its legitimizing national roots in state territory and use essentialist criteria for defining national identity, such as a common language, ethnic or racial origin and political culture. Despite its relevance to interest groups in general, the politics of defining the nation in academic research, and the consequences of using certain definitions of the nation-state, rather than that of others, have not received much attention in debates around nationalism and in the social sciences in general. As this topic is a broad one, this chapter is confined to the academic interpretation and definition of national symbols and the political and unintended consequences of 'mobilizing the dragon' in a Chinese context.

The politics of national identity marking

In debates on the coherence of national identity, it has been argued that a contradiction between criteria of inclusion is responsible for a weak sense of national identity, making a nation-state liable to crises of identity (Dittmer and Kim 1993: 29–31; Pye 1996). But why do contradictory criteria of national identity assume national proportions in the first place? Only when cultural markers and criteria have been *made* into a political national issue, nation-state identity becomes an arena for fighting out a host of apparently contradictory criteria. The job of turning symbolic markers into political issues has been and is likely to continue to be filled by nation-oriented academics. In their work the boundaries of the nation are shifted, cultural markers are redefined, and national identities linked up with knowledge of a world of nation-states.

In their quest for legitimizing nation-state authority, or their interpretation of it, some academics look for analytical criteria to justify the correlation between characteristics of the dominant nation in a nation-state and the territory that rulers claim theirs.[2] Such circular claims to national sovereignty

The power of national symbols   19

are propped up by historical narration, and selections of cultural, ethnic and environmental markers, none of which can consistently explain the state's sovereignty over all citizens and territory between state borders, but nevertheless may be convincing enough to lend authority to state rulers. The intelligentsia plays an important role in the manipulation and redefinition of nation-state symbolism. They are presumed qualified to interpret its canonical texts, collect meaningful national experience, and diagnose the national psyche. Nationalists regard it as natural that only native intellectuals can perform this task. Widely accepted images of, for example, China as a proletarian state and Japan as a middle-mass society are thought by some to defy the intellectual faculties of sceptical outsiders, who are believed incapable of understanding the true spirit of the nation (cf. Fitzgerald 1996; Murakami Yasusuke 1982).

Criteria and categories of differentiation alone do not sufficiently explain the force of nationalist ideology. It is the force behind the meaning of symbols – through which people collectively identify with a nation – that gives categories of difference their dramatic effect. A rationalist approach to understanding symbolic manipulation can hardly appreciate the zest with which symbols are presented, and easily passes over the contributions to symbolic life made by those who receive, internalize and alter them as they are applied in day-to-day affairs. The symbolical approach of Mary Douglas argues that highly charged symbols might be emotionally manipulated for political purposes with consequences that pervade everyday life. This also holds for 'natural symbols' such as race, blood and kinship (Douglas 1973). The familial and bodily symbols of nationalism are not simply metaphors; they are powerful emotive instruments of mass persuasion. The family provides an easily understood model for the loyalty and collective responsibility toward the state. Herzfeld argues that the bureaucracy draws on resources that are common to the symbolism of (Western) nation-states and to long-established forms of social, cultural and racial exclusion in everyday life. Symbols also provide members of the public with a means of conceptualizing their own disappointments and humiliations (Herzfeld 1992: 13). This process diminishes the ability of people to perceive problems not conducive to categorization in terms of accepted models of inclusion and exclusion.

The scale of symbolic power

But how do natural metaphors taken from common family institutions evoke such powerful emotional effects when employed at the macro-level of the nation-state? Douglas showed how taxonomic systems seem to push further and further away from grounded reality toward an all-consuming abstraction, even though these systems may continue to be manipulated by canny actors (Douglas 1987: 21–30). Douglas argues that scale is not particularly relevant to the centrality of symbolic classification. Institutional constraints on cognition do not disappear when the institutions themselves are larger

20 *Framing the nation*

– their 'modernity' or 'rationality' does not weaken their symbolic and personal value. Benedict Anderson's thesis on imagined communities describes this up-scaling of the level of daily relations as a process in which people move from a social to a cultural understanding of loyalty (Anderson 1995). It is a process of progressive reification, in which social immediacy makes room for cultivated imagination (Anderson 1995: 37–46). At the level of state policy, systematic and large-scale organizations are liable to such reification. For example, the creation of a national language from a dialect that has adapted successfully is an effective tool and symbol of unification. It is a shift from social relations to cultural images. Here Anderson's thesis, unlike Douglas' argument, makes scale a central issue; not on the basis of some presumed correlation between size, efficiency and reason, but on that of the semiotic technology required for maintaining a sense of cohesion.

Douglas' analysis seems to imply that symbols themselves are powerful and therefore effective no matter on what scale. However, the symbols themselves are not so much the carriers of magic as the triggers of effects. What makes symbols powerful rather than the belief in the symbols themselves is the belief in the effectiveness of their mobilization. This is why symbols are accompanied by narratives that 'explain' the effectiveness of the magic force in terms relevant to the memory and experience of the public. For example, a rocket named Long March embodies a particular history of Chinese struggle and triumph. Another example is the symbol of the Chinese family. It is no coincidence that in nationalist ideology the notion of fictive kinship is frequently used to symbolize the nation. The family in many communities is associated with unity, closeness and belonging. Its mobilization is associated with co-operation and survival. It uses the power generated and mediated by the family spirit and its strength based on shared blood. However, the specific associations made with the family symbol differ across cultures, from an emphasis on fraternity and loyalty to an emphasis on hierarchy. Similarly, the example of the dragon as a Chinese national symbol illustrates the importance, not of a fire-spitting ugly monster, but of a good-natured powerful animal. Scholars now replace explanations of symbols elaborated and passed on by many generations of folklore by academic explanations of their true meaning and effect. To illustrate this point, I briefly discuss the Chinese dragon, its symbolic value, the diversity of its forms and the role of nation-centric research in propagating the unifying force of the dragon.

The might of a multiple interpretable dragon

Many interpretations of the dragon are related to its symbol meaning for the East. For instance, according to some scholars of the ancient past, the notions of East and West were symbolically associated with the worship of the dragon and the phoenix and, according to others, with that of the dragon and the tiger (Tan Xuechun 1994). The 'descendants of the dragon' (*long de chuanren*), a metaphor referring to Chinese nationals, is meant to root the powerful spirit of the Chinese people firmly into the past. Although, according to Sautman, a critical China observer, the dragon was never regarded as an ancestral symbol of all Han Chinese, it did not discourage scholars from discussing its relevance to all Chinese today. Even though the dragon was considered to be the progenitor of ancient rulers only, the dragon is felt, including by Marxists scholars, to symbolize the power behind contemporary secular rule. And though from the Yuan dynasty onwards, common people were forbidden to associate themselves with the dragon in design and decoration, socialist rule has no scruples in feeding its symbolism to the workers of today. Therefore, the dragon appeared on the flag in the Qing dynasty and not on the gowns of the people, and only since the 1970s have ordinary people begun to identify themselves with the dragon. Nationalities other than the Han have myths that take other animals as their progenitors, the wolf among Mongols, the monkey among Tibetans and the bear among Koreans, Ewenki and Oroqen (Sautman 1997: 76–7).

The totem dragon

In his summary of Chinese totem culture (1990), He Xingliang, from the Institute of National Minorities at CASS (Chinese Academy of Social Sciences), claims that the existence of Chinese totem culture has always been denied or ignored by the West. This is why the dragon has not been recognized earlier as the common totem of China. He Xingliang argues that in the Paleolithic period, China, just like the West, was in possession of a flourishing culture of totemism. Only, for a variety of reasons it did not leave any traces, or rather the traces have not yet been discovered. The Neolithic age, in general, is the era in which totemism was in decline, but in China archaeologists have found a number of traces of totem culture. This means that Chinese totemism has been unique in its persistence in time: it persisted from ancient times down to the modernization of the 1950s. Its continuity has several causes. First, because totemism had great authority, it adapted to the new circumstances of different eras. Moreover, in tribal societies, totems served as ancestor deities and provided the tribes with great coherent power based on lineage. Rulers of feudal society used this power of coherence intentionally in order to enhance their authority. Totem culture was prevalent particularly in minority cultures where totemism was employed against the threat of their assimilation into Han culture. Thus, every region has its totem, worshipped by a small number of nationalities, for example, the wolf in the north-west, the bear in the east, the dog in the mid-south and south-east and the snake in the ancient south and south-east. However, according to He, the Chinese nation as a whole has a totem in common, too: the dragon. There is no regional variety in the view of the dragon as a unifying totem, argues He. For some thousands of years, every nationality regarded this dragon totem as a God-spirit, worshipped it, and dedicated to it ceremonial offerings.

22 *Framing the nation*

Therefore it is the emblem and symbol of the *Zhonghua* (Chinese) nation. Its continued importance, concludes He, lies in the fact that royalty used the dragon to base its authority upon, thereby strengthening its rule. Additionally, dragon worship contains some elements of the worship of nature, in particular, the worship of the dragon as the god of the weather (He Xingliang 1990: 37–9).

What He is doing here is exploiting an, in fact, old discussion of totemism in order to prove the unity of China by turning the dragon into a national totem. Thus, a claimed Western denial of Chinese totemism becomes tantamount to denying China its unity. Here, ethnological and historical materials are employed to provide the cognitive evidence in support of giving credence to the national symbol of the dragon.

The dragon as an oceanic giant python

In contrast with He Xingliang, who does not consider the dragon as a biological being, Yang Xiulu, an official at the Literature and Art Research Institute of the Qiandong Nan Miaozu Dongzu autonomous prefecture, asserts that the dragon must have been a real animal. However, at the same time, the dragon functioned as a totem symbol of the ancient eastern barbarian clans (*dongyi shi*). Yang believes that it is impossible for the dragon to just have been a fictitious animal, as is implied by the famous 'dragon-is-totem' thesis by Wen Yiduo. Primitive people, Yang argues, used to live in the midst of nature and could not make a clear distinction between themselves and their surroundings. In fact, the 'dragon' used to live in a tropical period after the last Ice Age, 7 to 10 thousand years ago, in the Bahai region (*Bahai Qu*) (Yang Xiulu 1990: 83–6).

And later on, as a result of the workings of the principle of natural selection, the 'dragon' was left in the interior as an oceanic giant python (*haiyang jumang*). During that time, the primitive people who were in awe of the giant python began to use it as a tribal totem. Later still, when tribal society entered class society during the Shang and Zhou dynasties, it was only natural that the dragon was mythologized and beautified, especially as chiefs used the dragon as their symbol. Yang can also explain how the dragon could have been found even at the northern latitude of thirty-five to forty degrees. Yang relates that, during the post-glacial period, the sea level was much higher and the whole world plagued by floods. Before the Xia and Shang periods, subtropical animals reached as far as the central plains and the areas of the middle and lower reaches of the Yangtse river were richly endowed with a habitat suitable to the large appetite of giant pythons (i.e. dragons). When climatic conditions deteriorated, many subtropical animals became extinct and only a few retreated to the south. But the giant python was not seen again (Yang Xiulu 1990: 86–90).

This realistic interpretation of dragon history is rooted in the contention that a history that can add some scientific plausibility to the former existence

The power of national symbols 23

of the dragon by placing it in a context of anthropology, biology, geology and climatology makes the dragon somehow more convincing as a symbol of power. Unlike He Xingliang, Yang finds it offensive that the dragon is regarded as merely a totem and puts effort into making the dragon into a real being that was assimilated by tribal societies into their primitive cosmologies. Although the meaning of the dragon as a totem has changed the significance of the, originally, historical animal, the dragon is proved to be rooted in material reality and, in ancient times, it is shown, the dragon was prevalent all over China, even in places one would not expect it.

The dragon as an embryo

Unlike He who regards the dragon as a totem, and Yang, who regards the dragon as a giant python, Su Kaihua, employed with the Nanjing Academy for Officers of the Land Force, argues that the dragon originally could not have been a sea snake, crocodile or whale. Instead, he maintains it derives its meaning from the embryo, as an early attempt at rationally explaining the origins of human life. The symbol of the dragon, Su argues, fulfilled the function of conveying a message about the origin of man. It is an early (scientific) thesis on the evolution of man, as the bottom half of the image of the dragon that was passed on was shaped as an animal (snake) and the top half carried a human head. Therefore the dragon cannot have been a totem. It expresses one of the earliest theses on human biological evolution from animal to *Homo sapiens*. Furthermore, the dragon does not originate in Dongyi (Longshan) as has been argued, but in Xibei (Gansu–Qinghai region) (Su Kaihua 1994b).

Su also explains why the dragon cannot be a totem in origin (Su Kaihua 1994a: 117–20). In the first place, totemism is based on the worship of animals. But the worship of animals in China preceded totemism. It was because man and animal in primitive society were still one, that man trying to explain birth, erroneously assumed that the animal spirit penetrates the stomach of the female. This idea brought them to worship the dragon. When human society became matriarchal man entered a stage at which he wanted to find his progenitors, and discovered that they could be found in women in the form of the embryo.

Su is not a supporter of the thesis that claims the dragon to be a totem. In contrast to He Xingliang, Su believes that the Chinese somehow have been misled into thinking that the dragon is a totem. The 'dragon-is-totem' thesis was defined and defended by the famous Wen Yiduo.[3] The thesis claims that the dragon was a synthesis of a great number of different animals. In all its different forms and shapes the dragon was worshipped by tribes in ancient China. According to Su, many foreign and Chinese researchers set out to prove that their worship was identical with totemism. Su disagrees for the following reasons. First, usually, a taboo rests on speaking about the animal that represents the totem, but in ancient records it says that the dragon was

24 *Framing the nation*

fed and killed. Second, a totem is required in wedding rituals as it was thought to enhance fertility. The totem in matriarchal cultures therefore disappears from the range of available fetishes when society becomes patriarchal. In China, however, the worship of the dragon continued for thousands of years, which is an indication that the dragon could not have been a totem. Third, in hunter societies the totem is usually a real animal. Out of all the different dragon shapes, which animal represents the real dragon? Fourth, a totem is usually not worshipped as a supra-national force. The dragon, therefore, seems to have uncommonly great authority. Fifth, totemism has followed the historical development of ancestor worship and disappeared together with it; the worship of the dragon, however, has become stronger in time. The dragon was not confined regionally, as were totems. Instead, its authority spread over the entire country of China. Sixth, the totem animal in prehistoric times was associated with the name of a tribe or served as its emblem; in China it only became the symbol of tribes. Seventh, totems usually are rejected by other tribes and exert a repulsive force. Dragons do not (ibid.). Su's argument is strong, complex and well thought through. It is clear that he is extremely adamant to prove his case against the totem thesis.

The modernization of a Taoist dragon

He, Yang and Su show their dragon politics only indirectly. By contrast, Hu Fuchen, a researcher of Taoism in the Institute of Philosophy at CASS, clearly expresses his antipathy for Confucian influences on the Chinese dragon and China's socialism. Hu also criticizes Wen Yiduo's thesis in his 'Talk of the Dragon and the Phoenix' (Hu Fuchen 1987). According to Hu, Wen used to regard the dragon as a totem worshipped by primitive clans. Other clans had their own totems, such as that of the horse, dog, deer and fish. They were combined with the snake (dragon) so that the dragon totem appeared in all forms and shapes. In ancient times people did not understand the causal relationship between sex and pregnancy and were superstitious. Thus, if a mother saw a bear, a dog or a horse on the day of birth, she would believe the child to have come from ancestors that had the shape of the particular animal breed she had spotted or encountered. This is also why clans were named after animal species, which explains too why descendants were left under the impression that this superstitious belief indicated the presence of totemism or ancestor worship.

According to Hu, however, the dragon cannot be both a totem and the name of a clan ancestor at the same time. Although from an early stage onwards totem symbols were used as clan names, historical records do not mention the dragon as the name of a clan (Hu Fuchen 1987: 71–2). Instead, Hu hypothesizes that the origin of the dragon lies in the sound of thunderbolts. Hu explains that when in ancient times pregnant women met with storm and thunder during a walk, they could have had a fright and given birth to a child. The birth of the child they explained by the call of the dragon.

The power of national symbols 25

To support his argument, Hu points out that the pronunciation of the written character for (thunder-) 'rumble' (*long*) is similar to that for 'dragon' (*long*). Moreover, the word for lightning (*lei*) in Tibetan refers to the sound the dragon makes (Hu Fuchen 1987: 73). Legend has it, Hu maintains, that the clan symbol of the emperor is the dragon. And it is precisely the emperor's dragon birth that betrayed the secret of the dragon: 24 months after the emperor's mother saw the lightning she gave birth to the emperor (ibid.).[4]

Primitive peoples, Hu explains, thought up the shape of the dragon, whose separate animal models formed its blueprint. They put the dragon together by using the snake's body as a base, and added the horse's head, the tail of a rat, the horns of a deer, the paws of a dog and the scales of a fish. Because the dragon can swim it must have been some kind of amphibious reptile. The creation of the dragon, Hu believes, was the first 'Copernican revolution' in 'Our' (Chinese) primitive thought: it is a remarkable result of using intuition and insight, resulting in the discovery of the concept of evolution. This, Hu explains, is one of the reasons that from ancient times onwards the epistemology of Chinese philosophy has been based on a tradition of intuition and insight. In a similar way the phoenix (*fenghuang*) was modelled on the peacock (*kongque*) not the wind (*feng*). Over time, totem societies changed into kingdoms and, later on, formed an imperial state. The dragon and phoenix became the symbols of the Imperial dynasty, and were invested with rich social meaning (Hu Fuchen 1987: 73–4). At the same time, they are also the symbolic expressions of thousands of years of patriarchy and feudal tradition. The dragon and phoenix mode of thought thus regards about everything in terms of family structures. Using the relationship between husband and wife as an analogy, the dragon and phoenix were also to be employed in theories and discussions of the correct relations between ruler and ministers, yin and yang and rulers and ruled.

The secret of Eastern autocracy, according to Hu, lies hidden in the notion of the family. The family in the autocratic model stands as a symbol for the entire empire. In 1853, Hu argues, Marx had already exposed the secret of Chinese traditional social structure. He regarded this kind of political structure as a patriarchal power. In this kind of system the ruler is always seen as the father of the country. This practice originates in the ancestor worship of ancient times. And because imperial power is mediated through the dragon in the heavens, the ruler also takes the position of God. This is why, Hu asserts, this structure can never change into that of Western Christianity, a belief in which God is placed above the monarch.

Hu regards Confucianism to be the monarchical centralism of the dragon and phoenix culture. The *lixue* of the Song and Ming dynasties is the symbol of its final completion, Hu argues that 'It (*lixue*) has become the opium of our race, and the patriarchal system runs through our blood' (Hu Fuchen 1987: 75).[5] Hu concludes his sharp critique of *lixue* with the observation that the reason that the slave system in the West could lead to an early rise of capitalism was that the step from a weak slave system to capitalism was

26 *Framing the nation*

very small. In China, however, feudalism strongly took root so that it could not easily transform into capitalism. But when it took its first steps, it found its way to socialism in one giant leap. Unfortunately, Hu argues, not all concepts of the feudal patriarchal tradition have disappeared with the momentum of the leap. For that reason, it is necessary for a healthy socialism to be established soon. Although the democratic rights of the people have been guaranteed, Hu argues, there are still people who use the Confucian classics to twist the meaning and significance of Marxism, and then mis-apply it to China's national situation (*quoqing*). This shows, Hu points out, that it is not easy to turn the descendants of the Chinese dragon into a true Marxist people. Despite the havoc caused by Confucian misapplications of the dragon, the function of the dragon has not just been to oppress the people. The function of the dragon is closely related to that of fire. Fire also used to be employed in ceremony and to 'melt stone to stop the gap in heaven' (Hu Fuchen 1987: 77). This practice, according to Hu, led to the scientific tradition of the Chinese nation. In order to exploit this tradition to the full, Hu declares that:

> We must embellish the flames of the hope of the people and use the flood of the reforms so as to sweep away the thousands of years of accumulated dirt and pollution, stuck to the body of the Chinese dragon, and to cause the rise of the socialist modernization of the Chinese people of the Eastern world.
>
> (Hu Fuchen 1987: 77)

Here, we observe the political use of the dragon by a Taoist philosopher under a Marxist regime. Hu links the dragon symbol to childbirth, the birth of the nation and the emperor system. Although the dragon still wears the dirt of a feudal past and the danger of a Confucian misreading of Marxism is still lurking around the corner, the true scientific nature of the dragon ultimately forges together all Chinese peoples, ready for a new era of modern socialism. Hu intends to show the damage caused by the family metaphor, but also feels it is his duty to point out its strength.

Symbols as effective triggers of associated sentiments in linked contexts

From the points of view of various perspectives and disciplines rationalist explanations provide the newly created academic contents of the dragon symbol, instead of the narrative explanations from folklore and myth. The question of whether these rational explanations are 'good' ones is beside the point. The academic efforts described above concentrate their attention on the different symbolic logic and forms of the nation that time after time repeat the same symbolic message of national unification.

The power of national symbols 27

A totem, Su Kaihua concluded, is a universal phenomenon prevalent in primitive cultures all over the world, but the Chinese dragon is a cultural phenomenon unique to China. He Xingliang, however, defends the status of the Chinese dragon as a totem. Whereas He seems to imply that foreigners have done their best to deny China its very own totemism, Su criticizes foreign and Chinese researchers for setting out to prove the Chinese dragon was a totem and not a uniquely Chinese phenomenon. He insists that the dragon is a totem, valued for its authority, Yang Xiulu believes it to be an oceanic giant python, mythologized by rulers in class society. Su, however, concludes that the dragon was regarded as an embryo, and a first attempt to explain human evolution. All of them, however, also define the dragon as the unifying symbol of China and try to prove it, employing their persuasive powers in the argument and appealing to the common sense of the reading audience. Almost in spite of one another, various academics provide a scientific explanation for something they can only believe in because it works as an explanation for the symbolic unification of China.

Hu Fuchen shows his politics more directly, and clearly expresses his antipathy for Confucian influences on the Chinese dragon and China's socialism. Although, according to Hu, neo-Confucian Yin-Yang thought has been the root of much corruption, feudal practices and patriarchy, the dialectic of history and the unifying strength of the dragon are still to bring socialist modernization to China. In other words, Hu's belief in his scientific explanation of the origin of the dragon politically justifies scientific socialism. Hu's academic argument, carefully attached to the symbols of the nation while appealing to the common sense and everyday experience of the audience, makes the power of the symbolic dragon real and effective. Both rationally and affectively, the mobilization of the Chinese dragon makes political sense.

In Japanese nation-centric research, the 'Japanese' macaque is frequently quoted as emblematic for Japanese cleverness and co-operation, and their closeness to nature, not with silly monkey business (Kawai Masao 1993).[6] The symbols seem to evoke strong emotive effects because of thought associations made on a micro-level about their effectiveness. Additionally, they gain new associations of meaning in their capacity of symbols on a macro-level.

It is only when symbols gain meaning as effective triggers of associated sentiments in many linked contexts, including that of daily life, that they become worthwhile laying down one's life for. The repetitive and wide use of national symbols in state propaganda may have a powerful effect in mobilizing good will and loyalty from national subjects, but only if its legitimacy has already been institutionalized through other means as well. But it takes more than just symbolic artefacts to attract citizens to nationalist ideology, even when semiotic technology is used to facilitate the process. Attention for more worldly issues is required in explaining the strong collective reactions to national symbols. Here, I do not just refer to the wide reach of state

28 *Framing the nation*

functions, such as assumed in education, transport and the media, all of which may have persuasive powers of popular mobilization. Rather, it is what is perceived as the *proved* ability of the state to correct disobedience to its rule and violation to its sovereignty that commands commitment and loyalty, necessary for state symbols to become effective.

Possessing a monopoly on the instruments of violence, the state can exact personal investment by claiming national subjects for the nation in battle, by demanding taxes, making people forego their procreative rights, by expelling them or by withholding support from them in the form of housing, pensions and employment. But it is not just the proof of the pudding that evokes national sentiments or makes people believe in the symbols of the nation. Fake evidence, academic argument, historical narrative and political threat make for a large share in the daily efforts put into persuading collective groups of the credibility and power of national symbols. As long as this link between symbol and effect can be made credible as a natural connection of cause and effect, by rational or irrational means, by folk narrative or academic theory, triggering the national symbol works in the mind of its believers. So while the state takes over functions of local communities and the family, it becomes possible for local feelings of belonging to be projected (in various ways) on to the nation-state. These projections include future aspirations that seem realizable only through the joint efforts of 'the people' and belief in the collective destiny of the nation. And as private and communal narratives of the nation are linked with state performance in clusters of mental associations, and as the nation has become functionally associated with the duty and rights of its citizens, national symbols become loaded, rituals meaningful, and their strategic and spontaneous use of great consequence.

Domestic state authority to a great extent is dependent on being acknowledged as a nation-state by the world community of nation-states. State leaders try to enhance their authority at home by staging and broadcasting official visits of foreign state leaders and their delegations. Thus the Chinese media daily report on the respect paid at state visits by state leaders from all corners of the world usually depicted as ravishingly successful and full of promises of success. Of great strategic importance are 'significant others', that is, international reference groups on to which powerful images of strength and morality are projected. Such reference groups can be both negative and positive. Positive ones provide legitimacy and authority to nation-state rulers, especially when negative reference groups, too, are willing to recognize them as legitimate representatives and accommodate to the rituals and symbols they claim to stand for.[7] When protest groups turn up just as foreign dignitaries are being received with stately honours, these groups are likely to be damned by rulers as a great nuisance. The success of the occasion (and the legitimacy of rule) is felt to be even more under threat if 'national traitors' claim to rebel on behalf of the nation. Such was the case when the then President Gorbachev visited Peking in 1989, and when the then Premier

The power of national symbols 29

Nakasone tried to talk Hu Yaobang into giving his assent to an official visit to the Yasukuni Shrine to honour the World War II war dead in 1985 (Nakasone and Umehara 1996: 90–2).

Contestants for nation-state legitimacy and dissatisfied citizens claim their own national narratives and employ their own sets of national symbols for demarcating their nation or their own homeland. Those excluded from 'the people' and banned from in-groups (dropouts) may try to overhaul prevailing criteria for the distribution of the rights and duties of citizens. Dissidents use various methods, such as terrorism, libel, counter-propaganda and co-operating with the 'enemy', to 'prove' current national symbols are empty. They can cause havoc in nation-states that rely heavily on the regular confirmation of symbolic force against potential competition. Access to information on how nations are ruled abroad can provide rebels with alternative sets of values and justifications of the rules they believe right, and give them new ideas for creating their own symbols of triumph or protest, expressed in, for example, clothing, hairstyle, art and academic discourse. The perception of a discrepancy between state symbolism and 'reality' may encourage disappointed subjects to demand changes in the system of national representation and state policies. National symbols to some may lose their significance if promised improvements in, for instance, the economy, conditions of employment and education, fail to materialize. Alternatively, the realization of promises of 'progress' could have an alienating effect on others who feel robbed of their national tradition by foreign forces (cf. Ivy 1995; Robertson 1994). If academic institutes are drawn into this political struggle, academics from the various social science fields become involved in continual fights over the current status of the nation, its political future and the manipulation of its symbols. It becomes an arena in which the contest between views of the nation stands in the way of any ideal of independent academic research that aims to solve problems without taking sides.

3 The coherent force of struggle and diversity in Chinese nationalism[1]

Nationalist discourse in Chinese academic circles of the 1980s is often associated with an emphasis placed on the uniqueness of China's national culture and the cultural homogeneity of its population. In the 1990s, however, the opposite trend developed. Various conceptions of 'coherent force', diversity and strife are strategically defined as factors that enhance unity, both from an evolutionary and cultural point of view. Cultural and racial conceptions of human groupings are employed alongside one another in 'proving' the uniqueness of the *Zhonghua* Chinese. In this chapter I show how both ethnic and naturalist categories such as culture and race serve to legitimate the delineation of the nation on a discursive basis of diversity and strife.

Natural group markers

Natural groups are groups constructed on the basis of markers such as gender, age, race, species, climate, geography, natural habitat and consanguinity. Such categories are employed to express the (human) unalterable nature of groups, as they are sources for the creation of 'natural' difference. Natural markers may facilitate symbolic manipulation on the basis of meanings extracted from what is perceived as natural, provide crude means of discrimination, and legitimize and consolidate rigid divisions in social organization and in the distribution of power over society. 'Natural' classifications of people are based on to humans unalterable factors, such as (quasi-) biological features (e.g. 'race', 'the primitive'),[2] environmental factors (geographical location, climate, natural resources) and/or kinship structure (clan, gender, blood, age). The point made here is not that these categories are determined by nature, for all mental perceptions of nature must eventually pass through the human mind. It is rather that these categories in the context of their application are presented and thought of as natural, and by implication considered unalterable, traditional and inclined to natural balance. For instance, if the marker 'race' is employed in ideological discourse to indicate unalterable difference between groups of people, then I regard it as a naturalist category. In some cases, however, the marker 'race' is regarded as alterable when, for

Struggle and diversity in Chinese nationalism 31

instance, Michael Jackson's nose job is discussed in racial terms. In, again, other cases, biological factors are used to emphasize the importance authors attach to cultural or ethnic difference. For instance, the concept of 'cultural gene' is often employed with that aim in mind.

The academic who makes predominant use of such natural categories in the analysis of social behaviour is bound to have rigid and static notions about the potentials of human development, and may regard cultural and political factors as a result of a 'natural' process of the development of human society. Such, mainly, 'natural' arguments often combine physical characteristics with environmental markers and categories of territory and descent. Of course, these notions also have implications for the ways in which culture is viewed. For example, sometimes the concept of *Zhonghua Minzu* (the Chinese race/nation) is regarded as a racial concept although in other contexts it is not. Therefore, I find it instructive to check if such a concept is used in the context of 'natural' theories, 'cultural' theories, or 'universal' theories. Even though the practice of labelling people can always be regarded in the light of the politics of producing difference, it is of great relevance to specify what kind of boundaries are erected between categories and therefore what kind of classification system is deployed.

The symbolic walls that are erected between different groups by the three classification systems of natural, cultural and universal categorization are of various heights, tenacity and hardness and of a different nature. This is not to say that the consequences of using one or another are less severe or that the use of one kind of marker is somehow 'better' than the use of others. As I discuss the three taxonomies in the context of nationalism, all three kinds of markers place undue, ideological emphasis on the differences between groups. But because their discursive domain varies, and with that the consequences of their employment, it is helpful to have an understanding of to which realm of categorization the applied concepts of discrimination belong. For instance, the use of some concepts of discrimination, such as the genetic differentiation marker, may convey an impression of cruel racial discrimination. On second sight, however, its usage may turn out to be based on a misplaced emphasis on cultural difference. The use of '*Zhonghua*' (China), for instance, apart from political, has both racial and cultural connotations, depending on the timing of its use, and the background and frame of thought of the author.

Origins, coherent force and consanguinity

Zhonghua is another word for China, and in the 1990s it was often employed to express racial political correctness. When writing about myths of Chinese origins, for instance, the Chinese descent from the dragon, the Yellow Emperor and Peking Man, scholars often use the concept of *Zhonghua Minzu* to point out the importance of *Zhonghua* as an organic unity between different clans and ethnic groups. The concept of *Zhonghua Minzu* is translated as both

32 Framing the nation

Chinese race and Chinese nation.[3] In Chinese there is no one word in referring to 'nation', as distinct from 'state' (*guo*).[4] Alternatives include 'people' (*renmin*) and 'race' (*minzu*), and its derivative 'Han race' (*Hanzu*) and 'Chinese race' (*Zhonghua Minzu*). The reformer Liang Qichao (1873–1929) complained that the Chinese people were unable to put a name to their country. The historical community was referred to by dynasty rather than by country, for example 'the great Qing state' (*da Qingguo*).[5] 'Zhongguo' (central country) had been used before the modern period but it designated neither the country nor the state itself; it referred only in the most general of terms to the place of the emperor at the centre of the world. '*Zhonghua*' first appeared in the formal designation of state as *Zhonghua Minguo* (Republic of China) in 1912 (Johnston 1985: 57).

In the 1990s, discussions of the origins of *Zhonghua* had links both with debates that stress political culture and with those that stress race, although the former clearly have gained the upper hand. Even though racial terms may be deployed in debates of both culture and nature groupings and both kinds of debate may aim to delineate China from the rest of the world, the paradigmatic context clearly differs. According to Jin Binggao (1992), for example, the concept of *Zhonghua Minzu* originates in the Wei and Jin dynasties. Jin argues that initially the concept was deployed in astronomy. The term *Zhonghua Minzu* forms an aggregate of the concepts of *Zhongguo* and *Huaxia*. In Chinese history, *Zhonghua* came to be used in history, astronomy, geography, culture, law, politics and ethnology. *Zhonghua* as a geographical name refers to units of national administration, such as provinces and districts. But in times of unity it refers to the entire country, and in times of separation it refers to the Central Plains (*Zhongyuan*). Therefore as a geographical term, Jin argues, 'Zhongguo' and '*Zhonghua*' are identical; and, as an ethnological concept '*Zhonghua*' was mainly used to refer to the Han nationality. 'Minzu' was translated from Japanese during the late nineteenth century and early twentieth century, and was used to express the meaning of 'race' or 'people'. Not long after, it was combined with *Zhonghua* into *Zhonghua Minzu* and became widely used. But at first, maintains Jin, the concept referred to the Han Chinese only; later on, it included both the Han and other ethnic groups (Jin Binggao 1992: 43–4).

There seems to be no agreement about when the term was first used and from what context it acquired its meaning. Chen Liankai (1992), for example, maintains that the concept only came into being in the twentieth century, although the notion of *Zhonghua* territory goes back to the 'original source' of the nation. According to most scholars, the term of *Zhonghua Minzu* became a commonly used concept only at the beginning of the twentieth century. Attempting to revive China, Sun Yat-sen used the generic terms of *Huaxia*, *Zhongguo* and *Zhonghua*. After the revolution of 1911, he spoke of the unity of the *Zhonghua Minzu* (*Zhonghua* race), which included only five ethnic groups (Heberer 1989: 18). Nevertheless, nation-centric

Struggle and diversity in Chinese nationalism 33

academics emphasize *Zhonghua*'s ancient roots. Chen insists that the origin of *Zhonghua Minzu* is located in *Zhonghua* territory.

Archaeology in New China (Xin Zhongguo) proved that no scientific evidence exists for the orthodox view, which locates the origin of China in the Central Plains, along the middle and lower reaches of the Yellow River. Nor is there any proof for the seventeenth century 'foreign thesis' which claims that the race of *Zhonghua* civilization entered China from abroad. Chen claims that there is evidence for the thesis that *Zhonghua* origins lie in what is traditionally thought of as China. However, until now, Chen argues, only on *Zhonghua* territory can one find fossils of all the stages of human development from ancient ape-man up to *Homo sapiens*. An evolution chart can be drawn of the development of the *Zhonghua* race on the basis of archaeological evidence, most of which points at an origin in south-west China. Moreover, after the discovery of Peking Man and Hetao Man, evidence was found that the features of ancient Huaxia Man were related to those of the Mongolian race (yellow race). The ancient Mongolian Liujiang Man, compared with the Mountain Cave Man, in the later stage of the development of *Homo sapiens*, already showed a considerable difference between northern and southern features (Chen Liankai 1992: 40). Furthermore, says Chen, the features of the Mongolian race are related to the *Zhonghua* in the Early Stone Age. This proves, Chen asserts, that ancient *Zhonghua* already harboured various racial groups. These ancient ancestors must have spread over *Zhonghua* territory to create man and generate historic culture. The difference between European development and that of China, Chen believes, is a qualitative one. Chen's conclusion clear favours the Chinese fashion of development above that of Europe. The strength of the European Empire, Chen argues, was based on military power. After it disintegrated, however, the pieces were no longer able to unite. Chinese history, by contrast, is characterized by a dialectical development of unity and differentiation. Each time it disintegrated, argues Chen, an even stronger unity was generated (Chen Liankai 1992: 41–2). In Chen's view, the Chinese capacity for survival is greater than that of Europe.

Much evidence is collected and attention paid to the competition between civilizations for a place at the beginning of history, as origin of the Chinese nation. Mu Hongli discusses materials that prove the 7,000 years existence of *Zhonghua Minzu* culture, placing its subsequent development into Hongshan civilization 2,000 years later, next to ancient civilizations such as that of Babylon and Egypt (Mu Hongli 1997: 89).[6] Unlike Chen Liankai, Mu traces the origins of *Zhonghua Minzu* to the northern Hongshan culture, a hierarchic clan society that has left traces of ceremony, nature worship and totemism. Mu argues that relics of ancient buildings, crockery and jade dragons show that the Hongshan influenced the culture of the Central Plains and indicate its unity with the culture of the north. Mu maintains that newly found evidence proves false the view that the culture of the Central Plains is the only cradle of Chinese civilization. According to Mu, the existence

34 *Framing the nation*

of other sources of *Zhonghua Minzu* proves that the civilizations of the Yangtze, the middle reaches of the Yellow River (*Huang He*) and Hongshan have started out separately and influenced one another later on, backing up the 'the unity of plurality-thesis' (Mu Hongli 1997: 91–2).[7]

Proof for the whereabouts of the origin of mankind is found in nature too. Jia Lanpo, the nestor of Chinese archaeology, from CAS (Chinese Academy of Sciences), takes a polygenic approach to human evolution, arguing that the earliest humans did not originate in Africa.[8] Jia believes that the earliest humans originated within the borders of present-day China, on the Qinghai–Tibet plateau.[9] Jia has noted that every country tries to expand its own history through the discovery of human fossil remains within its own territory. He believes Chinese scientists to be in competition with foreigners working in Africa. This not only implies that humanoids living in territories now part of China were somehow 'Chinese' but also that one purpose of palaeoanthropology in China is to reinforce racial nationalism by showing the antiquity of the pedigree of the contemporary Chinese people. The popular writings of Jia Lanpo have been officially commended for their role in patriotic education. Before the mid-1980s, Peking man was identified as the ancestor not of the Chinese only, but of humanity as a whole (Sautman 1997: 87–8).

'Coherent force' (*ningjuli*) is an important concept in knitting together the cultural, ethnic, developmental and territorial features of the development of the Chinese nation. This coherent force finds its expression in nature through the 'blood' and the interbreeding of the superior elements of various 'races'. Li Shaolian analyses Chinese history in terms of the three original Huaxia tribes: the Hua, the Yi and the Man (1990).[10] By treating history with respect, Li argues, it is possible to elaborate on the material basis and spiritual centre of the unity of China. This material basis and spiritual centre can be traced back thousands of years to the Huaxia clans. According to Li, China is one of the few nations in the world that has not yielded to foreign aggression, or internalized foreign factors and strength. Present-day China, Li asserts, consists of cultural and consanguine elements of the Huaxia, Man, Yi, Xu and Yi clans (Li Shaolian 1990: 106). China is a mixed body of races, Li argues, and therefore China forms a united multiethnic nation (*duominzu guojia*) with fifty-six relatively closely affiliated nationalities. Li describes how their struggle, assimilation and dialectical formation into one stable nation stimulated the historical function of Chinese civilization: national unity. The three tribes originate in a unique, primitive Chinese society, which came about approximately 7,500 years ago (New Stone Age). The area over which the tribes were spread covered a vast territory, and this ancient society was characterized by clear cultural traits, a fast pace of development and rapid social transition (Li Shaolian 1990: 108). Li's main question deals with how the three influenced the development of Chinese civilization. First, their coherent power stimulated the communication between primitive tribes of different levels of development and spread over a huge territory. It brought

Struggle and diversity in Chinese nationalism 35

about a united culture that in time met the necessary conditions for the establishment of the Chinese nation. Second, the Yellow emperor, who survived the wars among the three clans, transcended the power of the individual chieftain and became the sovereign, that is, the seed of national sovereignty. And, third, the cultures of the three clans became the basis of the nation by the dialectics of merger through struggle (Li Shaolian 1990: 108–10).[11]

Many socialist scholars, in contrast to Confucian academics, do not mind referring to Chinese history as one of violent Spencerian contention. In this view, struggle is not the agent of collapse but a natural source of becoming healthy, necessary to a dialectical development of self-strengthening, that is, evolutionary survival.[12] Thus, Li describes *Zhonghua* history as one of struggle and unity and, rather tautologically, as one in which the emperor survived. The apparent need to explain differences in the Chinese genetic make-up culminated in a 1997 article on 'The Origin and Development of the Chinese Nation From a Genetic Perspective' by Du Ruofu and Xiao Chunjie.[13] On the basis of a genetic frequency analysis on the genetic relationship between the Han and the national minorities in south and north China the authors conclude the following. On average, the blood relationship between the Han and the national minorities in north and south, respectively, is very close, while the genetic distance between north and south is relatively wide.[14] This proved, according to Du and Xiao, that the Han and the national minorities have very frequent consanguine communication. The implication is that the Han and the national minorities form an even closer family in their own half of the country than do the Han internally over the whole of China (Du Ruofu and Xiao Chunjie 1997). This conclusion forms a weapon against any appeal for ethnic separation and pre-empts any attempt by national minorities to create theories of ethnic uniqueness based on physiological particularity, environmental adaptation or consanguinity.

Coherent force: The dialectical unity of merger through struggle

In the genre of classifications based on natural criteria, a variety of discussions concerns questions of *Zhonghua* origin and forms of *Zhonghua* evolution. They have in common a tendency to:

- expand history into the ancient past, if possible, at least as far as that of other known civilizations;
- establish a continuity between the origin and the present;
- stress the enormous consequences of the birth of the *Zhonghua* nation for world civilization and its development;
- ascribe the present unity of the people and/or positive prognosis for future developments of the Chinese nation to longstanding forms of historical development.

36 *Framing the nation*

Although the ancient past in these debates is not always associated with positive meaning, the weight of time tends to evoke awe and is used for its extraordinary persuasive powers. The source of continuity between the nation's origin and the present does not necessarily lie in the carriers of national identity. It may be the mechanism of competition, struggle, inter-marriage, family-line, co-operation, the triumph of the Yellow emperor, or the gradual evolution from ancient ape-man to *Homo sapiens* that are assigned explanative authority in providing narrative proof of the nation's conquest of time. In the cases described above, the diversity of people, rather than a reason for considering national devolution, has become a crucial condition for the survival of the *Zhonghua Minzu*, especially in official Chinese publications. What matters here, however, is the authority borrowed from long periods and uncontrollable processes of genetic transformation. It is exactly because humans cannot control them, and because they inspire awe, that they are ideal as markers for the legitimization of nation-state authority.

The transition that took place in Chinese academic communities from cultural nationalism in the 1980s to other, materialist, forms of nationalism in the 1990s corresponds to a change in political emphasis encouraging an integration of cultural and materialist approaches. In this context, the 'unity of plurality' emphasizes the particularity of both *Zhonghua* and of its fifty-five official national minorities without setting the Han majority apart as the dominant group. In this sense, the 'unity of plurality' is both a propaganda instrument and an administrative reality in line with materialist conceptions of society that employ natural and cultural group markers in set patterns.

Without doubt, the new trend in national history writing will influence the next generation of students, and leave its imprint on the ways in which they discuss the essence of *Zhonghua*. Many Chinese and non-Chinese students of Chinese history in the past have argued that Chinese modernity can be understood only as a cultural entity, but at least as many have argued against it (Fitzgerald 1995; Sautman 1997). In fact, the debate whether China can be described in cultural terms, in terms of class struggle, imperialism or in terms of politico-administrative organization cannot be separated from its political implications. Especially in the 1980s a clear link between cultural historical interpretations and liberal political views and historical class analysis and orthodox Marxist views led to painful clashes, both in the intellectual field and in the field of academic politics (Goldman 1994; Sleeboom 2001).

The new trend of understanding *Zhonghua* in materialist terms is partly due to changing official policies toward academic debate in the period following June 1989. After the implementation of academic reforms in the beginning of the 1990s, radical academic approaches were discouraged by means of administrative and financial instruments of academic policy-making. This change is expressed in official guidelines for academic research and recruitment (cf. CASS Yearbook Editorial Committee 1992–2000; Sleeboom 2001). The outer limitations of debates with regards to characterizations of China were redefined by supporting only certain definitions of the system of Chinese governing, i.e. 'socialism with Chinese characteristics', providing limited space for culturalist interpretations of Chinese history and ample for materialist ones. In other words, a balanced approach that could explain China's cultural heritage in congruence with China's socialist progress in the world became a departure point for academic research programmes concerning Chinese society, history and culture (cf. National Philosophy and Social Science Planning Office 1997). It is doubtful that one or the other approach will dominate the debate in the near future.

Part II
Group categorization

4   Natural categorization

Distinctions made between groups based on what are perceived as natural markers are quite rigid, in the sense that boundaries are erected between units of comparison that are hard to overcome. After all, as sources for creating absolute difference, natural categories of distinction such as genetic make-up, climatic change and environment, the brain and blood, are chosen for their overpowering influence over human alterability.

Natural markers facilitate symbolic manipulation on the basis of meanings extracted from what is perceived as natural, provide crude means of discrimination, and legitimize and consolidate rigid divisions in social organization and in the distribution of power over society. The natural character of such categories refers to the way they are thought of as natural, and by implication considered unalterable, traditional and inclined to natural balance. Academics who habitually apply such categories to the analysis of social behaviour are bound to have rigid and static notions about the potentials of human development, and may regard cultural and political factors as a result of a 'natural' process of the development of human society.

Chosen peoples and codified brains

The importance of natural categories has been widely noticed by, for instance, critics of genetic determinism. I begin this chapter by pointing out how criticism of natural categorization could needlessly turn into exceptionalism. Carmen Blacker in her 'Two Shinto Myths: the Golden Age and the Chosen People' pointed out the difference between two principle myths, that of the golden age and that of the chosen people (Blacker 1988: 64–77).[1] Whereas the first type is common, the second, apparently, is confined to Japan where it flourished at the time of the Tokugawa Shinto revival movement among famous *Kokugaku* (national learning) scholars, such as Kamo Mabuchi, Motoori Norinaga and Hirata Atsutane.[2] Their works express the pure, spontaneous and innocent nature of the Japanese spirit (*magokoro*) of ancient times, the corrupting influence of the Chinese intruder, the magic purity of the Japanese language, the continuity of ancient ways through the line of the emperor, and the Japanese people as a superior race and chosen people.

42 Group categorization

This theory of the Chosen People, according to Blacker, cannot be found elsewhere. For the *Zhonghua* (Chinese) doctrine allowed other peoples to become civilized by becoming its subjects; the Jews were not created by a special act which made them superior; Calvinist doctrine held that all humans are equally tainted with original sin, while God saves certain people only arbitrarily. The chosen people myth re-emerged in the *Kokutai no hongi* (1937) and, Blacker concludes, lives on in Dr Tsunoda Tadanobu's neuro-physiological research (which is discussed in this chapter).[3]

Here, I believe, Blacker particularizes Japanese myth and ethnocentrism unnecessarily. Although racial discrimination, as a 'natural' system of classi-fication, makes for a crude means of inducing division between groups, encourages politics of difference and nationalist sentiment, it seems pointless to single out one type of racial discrimination as unique, or as the monopoly of one nation.[4] Many forms of racial, religious and cultural discrimination, single out one nation as being superior to others. This form of nationalism is bound to remain as long as problematic tendencies are automatically trans-lated into the problematic nature of certain nation-states. In fact, nation-centred theories of the 'chosen people' are widespread and take many forms. They make use of the concept of 'cultural gene' and the kinship metaphor. They also utilize various kinds of environmental determinism to give 'natural' explanations for cultural phenomena, and underline cultural sentiment by ascribing to it a 'natural body'. Concepts from nature and science (genes, climates, family ties) are employed to add to the notion of the nation a false sense of stability, long life, and extra survival power. Dr Tsunoda's neurophysiology is a case in point. Tsunoda provides a scientistic foundation for theories that link a unique Japanese brain (*sic*) to Japanese linguistic behaviour, thereby 'proving' the deeply rooted nature of Japanese identity. As Tsunoda emphasizes the brain in explaining the uniqueness of Japanese culture, his theory belongs to the category of theories that delineate the nation in terms of natural classification systems.

Although linguistic determinism is often associated with interpretations of the cultural environment, some academics look to science for an intellectual basis. For instance, Tsunoda claims that the neurophysiological functions of the Japanese brain are different from those of the occidental brain.[5] While consonants and vowels are handled together in the left hemisphere of Japanese brains, in occidental brains consonants are processed in the left hemisphere and vowels in the right. The left hemisphere of the Japanese brain unifies the perception of natural acoustic phenomena (linguistic, musical and natural sounds), whereas these are treated separately in Western brains. Thus European speakers process independent vowels – along with non-linguistic sounds, such as of machines, nature and expressions of emotion – in the right hemisphere of the brain, and Japanese process both independent vowels and non-linguistic sounds – except those of machines and musical instruments – in the left hemisphere. Since the left hemisphere performs logical and mathe-matical functions as well, in the Japanese brain *logos* and *pathos* are, as it were, integrated, in contrast with cerebral performance in the European thought process, in which logic and emotion are contrasted and opposed.

So-called neurophysiological proof for the difference between human languages and cultures constitutes an open invitation to racism and nationalism. As his theory is used as a scientific argument, referring to laws of nature, to prove an essentially cultural difference between the Japanese and foreigners, I regard Tsunoda's theory as a naturalist theory. This does not mean that nature and culture are not dialectically related. Thus, Tsunoda maintains that 'My investigations have suggested that the Japanese language shapes the Japanese pattern of brain functions, which in turn form the basis of creating Japanese culture' (Tsunoda Tadanobu 1985: vi). Japanese culture here is based on a racial factor, the product of the continued interaction between the neurophysiological particularities of the Japanese brain and the Japanese language. In other words, the national reproduction cycle of the Japanese people lies in the three-link cycle of brain–culture–language.

The evolution of Us cultural brains and Them civilized brains

Yōrō Takeshi has published a number of popular books and appears on television frequently. Trained as an anatomist, he made a name by writing on topics related to the human body, such as the brain, modernization and death. The way he used his medical experience as a pathologist in his work on culture and modernity drew the attention of culture scholars such as Umehara Takeshi, Morioka Masahiro and Kawai Hayao.

Yōrō Takeshi links his theory of 'brainism' (*yuinōron*) to the cycle that reproduces Japaneseness as an interaction between the collective memory of the brain, culture and language. For this reason I regard Yōrō's theory of brainism as a form of natural classification. Apart from informing the public on cerebral research and engaging in discussions on culture and the Japanese, Yōrō is an anatomist (*kaibōgakusha*) and professor at the Medical Department of Tokyo University. His work focuses on the human body and its relation to society. Yōrō is known for his view that the brain has to be returned to the Japanese body. According to Yōrō, globalization has led to universalizing trends of brainism which involves a strong trend in which the cultural body is neglected, leading to an overall alienation of people from the culture to which they belong. And as Japanese culture has roots in the unconscious (*mu-ishiki*), which is seated in the brain and expressed through the language of the body, it is necessary to reattach the function of the brain to its material seat in the cultural body of the Japanese.[6]

In information society the brain, according to Yōrō, has been allocated the role of creator of all artefacts, including cultural tradition, social systems and language: 'whereas cavemen used to live in nature, present man lives in the brain. Our history is saturated with the history of the brain. This we call progress' (Yōrō 1989: 7). Yōrō points out that environmental protection

44 Group categorization

movements that have emerged in fact are intuitive anti-brain movements. According to Yōrō, rather than opposing the brain, we must ask to what extent we allow ourselves to be governed by the brain. Our age is an age of 'brainism', according to Yōrō the reason why death is now conceived as 'brain-death'. We have been liberated from nature, but now we have to see whether we are really liberated with regards to the brain. Science and technology, skills, fashion, language, religion: all are attributes of the cerebral function. In society we exchange language, things, money, etc. This is possible because the brain is based on the same principle: the exchange of signals mediated by symbols (through air vibration, electromagnetic waves, etc.) (Yōrō 1989: 7–13).

Despite Yōrō's privileging of cerebral structures as his object of study, the expectations he harbours of the long-term development of the brain and his views on its functions show that he does not exclude from his theory the notions of time and purpose. Time, according to Yōrō, has two fundamental characteristics: change and repetition. Without change or repetition, there can be no time. In biology optic time is intimately related to movement and changes in the direction of time units (differentiation), while audile time is related to rhythm and the repetition of units of time (frequency). Then there is cultural time, in which, for example, a pyramid or the emperor system is visualized as eternal in nature. Differences in the perception of cultural time cause cultural conflict: cultural time determines our memories in various ways.

The awareness of one's identity develops parallel with the awareness of time: the two are integrated in the architecture of the brain. Natural selection, Yōrō argues, tends to keep memory from becoming tangled by means of 'the selection of the fittest awareness'. The correctness of awareness is subject to the same constraints as logical positivism: awareness that does not concur with reality is unfit and becomes extinct. Fitness, here, according to Yōrō, does not refer so much to the transformation of brain structures, but rather to the ways in which their functions fit their carriers: the human body and culture. One should not base evolutionary principles on the way in which organisms change in shape in the Darwinian sense. For apart from the sense of vision on which our perception of shapes is based, there are other senses that could serve as the basis for criteria of selection in evolution (Yōrō 1989: 202–18).

According to Yōrō, Darwinism sprang from transcendental religion, as it rejects the question of why Darwin was thinking about natural selection. Yōrō's preference lies with the evolution theory of Imanishi Kinji: the Japanese classical theory of evolution.[7] Imanishi's concept of evolution is based on the historical consciousness that projects nature on to change, and regards it as an 'eternal becoming'. In this view of evolution, species change when they ought to, and if one member of a species changes, all change so that a new species emerges. Yōrō is aware of the influence the pre-war Kyoto school, of which Imanishi is considered to be a crucial member, exerted on

Natural categorization 45

the creation of the 'Fundamentals of Our National Polity' (*Kokutai no hongi*).[8] He also understands the racist implications of Tanabe Hajime's use of the concept of 'becoming' in his 'The Logic of Species' (1969). Moreover, Yōrō directly points out that Imanishi must be regarded as a product of his time, and that species should not be interpreted as a national group. Nor should the nation be regarded as the absolute mediator between the individual and the world. Nevertheless, Yōrō points out, the famous socialist historian Maruyama Masao in 'The "Ancient Stratum" of the Historical Conscious' made a very similar point.[9] Maruyama argued that the *basso ostinato* of the Japanese consciousness is expressed in the meanings of Japanese written characters such as that for *umu* (giving birth; to be born; Ch. *sheng*), which all may be interpreted as 'becoming' (*naru*) (Maruyama Masao 1972). 'Becoming' is the archetypal form of historical consciousness and reflects the external factor of vegetational growth. It is a timeless eternal becoming and therefore a mode of being. It is a concept very close to that of nature in Imanishi Kinji's theory of evolution (Yōrō 1989: 212–20). Nature, in Yōrō 's view, contains purpose reflected in the human brain. Human behaviour cannot be explained by reference to mimicry, he argues. It is related to the innate purpose of the brain. The brain knows how to deal with the senses, which are activated by external stimuli. It also has the function of producing consciousness of motion, albeit a summary of it. For if our brains were aware of all details and motion, the cerebral programme of our brains would explode. We need a degree of awareness if we want to think up a purpose or do something new. Most of this awareness is retrieved from our innate memory and unconscious (Yōrō 1989: 234).

Japanese society, according to Yōrō, especially since the war, has strongly emphasized the brain over the body. But traditional society, too, has concentrated on the brain's function to control the body. That is why 'our society' has built the world's most peaceful era, which lasted longer than Rome. On the other hand, 'We' have problems with kidney transplantation and brain death. In other words, the brain is deployed in manufacturing and artificial intelligence but not as a means for sustaining the body; Japan has a brain for control and regulation but none for the Japanese body. Not much can be done about it, apart from giving back the brain to the body by, for instance, not accepting hearts and kidney from other countries. Although this, of course, is a form of discrimination, it is at least in line with Japan's inherent traditional social structure of discrimination (Yōrō 1989: 260).

According to Yōrō, in Japan the body was not consciously thought about (*shisō to shite no karada*) before modernization. The Japanese followed cultural standards unconsciously and used to 'live for the flesh'. Instead, now, the Japanese (We) have become the world's number one and produce cars, cameras and calculators. The body is being neglected. Witness the countless offerings to the Guardian of Children (*jizō*) to be found at the temples of Kamakura: procured abortion has stunted the growth of the population

46 *Group categorization*

(Yōrō 1989: 261). Similarly, Yukio Mishima died because he had lost the brain for his body. Since ancient times, this country has been brainy, Yōrō argues, Japanese students in schools abroad are all said to have excellent marks. 'Our' society is built on the aggregate of 'Our' people. But, Yōrō observes, 'We' had Kamikaze pilots but no individualism (*kojinshugi*). It is the result of 'Our' weak physique, Yōrō believes. There have always been ways to compensate for it through education or by using the forces of nature (Yōrō 1989: 263). Now, however, nature has lost its power. The only thing to be done, according to Yōrō, is to take away the taboo on the materiality of the brain.

Yōrō's theory of brainization does not advocate brainization; it merely confirms its evolutionary role and argues for a development of the brain in tune with the body, that is, the cultural body. Here lies a crucial role for the distinction Yōrō upholds between civilization and culture. Civilization and culture are different, Yōrō argues, in that civilization is something we are aware of, while culture is an aggregate of the conscious and the unconscious of a people. Only the former can be transplanted (which is what is meant by *wakon yōsai*),[10] and is apparent in the process of globalization. Yōrō believes that the 'globalization of Japan' would be more suitably expressed as the 'urbanization of Japan' (Yōrō 1997: 3). As for culture, Yōrō makes a distinction between music and painting, and language (in the sense of *langue*). The latter is processed by the brain in the left cerebral hemisphere, which has become increasingly specialized and is concerned with the conscious processing of information. Music and painting, by contrast, are recorded in the right-hand hemisphere. The information in this half is not processed, cannot be expressed through language, and affects the unconscious.

Defining 'unconscious expressions' is a problem, of course, but in the narrow sense of the notion, unconscious expressions include physical expressions (Yōrō 1997: 5–8). For example, the naked body is taboo at most social gatherings. Why? Because the body as nature is not a product of the conscious but also expresses the unconscious. Furthermore, it expresses unconscious urges that cannot be controlled by conscious awareness. Just like the naked body, cultural expressions are not necessarily conscious or expressible in language. Therefore cultural theory is somewhat of a contradiction. Especially in cities the ('natural') naked body is replaced by attires that express the unconscious on the basis of shared cultural criteria. Certain kinds of clothes or uniforms express people's occupation. Such equipment puts people at ease. In Japan 'form' (model) (*kata*) is very important and sensitively expressed by the body. Its original meaning emphasizes 'form' and the correct way (art) of doing things (*dō*). Form has not died out, because it is a product of the body, and the body remembers it. Therefore the way is expressed in all Japanese art. In general, the topic of form has been discussed very little. Apart from the difficulty of expressing form in language, there is another, still greater, difficulty: the Japanese traditional expression of form follows the rule of 'act in silence', that is, the endless

Natural categorization 47

repetition of action until one is one with its form. This oneness is thought to be a direct expression of the unconscious (cf. Suzuki Daisetz 1991).

Culture is disappearing because of urbanization, that is, civilization and brainization. Or, rather, brainization is in conflict with culture. Yōrō regards this process as one of the universalization of awareness. For this reason, he does not trust the study of comparative culture: culture is not translatable as, at least partly, it is an expression of the unconscious. Moreover, culture is not always expressed in language. And even so, before one can discuss an alien culture, it is necessary to become aware of one's own culture. And especially in the case of a tradition that is expressed in (unconscious) bodily control, such as that of Japan, it is very difficult to become aware of culture. The work of Yōrō exemplifies a contemporary method of projecting natural categories (such as brain and body) on to society by defining culture partly in vague terms of 'unconscious' functions of the brain and partly in terms of the movement and bearing of the body. To Yōrō, the West, globalization, civilization and urbanization, all cause the brain to increase its conscious functions of regulation and control, while the space left for culture and the unconscious activities of the brain is reduced. In Japan, only the arts remember Japanese culture through the bodily expressions of the unconscious. Yōrō's affiliation with Buddhism seems to have extended his cultural region from the confines of Japan to the Buddhist region, where he can feel at ease as well. In the 'Christian West', however, he always feels some kind of tension. This tension he attributes to the effect of unconscious cultural differences, that still find their physical expression through the mind and in the body. The rift between Yōrō's cultural region and others cannot be bridged, unless the entire world becomes urbanized and brainized. Otherwise culture is untranslatable: the body anchors it in the unconscious, and cultural memory is carved out in the brain for thousands of years. Only for a relatively short period, since the Taishō period (1912–26) the process of becoming self-aware has started to accelerate in Japan (Yōrō and Morioka 1995: 202). And the only way for the Japanese to keep their cultural body is to become aware of the corpses that embody the material substance of this most brainy of races. Only then, may the brain be readjusted to its cultural self. Yōrō's work, therefore, shows how a combination of an extreme form of cultural relativism, material culture and teleological evolution model can lead to a racial gap between 'we cultural brains' and 'they civilized brains'.

Instinctive distancing: Are we closest to macaques or Ōbei-ans?[11]

One type of naturalist classification of national identities makes the ability and desire to be part of nature contiguous upon national or regional origin. The use of Imanishi Kinji's theory of group evolution, Tsunoda's linguistic brain thesis and his own primatology enable Kawai Masao to define the

48 *Group categorization*

Japanese as more natural than other ethnic groups, thereby isolating Japan from both China and the West.

The biologist Kawai Masao, the brother of Kawai Hayao, insists that Western people are severed from nature, and when they want to express their closeness to nature, they speak in anthropocentric terms of 'animal rights' and 'animal welfare'.[12] Whereas in the West, people stand in a hierarchical relationship between God and animals, the Japanese regard themselves laterally connected to animals. In Japan, many animals are close relatives of the Gods (e.g. fox, cow, pigeon and monkey). And, whereas in Japan, animals and Gods share the same world, the West worships the trinity in heaven (Kawai Masao 1993: 62). When staying among monkeys to conduct research, relates Kawai, the Japanese can easily individuate monkeys' faces, remember their names, and tell their family members; Westerners, by contrast, are unable to individuate monkeys. So Westerners accuse the Japanese of disturbing the monkeys and creating feelings of incongruence (*iwakan*) among them, especially in the case of the Japanese macaque.[13] For instance, a Japanese researcher studied 306 baboons in Ethiopia and remembered a hundred of them, while an Englishman could only remember the eighteen male leaders he had studied. It is said, Kawai believes, that the Japanese have an unusual capacity for individuating monkeys. The Ōbei-ans, Kawai asserts, tie a collar around the necks of wild monkeys or chalk numbers on them as if they are prisoners: in prison the individuality of all members is neutralized and the prisoners are recognized by their numbers only. By contrast, Japanese research progresses through the close relation between the Japanese culture of the researchers and the monkeys (Kawai 1993: 63–5). Invoking Tsunoda's thesis on the Japanese brain, Kawai believes the Japanese have a unique feeling of natural aesthetics, especially with regard to birds and insects. The Japanese process their sounds by the left hemisphere and Europeans by the right hemisphere (Kawai 1993: 67).

Nowadays, Kawai argues, Ōbei places stress on 'animal rights' and 'animal welfare', and sensational voices are raised against killing whales. Japan is different as it upholds a more fundamental animal rights and welfare movement. Furthermore, Kawai adds, the idea of concluding a contract, taken from the Bible, is very strong in Ōbei. Now it is thought that the contract between animals and humans has to be revised. In Japan, Umehara ('my respected teacher') advocates going back to the ancient Jōmon ways of hunting and gathering (see below). Abroad, Kawai concludes, this kind of thinking is gradually emerging as well (Kawai 1993: 73).

The use of Imanishi's theory of group evolution and Tsunoda's linguistic brain thesis enables Kawai to isolate Japan from both the West and China. On the one hand, Kawai creates a greater distance between the Japanese and Ōbei-ans than the one he claims to exist between the Japanese and macaques. The latter pair understands one another intuitively and instinctively, while the rift between Western individualism and Japanese group behaviour separates the latter. For Western individuals can only think in rational terms of laws and numbers, while the Japanese, due to their instinctive group behaviour, have reached a relatively higher level of communication in the evolution of species. On the other hand, in his hurry to distance himself from the West, Kawai invokes Tsunoda's linguistic brain experiments. These, however, do not only show a difference between the sound processing of Western and Japanese brains, but also between the Japanese and Chinese and Korean brains, as the Chinese and Korean languages do not belong to the vowel-abundant Japanese and Polynesian tongues (Tsunoda 1985: 138). In Kawai's theory, therefore, the barrier between cultures has been fortified by biological, psychological, linguistic, aesthetic and social factors. It makes one wonder to whom is Kawai trying to explain his ideas.

A Japanese solution to climatic deterioration: Animism renaissance

The following examples do not only show the ambivalent use of concepts of nature to characterize culture in a politically meaningful way, but also how long-term histories can be mobilized in support of characterizations. It is especially phenomena that seem to be above human control, such as the climate and evolution, that are mobilized in such manner.

Yasuda Yoshinori,[14] a scholar much influenced by the *fūdo* theory of Watsuji Tetsurō,[15] employs such a climatic determinism in his characterization of East and West. With the help of pollen analysis, Yasuda found that the origins of the Eastern and Western *fūdo* go back 730,000 years, when the atmosphere of the Himalayas brought about a climatic difference between them. At the same time, in humans a great evolutionary change occurred: *Homo erectus* emerged. It was the time that Stone Age man began to show progress in his stone tool-making techniques, when man started to make fire and developed the capacity of thinking through language. In Asia, *Homo erectus* appeared around the same time (Yasuda 1993: 153–5). Thus, when the climatic contrast between East and West was formed, *Homo erectus* came into being.

Yasuda points out that the culture of the ancient Stone Age of *Homo erectus* shows clear regional differences between East and West: the West's ancient Stone Age culture centred around the stone axe, while that of the Eastern region made use of chopping tools. The climatic background of this polar difference was the wet East and the dry West. In a *fūdo* with an abundance of forests and a high level of moisture, the birth of the chopping tool culture was highly probable, while in dry areas with steppes the axe culture was likely to come about. Climatic and vegetational differences were reflected in the different kind of Stone Age culture of East and West. About 500,000 years ago, *Homo erectus* in the West evolved into *Homo sapiens*; in the East, this transition occurred more than 200,000 years later. According to Yasuda, the reason for this can be found in the wet climate and the forests of the East and the droughts and steppes of the West. The Eastern *fūdo* provided

50 Group categorization

the circumstances in which Eastern man could evolve more gradually compared with Western man. This difference presented itself again in the physical development of Eastern and Western humans (Yasuda 1993: 156–8).

Yasuda argues the different evolutionary roads taken by Eastern and Western culture on the basis of long-term historical changes in world climate. As a result of climatic warming, approximately 15,000 years ago, there was a large population increase, which caused food shortage. This induced a large population decrease during the last major Ice Age (Pleistocene, c. 2 million to 10,000 years ago). When 13,000 years ago the climate started to warm up again it caused enormous tidal waves, also in Japan. Melting snow caused floods and food crises resulted. Necessity induced the invention of new tools, marking the beginning of agriculture (Yasuda 1993: 159–60). Pollen analysis shows that in areas of steppe the *fūdo* was most conducive to the growth of wild grasses, ultimately leading to the cultivation of wheat and millet, and animal husbandry. This happened first in north-east Syria, while around 7,000 years ago, in China, along the Yangtze valley the marshes and forests gave birth to rice cultivation.[16] In East Asia, the late Pleistocene also stimulated the development of agriculture and caused great environmental changes in Japan. Below forty degrees northern latitude, falling broad-leaf forest started to expand. This is the area where the ancient pottery culture of the Jōmon was found. The Jōmon lived on nuts (chestnuts), acorns, mountain crops and fishing. The people first settled in Japan about 12,000 years ago, and used the forests as means of subsistence. The wet forests of east Asia and the dry steppes of west Asia gave rise to the entirely different *fūdos* of rice and of other grain crops, such as wheat (Yasuda 1993: 163–6).

When in Europe the climate became harsher, relates Yasuda, people started to subjugate nature to their wishes. They used science as a weapon against nature without taking into account the *fūdo* and, later, even started to call it environmental determinism (Yasuda 1993: 178). As a result, Eastern thought, based on the *fūdo* of the forests, has the task to rescue the world, which is being destroyed by modern Western technology (Yasuda 1993: 182). In dealing with issues of the global environment, Yasuda recommends, Japan needs to be aware of monsoon Asia (including Japan) as described by Watsuji Tetsurō: 'because of the violence of nature, people did not choose to control nature, rather, they chose to be passive and persevere'. Yasuda concludes that, 'We need to study once more the potential role of Monsoon Asia in establishing a grand model.' He urges more 'actively engaged' research as 'the world in ten years time may no longer need a grand model'.[17] In order to resuscitate the forests, Yasuda presents us with the concept of 'animism renaissance', which explains how man fell from forest life, and how to revive its spirit. Yasuda's 'genealogy of the civilization of deforestation' describes how the people of Europe inherited the civilization of Mesopotamia, around 5,000 BP.[18] The philosophy of Christianity he regards responsible for the expansion of this 'civilization of deforestation'. The German and Celtic gods of animism were eliminated by the invasion of Christianity, and the trees,

Natural categorization 51

sacred to these gods, were cut down by the Christians. The ideology of this 'civilization of deforestation' invaded primitive civilizations, which were peaceful and part of a system of harmony between man and nature. Yasuda concludes that the invasion and expansion of Christianity destroyed the world of animism.

By contrast, forest civilization, which owing to isolation still survives in Japan today, is based on the harmony between man and nature. Yasuda tells its story: the origin of 'forest civilization' in Japan can be traced back to 12,500 BP, when the climate softened at the end of the glacial period. The hunters and gatherers of Japan's neolithic Jōmon culture developed by utilizing the plentiful resources of the forest. Because the forest was thought of as essentially mysterious and divine, Yasuda calls Jōmon man animistic. Animism was able to survive after the introduction of agriculture because traditional Japanese rice cultivation was not plagued by domesticated animals that eat the leaves and bark of trees. Instead, Japanese rice cultivation was closely linked with the resources of the forest. According to Yasuda, animism survived until recent decades, maintaining the traditions begun by Jōmon culture. Shinto played an important role in preserving animism, he argues,[19] 'as the trees sacred to the gods survived in the consecrated precinct of Shinto shrines'. But Yasuda regrets that in the past 20 years people have forgotten the gods of the forest, which have been replaced by the gods of computers. He observes a parallel between the severe destruction of nature and the disappearance of animism. As a contribution to the future of mankind, he recommends a revival of the more pragmatic aspects of animism and their application to modern society.

What to some academics seems like a simplistic generalization, to others appears to be an elegant hypothesis. Which aspects of this long-term approach do we take seriously? In forming a view on Yasuda's animism renaissance, short of becoming climatologists and archaeologists ourselves, we can check out the adequacy of the units of research and the time-scales employed in such long-term approaches to large research entities. For instance, the two genealogies of Shinto and Christianity are equated with a forest civilization and with a civilization of forest destruction. In turn, these are equated with Japan and the West, as if there are no environmentalist movements in regions tainted by the Abrahamic religions; and, as if Japan is not a large consumer of, especially, imported timber.[20] This seems problematic.

More remarkable, however, is how political advice on specific cultural behaviour is drawn from findings based on long-term studies of the climatic environment, which involve units of measurement larger than 10 thousand years. The assumption that cultural change follows transformations in the climatic environment and can be objectively measured over periods of thousands of years makes sense only if you want to investigate trends in climatic transformation over long periods of time and make inferences about long-term changes. If, however, an analysis of environmental change over millennia enables only some humans of a specific nationality to steer

52 *Group categorization*

the course of world history away from a Western, problem-ridden modernity, we seem to be dealing with an ideological quick-fix solution aimed at an escape from the modern time warp. If this forest-spirited nation is to succeed in leading the world back into the past (such as to the forests life of the Jōmon) it means that the control of humanity by only a few can been realized. This in itself could be considered to be against all odds, for how can the political culture of just a few people succeed in planning changes in a history that is measured in time units of millennia and steered by its *fūdo*? If, on the other hand, humankind would realize a spontaneous return to natural life for the next few 10 thousands of years, a planned organization seems to be redundant. In any case, a short period of human steering of mankind seems an extraordinary defeat of statistical chance in an eternal period of natural law. It would be interesting to see how many long-term theorists over the centuries have pressurized their 'too modern' contemporaries into a speedy return to the time-tested ancient ways of 'natural' life.

The king's fall from the forest and Western Cartesian thought

Umehara Takeshi is even more zealous in advocating the revival of the spirit of the forest than Yasuda.[21] Umehara advises research into the change of the environment, not just by means of the reliable data of science, but also by means of social science, as he believes it is linked up with human fate. Moreover, social science and the humanities are also to take part in saving the world from science. The origins of modern Western thought, Umehara argues, lie in the science of Bacon and Descartes. In their turn, they were influenced by the traditions of Christianity and Greek thought. Despite the impression one may form on the basis of his oeuvre, which for a large part criticizes what he regards as the West, Umehara made explicit his intention not to polarize Western and Eastern thought (Umehara Takeshi 1993: 10–16).

Despite his oeuvre, Umehara regards Heidegger as the greatest philosopher of the twentieth century owing to his views on Western thought, which Umehara found subjectivist and anthropocentric (Umehara 1993: 17); but also because Heidegger greatly valued forests.[22] Umehara explains where the West went wrong. The West, Umehara associates with Christianity, which derived through the Greek and Egyptian civilizations from Mesopotamia. In turn, Mesopotamian civilization succeeded the society of hunters and gatherers. When agriculture was introduced to Mesopotamia, man began to control nature. It led to the first urban civilization, the Sumer, created by King Gilgamesh of Uruk. The king had killed the god of the forests, Chumbaba, who was a snake. This act of killing changed the fate of forest civilization. Killing the god of the forest meant felling the forests to build 'urban civilization'.[23] And in the remainders of these civilizations, today, no forests are left: they were swallowed by desert.

Natural categorization 53

After urban civilization moved to Europe, the industrial revolution gave birth to a new form of knowledge. This science became an even stronger weapon against nature than urban civilization had been. The new modern civilization did not just destroy the forest in its own countries but also the rain forests in Asia and the Amazon region. Umehara believes Western philosophy played a main role in rationalizing the means by which to destroy nature. In its stead, Umehara advocates a New World philosophy in which Japanese philosophers play an active part (Umehara 1993: 20–3). For example, Nishida Kitarō criticized the Cartesian duality between subject and object, and united them;[24] the famous environmental (*milieu*) philosopher, Watsuji Tetsurō, developed the concepts of *fūdo* and *aidagara*. *Aidagara* embodies an ethical relationship between people, just as is the case in some Buddhist concepts.[25] From the points of view of Nishida and Watsuji, according to Umehara, it is possible to develop an original (Japanese) theory (Umehara 1993: 23). The *fūdo* of the monsoon region developed in east Asia is very different from that of steppes and deserts. According to Umehara, Watsuji's *fūdo* theory is not Eurocentric but universal, and an achievement of Japanese philosophy. The only thing Umehara finds unconvincing is the absence of the forest in Watsuji's taxonomy of *fūdo*. Watsuji compared the different regions of the world by making a distinction between the *fūdo* of the steppes, the desert and the monsoon. The first two, Umehara argues, are ecological–environmental concepts while only the latter focuses on climate. From the start, Umehara opines, Watsuji should have selected the *fūdo* of the forest instead of that of monsoon. In the contemporary world, he argues, *fūdo* theory will be extremely useful as an ecological lead for the world to follow (Umehara 1993: 24–5).

Another lead is that of rice civilization. Rice civilization, according to Umehara, exists in symbiosis with the forests: it was born from the forests. Although trees were felled and plains were used as fields for paddies, a part of the forests was left untouched, and functioned to hold the soil together and retain water necessary for the irrigation of fields. In Japan, Umehara maintains, agriculture arrived quite late, around 2,000 years ago, and it did not start with wheat but with rice cultivation, a legacy from the forest civilization of hunters and gatherers. When agriculture and animal husbandry were introduced, man interfered with the relationship between man and nature. At present, Umehara concludes, we can do nothing but return to the forest civilization of hunters and gatherers. Umehara believes it is feasible to return to nature from a development stage of ultra-sophisticated technology. He therefore underlines the words of Fukui Kenichi, a Nobel prize-winning scientist, who advocates employing science and technology in our respect for and worship of nature (Umehara 1993: 26–7).[26]

In the theories of Umehara and Yasuda the influence of climate on the evolution of nations and world regions is immense and, similar to biological evolution, its relationship with culture is ambivalent. The concept of *fūdo*, however, is even more intricate than that of evolution because it also

54 Group categorization

incorporates aspects of culture. To users and protagonists of the concept and ideology of *fūdo*, however, its validity reaches beyond the scope of human individuals and groups. Even before *Homo erectus* could walk upright, it constituted the environment that, long before its realization, staged specific kinds of human behaviour, such as axeing or chopping. Furthermore, *fūdo* constitutes both cause and effect, which makes it an ideal model for theories that use descriptions of nature to provide prescriptions for human behaviour. Which is cause and which is effect? Killing the god of the forest is as much an effect of making the step to urban civilization as it is the cause of its downfall. Or rather should we ask the symbolic question of whether the king had a choice to kill Chumbaba? Do contemporary academics, according to Umehara and Yasuda, face a similar choice? For the most important characteristic of *fūdo* seems to be its continuity, which favours a people submerged in the right kind of *fūdo*, that is, the forest. The future of this people is blessed with a favourable *fūdo* endowment, unless they come to violate it.[27]

Digging up genetic roots: The reappropriation of the past

Considerable efforts have been put into finding the roots of the Japanese people, as is witnessed by the numerous *nihonjin-ron* publications on the origin and essence of Japaneseness. In this context, the case of the Ainu has proved to be one of great cultural complexity and political sensitivity.[28] Generally, the Ainu nowadays are believed to be the aborigines of Japan, and, according to some academics, they therefore are more Japanese than are the Japanese.[29] However, it has taken much time and trouble for them to obtain recognition as a minority culture.[30] Although the origins of the Japanese have been the object of long and heated debate, most researchers now agree that the Ainu are the aborigines of Japan, and that the 'later' Japanese came either from Southeast Asia or north-east Asia. In this debate Hanihara Kazurō proposed the 'dual-structure model' to explain the population history of the Japanese, including the Okinawa islanders and the Ainu. The model assumes that the first occupants of the Japanese archipelago came from somewhere in Southeast Asia in the Upper Palaeolithic age and that they gave rise to the people in the Neolithic Jōmon age, or Jōmonese. A second wave of migration from north-east Asia followed, which ushered in the Yayoi era. However, the populations of the various lineages intermingled only gradually. As a consequence, the dual-structure model assumes that the population intermixture is still going on and that the dual structure of the Japanese population is maintained even today. According to Hanihara, both physical and cultural regional differences in the Japan, for example, between eastern and western Japan, are explained by the varying rates of intermixture from region to region. In his view, the dual-structure model generally agrees not only with physical and cultural evidence but also with

Natural categorization 55

non-human evidence as revealed by research on the genetic make-up of Japanese dogs and mice (Hanihara Kazurō 1991).

In 1970, Omoto Kei'ichi's research on blood types and proteins showed that the Ainu who, on the basis of the texture of their skin and the shape of their bones, were thought to be related to Europeans, actually used to live on the main island of Honshu. Thus, they have the same Asian roots as do other Japanese (Omoto 1996). Omoto rejects Hanihara's 'dual-structure thesis' that the Jōmon (who were short of stature, possessed deep facial features and roundly shaped faces) came from Southeast Asia and that the Yayoi (who were tall and had flat faces) came from north-east Asia. In fact, maintains Omoto, genetic research shows that the Ainu came from groups similar to those of north-east Asia, but arrived in Hokkaido earlier than did the Yayoi. Omoto's thesis is that the Jōmon's ancestors came from north-east Asia, and that, thereafter, new groups entered Japan from north-east Asia to form the Yayoi by mingling partly with the old Jōmon groups. It also explains that the Ainu are genetically close to the Okinawans and that the Hondo (main island, Japan proper) Japanese are genetically close to the people from the Korean peninsula.[31]

But how do we explain the drastic differences in facial appearance and the area of hair coverage between the Ainu and *Wajin* (lit. 'peace people')? In the late Palaeolithic period, populations with generalized morphological features, proto-Mongoloids, inhabited East Asia. During the last glacial age, which peaked some 20,000 years ago, populations of north-eastern Asia suffering from extreme coldness sustained a drastic phenotypic change due to adaptation. The results of this change include the flattened face, a stocky build, the flat eyelid with Mongoloid fold and hairlessness. The populations isolated in the Japanese archipelago did not suffer from this extreme cold, and therefore did not undergo the same alterations. After the glacial period and, by then, aftermath of the neolithic revolution, the so-called neo-Mongoloid populations of north-eastern Asia experienced a drastic population expansion, and some of them migrated into Japan through the Korean peninsula. In contrast with the newcomers, the Ainu may have been the last of the native population of Japan who were phenotypically the least affected by the glacial period (Omoto 1992: 142).

The question of the relationship between the Ainu and the 'Japanese' is very important to contemporary debates on the origins of Japan, especially to Umehara Takeshi. Because for a long time the Ainu were believed to constitute a branch of the Caucasian race, Umehara argues in conversation with Hanihara, anthropologists, archaeologists and linguists had neglected them. Therefore, it became impossible to establish a proper *nihonjin-ron* (Umehara Takeshi and Hanihara Kazurō 1982: 102–3). In order to explain the continuity and differences between the Jōmon and the Ainu, according to Hanihara, the concept of 'small evolution' is required (Umehara and Hanihara 1982: 130). Erroneously, the Kinki people, who occupy the region around present-day Kyoto, for a long time had been thought to be the centre

56 *Group categorization*

of Japanese culture but, racially, they now appear to be the 'least Japanese' and rather like 'foreigners' (*gaikokujin*) (Umehara and Hanihara 1982: 139). Even though it is not entirely sure that the Ainu and the Ryukyuans belong to the same race, Hanihara reasons they probably have preserved characteristics of the people of the Jōmon era. In other words, Umehara opines, it would be better to think of them as the race that has preserved the characteristics of the ancient Mongolians (Umehara and Hanihara 1982: 150). Hanihara confirms this, believing it is highly probable that the proto-Mongoloids moved to Japan during the diluvial epoch to avoid the cold (as they were not yet cold resistant). Hanihara points out, however, that the proto-Mongoloids probably evolved into neo-Mongoloids by acquiring new traits (small regional evolution) (Umehara and Hanihara 1982: 154). Judging from current research, Hanihara claims, the people from the Jōmon age, in the absence of much interbreeding (*konketsu*) or population replacement, have undergone a 'small evolution' into the present Japanese under the influence of the environment and culture. Therefore, it is not appropriate to revive the thesis that 'equates the Jōmon era to the Ainu', that is the 'inbreed thesis' without redressing it with the concept of small evolution first (Umehara and Hanihara 1982: 155–6).[32]

The theories of Omoto and Hanihara show there is no agreement on where exactly the Japanese come from and in what order the various groups of migrants have entered Japan. Omoto argues that the different groups have all come from the north, while Hanihara thinks the first groups came from south-west Asia. In order to support his dual-structure thesis, Hanihara inserted a 'small evolution' theory to explain that the Ainu have evolved since the Jōmon era without having interbred with the Yayoi people. In this way, according to Umehara, the Ainu could have evolved biologically and at the same time preserved their proto-Mongoloid traits, representing the native population 'least phenotypically affected'. Thus the Ainu and Ryukyuans are not only the newly found ancestors of the Japanese but also turn out to be the only peoples to have preserved the characteristics of the proto-Mongoloids. Umehara even appoints the Ainu and Ryukyuans as the ancestors of the entire Mongoloid race. For not only do the Ainu and Wajin (Japanese) have the Jōmon as ancestors, somehow the Jōmon also are the offspring of the ancient Mongoloids, whose features have been preserved in Japan in the Ainu and Ryukyuans.

Natural group categories in short

In this chapter I argued that forms of natural discrimination and classification make for a crude means of inducing division between groups that encourage politics of difference and nationalist sentiment. However, it seems pointless and politically suspect to single out one type of racial discrimination, such as that of non-chosen people, as a unique or exclusive practice of one nation.

Both obvious and subtle expressions of racialist discourse may affect public

Natural categorization 57

debate on cultural issues. Racial explanations of human behaviour refer to physiological features, even though other factors may be more plausible. Ideology might blind us to the possibilities of other explanations, because ideology reduces our field of vision and limits the categories available to us when we observe and deal with the problems around us. Becoming aware of the fact that we observe the world through categories and that we need to discriminate between the things we experience in order to create categories may help us to make up our minds about which categories we find harmful and helpful.

The brain theory of Tsunoda makes a racial distinction between the brains of linguistic groups, which Tsunoda regards as a result of the continued particularity of the neurophysiological characteristics of the Japanese brain and the uniqueness of the Japanese language. While the racial link in Tsunoda's theory constitutes an indelible imprint of linguistic culture on the brain, in Yōrō Takeshi's more subtle theory of brainism the link between brain and culture is gradually eroded by processes of urbanism and globalization. In order to reverse this trend, Yōrō advocates a life of harmony between the cultural mind and the natural body. This involves a rerooting of cerebral activities into the cultural body of the Japanese. Kawai Masao discovers the greater likeness between the Japanese instinct and that of macaques to that of Westerners. Kawai's use of physiological traits isolates racially the Japanese from the Chinese and Western individuals. The use of Imanishi Kinji's theory of group evolution, Tsunoda's linguistic brain thesis and his own primatology enable Kawai Masao to define the Japanese as more natural than other ethnic groups.

While some academic framers of the nation find the root of difference between East and West in the human brain, genes, instinct and linguistic behaviour, others discover it in the environment. In my discussion of Yasuda's climatic determinism, Umehara Takeshi's nativist Jōmon theory of forest life, and in Hanihara Kazurō's and Omoto Kei'ichi's respective quests for the genetic roots of the Japanese, I elaborated on the fallacy of using universalistic long-term approaches for providing cultural short-term solutions.

The idea that 'Japanese' ancient cultural features, social forms, hunting habits, art and language have been preserved over long periods of time in the Ainu has inspired contemporary artists and academics in their work.[33] In Umehara Takeshi's work, the recognition of the Ainu as a biological link with the past, have provided the formerly rootless Wajin (Japanese) with a new narration of human origin and with a racial link, as Mongoloid predecessor, to China. Interestingly, the Japanese academics that tend to fraternize with China, such as Umehara and Yasuda, are hesitant to point out the shared background of Confucianism, Buddhism, Taoism, Zen and Chinese characters as the basis for a shared culture. The relevance of these links is denied by merely referring to their indigenized forms, although rice cultivation is marked as the basis of the historical and cultural identity they have in common. Thus, joint archaeological research in south-western China

58 *Group categorization*

(Sichuan) contrasts ancient Chinese civilization, based on rice culture, with the northern heartland along the Yellow River, where wheat cultivation (and other grains, but without rice as a staple crop) and animal husbandry are more common.

As for the animistic and Jōmonese methods for escaping the modern time warp, it is hard to see, however, how the rice-growers can succeed in persuading the 'West' to return to the forest. After all, according to the logic of *fūdo*, Western climate, Cartesian thought and the disappearance of the forests hamper the West's acquisition of a profound understanding of nature. Nor is it easy to see how, at present, Chinese modernizers could abandon their efforts for the way of the forests, even though Chinese tradition serves as a source for finding environmental friendly ways to modernize. Many a scholar would argue that a clue to solving the country's environmental problems lies in further modernization rather than in less.

Although climate influences the ways in which communities are organized, in studying society we need to differentiate climate from other influences. We also need to think about where, how and why we draw boundaries between (e.g. national, regional and local) communities when we try to solve societal problems by means of comparative approaches. Any advice given on short-term human action based on laws deduced from long-term environmental observations of nature seems to beg the question: why did nature allow man to stray? In fact the issue belongs to a genre of questions that are religious in nature as they build upon a belief of unspoilt origins, man's fall from paradise, chosen people and the redemption of mankind. In the examples above, the origins of man lie in the forest, the fall from paradise is symbolized by the king killing the god of the forest, and rescue from modernity, that culmination of alienation from nature, can be found in the Japanese preservation of ancient instincts over time. The revival of animism here means the escape from the modern time warp, the temporal mistake.

This environmentalist fallacy flourishes in the *nihonjin-ron*, but it is shared by any long-term historical approach that tries to dictate short-term answers to cultural and political problems. Turning minorities into national ideal types, and anchoring the past in their genes, language and culture are examples of producing national identity by misappropriating the past. It constitutes a detemporalization of human history, for time becomes essentialized in timeless essences, such as in eternal laws of environmental change. Thus, the celebration of the ascribed characteristics of a minority culture, such as the Ainu, seems quite obscene. The group is weakened to such an extent that its language must be sustained by academic journals, its rights defended by lawyers and academics, and its lifestyles are appropriated by contemporary nostalgic trendsetters. Judging from these attempts to go back in time, it seems that our return tickets are no longer valid.

5 Culturalist categorization

This chapter starts out with an exploration of cultural definitions of nations and world regions validated through notions borrowed from both science (ecology and biology, such as the environment, gender, genetic law and cerebral functions) and the humanities (language, psychology, history). I show how the use of natural and scientific symbolism, instead of celebrating the world's cultural diversity, obstructs cross-cultural communication by rooting cultural differences in various notions of nature.

Cultural systems of classification are often thought to be politically harmless. After all, classifications created on the basis of learnt culture, short of absolute forms of cultural relativism, proceed from the idea of the basic similarity of human beings. Some cultural classification systems, however, facilitate extreme forms of cultural relativism, thereby excluding some peoples by attaching crucial meaning to 'natural markers' in definitions of culture.

Finally, I show that the structure of culturalist argumentation and the 'scientific evidence' in the work of four academic researchers (two from China and two from Japan) are unrelated to the specific claims of national particularity. Thus, similar functions are attributed to notions of East and West, the left and right cerebral hemispheres, femininity and masculinity, while in fact application of these concepts varies according to the political and disciplinary background of the author, rather than their nationality.

Academic theories that routinely proceed from cultural group classifications (cultural groupings) contrast with those based on the classification of groups borrowed from nature (natural groupings) as the latter pretend to have universal implications. Theories based on cultural groupings identify people as collectives primarily on the basis of spiritual and cognitive factors, which are thought to be native to their 'home'. Cultural groups are assigned traits on the basis of cultural markers, such as shared history, customs, language, cultural knowledge, group-psyche, particular forms of family organization and traditions of work division. These features are usually believed to originate in an ancient cultural source or to have emerged a very long time ago, having grown into stable structures embodied in, for instance, the national psyche and language.

60 *Group categorization*

Cultural systems of classification are often assumed to be politically harmless as classifications created on the basis of learnt culture, short of absolute forms of cultural relativism, proceed from the idea that inter-human communication and understanding is possible if we are prepared to be open to other ideas, customs and experiences. Although overcoming cultural differences may require much effort, at least it makes possible, in principle, communication between various groups of people. Some cultural classification systems, however, facilitate extreme forms of cultural relativism, thereby excluding some peoples from interhuman communication by attaching 'natural markers' to cultural definitions of human groups. The meaning of culture in such theories is ambiguous bordering on extreme forms of cultural relativism and in some cases racism. Thus some cultural categories of humans are alleged to have a particular kind of brain or instinct as the result of a long-term historical development of the cultural traits inherent to their particular ethnic make-up. For example, the 'cultural gene' argument claims that the brain has been altered and shaped by certain linguistic habits formed over long periods of time. Alternatively, it attributes certain kinds of behaviour to language acquisition, creating differences between social groups that are virtually impossible to overcome.

The examples below derive from academic communities in China and Japan, where debates of national identity based on dualistic contrasts between East and West thrive both as tools for international policy-making and conducting academic argument at home. The structural frame in which arguments are moulded, constituting contrastive and dualistic notions of the nation-state, East and West, yin and yang, and left and right hemisphere, male and female, English and Japanese/Chinese, seems to betray their outcome. By not adequately taking into consideration empirical evidence, such frames constitute an open invitation to politics, turning the personal into politics and encouraging the formulation of political issues in imprecise concepts and symbolically laden notions of international relations.

To make clear the ambiguous relationship between the universal and particular in culturalist theories I use examples taken from the works of academics with strong political convictions, which they do not clearly separate from the academic theories they try to convey. Solutions to world problems (usually blamed on Western modernity) are found in cultural sources that derive from the East. In the first three examples the suitability of these cultural sources from the East is justified by referring to evidence from modern science, while the last example borrows concepts from Jungian analyses of the unconscious.

The universality of primitive forest culture: Umehara Takeshi's Jōmon

Academics use various academic disciplines in claims about the unique nature of the nation. Religion, ethics and environmental studies are all mobilized in

Culturalist categorization 61

support of the particular moral standards of the nation, its longstanding history and contributions to science. They frequently point out the value of interdisciplinary approaches to the comparative study of nation-states. Thus the interplay of religion, biology, archaeology, anthropology, sociology, psychology and ethics is exploited in the colourful oeuvre of Umehara Takeshi, the founding director of Nichibunken.

Umehara Takeshi is known in international environmental circles for his stance on world ecological problems. Part of his mission is to incite the world to emulate ancient forest cultures. In Japan, Umehara is known for his views in the fields of religion, philosophy and literature. He champions a brand of Japanese Buddhism, which, he argues, has been shaped under the influence of the ancient culture of the Jōmon.[1] The Japanese, Umehara asserts, possess an 'intuitive ethical sensibility', causing them to have certain feelings of doubt about issues such as homosexuality and brain death. Umehara explains: 'No doubt the great majority of Japanese feel that homosexuality goes against the natural order of things in the same sense that castration and foot binding do. Apparently they view organ transplants with a similar suspicion (Umehara 1989b: 79–80).[2] Umehara believes that brain death, regarded as the medical and legal definition of death, is the ultimate vindication of the Cartesian human-machine dichotomy: 'Attempting to legitimise murder with the expedient concept of brain death is the worst sort of self-deception. This is the kind of fraudulent logic one must use to justify transplants if one interprets the procedure within the framework of Cartesian thinking' (Umehara 1989: 80). Instead, Umehara recommends the idea of reincarnation, according to which the spirit travels to the nether world, abides there for a while, and then returns to this world as one of the descendants of the deceased:

> This concept, primitive though it may sound to us now, contains an important scientific truth: *the idea that genes do not die*. If we interpret the 'spirit' as genetic information, the ancient Japanese belief accords with the findings of modern science.
>
> (Umehara 1989a: 81)

Using the idea of reincarnation, in Umehara's view, facilitates the realization of self-sacrifice, as in nature self-sacrifice for the survival of the species is a common phenomenon. Mahayana Buddhism in particular stresses such behaviour, Umehara explains, because the bodhisattva is a being of infinite mercy, sacrificing everything for the benefit of others. In a famous ancient story, a young prince – Gautama Buddha in an earlier incarnation – throws himself down from a cliff to allow a starving mother tiger to feed on his body.[3] The donation of organs should be undertaken in this spirit, Umehara advises. A part of oneself will live on in another human being, sustaining the cycle of death and rebirth. The recipient must accept this gift with boundless gratitude, as organ exchange should not be done in an impersonal manner.

62   *Group categorization*

Instead, Umehara argues for establishing a society of bodhisattvas for doctors, who follow the example of selflessness, set by people like the Japanese surgical pioneer Hanaoka Seishū (Umehara 1989b: 81).[4]

In Umehara's mind religion (Mahayana Buddhism) and biology (Jōmon intuition, survival of the species) have become intertwined in an explanation of the Japanese ethical view. This bio-religious determinism makes it particularly difficult for a critic to form an academic counter-argument as the theory precludes communication between cultural groups from the start. A critical argument against the presumption of the inheritability of group intuition in biological terms can always also be met by an argument that 'proves' the same argument by couching it in the ethical notions that support the biological presumption in the first place. Such intertwining of religious and biological factors is not particular to Umehara's work, but is common in academic works that do not subscribe to an *impartial* principle of evolution and aim to prove the national particularity of the biological nation. An environmental determinism based on the notion of *milieu* (*fūdo*) equally erects cultural boundaries that set the Japanese apart from other 'species'.

The point here is that Umehara at once argues for the uniqueness of the (what he calls) Japanese view and for its universal nature, trying to convince the world of the validity of his philosophy. The Japanese view of the nether world, Umehara says, is an extremely primitive one, probably of Palaeolithic origin, and represents the primordial concept of the afterlife. It admits no distinction between heaven and hell and thus lacks such concepts as final judgement, karma and retribution. The differentiation of Japanese concepts into realms of light and dark and the notion of a moral reckoning were superimposed later, when the Japanese started to abandon forest life. And as urban civilization developed, the ancient values of the Jōmon were projected on to the world beyond, just as were the values of other primitive peoples. From this Umehara deduces that the prototypical Japanese view of the nether world was at one time a universal concept, shared by many primitive peoples. In most parts of the world, however, it was unable to survive the shift to agricultural and urban civilization. But, claims Umehara, it persisted in Japan because hunting and gathering were superseded by wet-rice cultivation at a relatively late date and, even then, many elements of the earlier Palaeolithic culture were kept.

Ultimately Umehara tries to convince his audience by scientific authority for his argument that modern scientific truths were hidden within the so-called primitive religions all along. To the world's great religions with their anthropocentric orientation, Umehara argues, the notion that humankind is one with the rest of nature may seem backward and childish. Yet, he asks rhetorically, does not this view prefigure the scientific principles revealed by modern biologists since Darwin? Over the past century or so it has become clear that living creatures were not created one after another by an anthropomorphic god, as the Old Testament claims, but emerged from one vast evolutionary flow. It also showed that life is inextricably bound up with the movement of the universe as a whole. Thus, Umehara concludes, the view inherent in animism – the idea that mountains, rivers, plants and trees all achieve Buddhahood – agrees in essence with the understanding of life arrived at by modern science.

Umehara's view of Japanese culture generalizes the Jōmon instinct to a universal level. Although he makes a point of being a philosopher, not a scientist, Umehara likes to see his views being corroborated by scientific means in print. To Umehara, the pure innocence of the Japanese has been preserved. However, as even in Kyoto, home to Umehara, it is hard to argue convincingly that the city has preserved the forest spirit, apart from in its temples, Umehara reverts to human intuition and instinct to which the Japanese mind is still intrinsically linked. Umehara's main message, however, is cultural and ethical. The racial and physical criteria Umehara uses in his argument are subordinate to the regional spirituality and morality of the Japanese, but its natural roots claim universality.

Yin–yang regulation of the two hemispheres: Ye Qiaojian

The following example culturalist categorization, which is based on yin–yang contrasts, shows how even subtle arguments by forging together natural and cultural categories may lead to simplistic and predictable results, as do unsophisticated ones. This is due to a general framework of oversimplified analytical and comparative units, which they share. Studies that compare East and West in terms of yin and yang are very marketable in both East and West. In the West, for instance, Fritjof Capra linked yin and yang through culture, science and religion with East and West, respectively (Capra 1992). In China, CASS professor Liu Changlin summarized the Chinese mode of traditional thought as the ten aspects of the 'cultural gene' (*wenhua jiyin*): feelings; interpersonal relations; function; the whole; cyclicality; symbols; synthesis; equality; time; and intuition. According to Liu, Chinese traditional culture forms a holistic unity and clearly is characterized by a tendency towards yin (the feminine). In his view then, the ten features correspond roughly to the psychological features of female thought (Liu Changlin 1990: 578–81).

Compared with such relatively basal argument, Ye Qiaojian's argument about cerebral functions is subtle. He is critical of the simplistic application of the notions of left and right cerebral functions to those of East and West. Ye's views are worth looking into because they touch upon important debates of interregional human difference. The way Ye nuances his arguments on the subject of cultural classification shows that he tries to avoid simplistic linguistic, cultural or biological determinism. However, despite his efforts to be rational, I argue that the way in which he deploys the regional unit in his comparative framework leads him to gross generalizations and an indirect cerebral determinism of the two world halves.

64 *Group categorization*

In his 'The Division of Labour between Left and Right Brains and Some Misunderstandings About Its Inferences' (Ye Qiaojian 1995: 71–6, 12), Ye criticizes the elementary attribution of analytical, abstract and cognitive thinking to the left cerebral hemisphere and the functions of synthetic, symbolic and visual thinking to the right. An extremely simplistic and unfounded thought association, he argues, is that between the right hemisphere with female attributes and the left with male ones. Ye especially stresses the fallacy of equating right hemispheric functions with the East, such as Jiang Qian did. Jiang asserts that, 'if we enlarge the asymmetrical functions of the two cerebral hemispheres to cover the world, then it would overlap with the difference in the national/racial modes of thought between East and West' (Jiang Qian 1993).

Ye points out that in Chinese tradition we can find plenty of instances of practices that are attributable to the left hemisphere, such as dissection in Chinese medicine and mechanical physics in Chinese agricultural studies. Conversely, creativity in Western art can be attributed to the right cerebral hemisphere. More plausible as an explanation for a correlation of cerebral functions with regional differences in East and West, according to Ye, is the process of growing up in the Chinese-character region (including Japan, Korea and Vietnam). The processing of characters is associated with concrete, spatial and holistic forms and that of the alphabet with abstract, temporal and analytical forms. Nevertheless, argues Ye, Chinese psychologists in the 1980s conducted experiments that show Chinese people do not have a superior left or right hemisphere. Instead, a great amount of evidence indicates hemispherical parity. The reason is, argues Ye, that the ideographic and phonetic aspects in the information processing of characters requires activity from both hemispheres of the brain (Ye Qiaojian 1995: 75). Therefore, Ye concludes, the difference between Eastern and Western people is that the brain of the former is characterized by equal parity between the right and left hemispheres, while the latter is not. Chinese traditional thought therefore is a little more feminine than that of Western thought.[5] According to Ye, Western people strictly separate abstract, and imaginary and symbolic thinking, while the Chinese regard them as mutually penetrating: 'Westerners can make a sharp contrast between rational and irrational thinking, while to the Chinese they are mixed like milk and water' (Ye Qiaojian 1995: 75). Furthermore, the Chinese make use of analogies and intuition in communication, and widely use this form of 'concrete rationality' (*juti lixing*) in traditional philosophy, art and science. While in the Western mind the links between whole and part are severed, in the mind of the Chinese they form a holographic whole.[6] Ye illustrates this by providing the examples of the 'correspondence between heaven and man' (*tianren-xiangying*), the similar structure of the family and the nation, and the metaphoric projection of the large in the small universe (*daxiao yuzhou*). Therefore, Ye observes, quoting from the medical classic, the *Huangdi Neijing*, one cannot blame former philosophers for saying that 'the wise examine the identical, the stupid the different' (*zhizhe cha tong, yuzhe cha yi*). In summary, Ye concludes that the difference between the modes of thinking in East and West is not one of bipolarity, not a simple difference between yin and yang, but a relative difference on a continuum, or a difference of yin and yang blending (Ye Qiaojian 1995: 12).

Yin and yang are confusing concepts as they sometimes function as analytical tools, and at other times as attributes of research objects (such as East and West). Saying that yin and yang features must not be viewed as diametrically opposed to one another is not the same as saying that the methodological tools of yin and yang are not diametrically opposed. By confusing the two, we end up measuring yin and yang by means of yin and yang. Ye complicates matters even further. After having argued that East and West do not represent yin and yang, but only possess yin and yang features, and after having measured them by means of yin and yang tools, he concludes that the difference between East and West is a matter of yin–yang blending. And as he considers the admixture of the East to be nicely balanced and that of the West as too yang, we are back at the beginning: the simplistic analogy between yin and yang and East and West. Thus Ye claims that with respect to pragmatic and technical invention on a low level, China and Japan, and other Eastern peoples have a superior tradition. On a higher level of abstract scientific invention, however, Europe and America and other Western peoples perform better. Of course, Ye warns, this difference cannot be deduced directly from the two hemispheres of the brain, because various cultural factors are involved. However, concludes Ye, the two polar tendencies of 'interflow and mutual blending' (*hutong-hurong*) and 'mutual exclusion and complementing' (*huzhi-hubu*) express the great disparity between Eastern and Western modes of thought (Ye Qiaojian 1995: 12).

Hu Fuchen: Taoist universality and Chinese scientific wisdom

Some authors claim that comparing cultures from East and West may lead to an increase in mutual understanding between the two and stimulate global dialogue. This cannot be said of Hu Fuchen's Taoist ideas (Hu Fuchen 1993: 87–99, 1995: 74–80, 1997: 8–10).[7] Hu uses his conception of East and West to draw the attention of other Chinese academics to Taoism. According to Hu, Western interest in Taoism expresses Western inferiority since it expresses a need for Taoism to make up for its defects (Hu Fuchen 1995, 1997). His claim of cultural superiority (if the West likes and lacks it, it must be good) is not so much a sign of chauvinism as a domestic sales technique for persuading opponents at home. He fortifies his concept of 'culture' with the weight of thousands of years of tradition, maintaining that 'tradition is the most inert and conservative force of a nation/race in society. (In the case of China) It coalesced for a historical period of ten million years, but the *minzu* (Race/Nation) cannot shake off cultural tradition' (Hu Fuchen 1995: 74).

66 *Group categorization*

According to Hu, the PRC has two traditions: the matriarchal and the patriarchal. Taoism carries the former and Confucianism the latter. In the Spring and Autumn period, Taoism was central in studies of peaceful rule. Confucianism, however, gained the upper hand. According to Hu, the cyclical transition of a matriarchal to a patriarchal society and vice versa, is predestined. Nevertheless, for the longstanding patriarchy of the Chinese nation/race (*Zhonghua Minzu*) there are geographical, economic, social and historical reasons.[8] The strength of Chinese tradition is apparent, Hu argues, from the brake it put on China's societal transformation. China did not make a transition to class society, for instance, because it had not experienced the turmoil of Ancient Greece, which had driven the region to forming a system of city-states. Instead, China used its lineages (blood relations, clans) to form a national patriarchate, a fact promptly noticed by Marx. This patriarchate lasted for 5 thousand years. At its top, the emperor held the position of the ruling father of the empire in which Confucian dogma held high the values of loyalty and filial piety. According to Hu, this system should be distinguished from the original teachings of Confucius and Mencius. The nature of Taoism was altered by the system, which turned into the way of Emperor Huang and Lao Zi (*Huang-Lao Dao*), a religious counter-weight to Confucianism. However, another form of government, legalism, became the instrument of the Confucian patriarchate. Since the Eastern Han, Hu explains, Confucianism became the way of the kings, and legalism the way of the chief's hegemony. Taoism no longer functioned as a political faction (Hu Fuchen 1993: 1–4, 1995: 74–7).

In exploring the coherence of the Chinese nation, Hu argues that Chinese culture may be divided into the elements of politics, economics, religion, philosophy, science, literature, art and ethnic customs. In the history of the Chinese race, Hu maintains, the cohesive powers they collectively emanate constitute the essence of the unity of Chinese culture. Thus in the blood of all Chinese nationals the genes of cultural traditions are passed on, and no one can cut off this endless line. Nevertheless, argues Hu, it is also true that foreign trees can be planted on Chinese soil as even tradition has the capacity to change. For example, Indian Buddhism and the May Fourth have fundamentally influenced the flow of Chinese history,[9] and so have calls for democracy, rule by law and human rights (Hu Fuchen 1997: 5–6). However, it is an age-old, conservative mechanism by which Chinese intellectuals were attracted to Marxism. Marxism and Chinese tradition have several elements in common, Hu observes. For example, the adage of 'the world belongs to everyone' (*tianxiaweigong*), the tradition of peasant resistance and Taoist dialectics are common to both. Furthermore, Taoism, too, was influenced by the West for certain elements were inserted (into Taoism) to overcome Western maladies. Therefore Hu urges China to watch over its treasures: 'Following the trend of increased communication between East and West, *we* (Chinese) must reconsider the significance of Taoism and Taoist culture for the present' (Hu Fuchen 1993: 6–7).

Culturalist categorization 67

Hu not only advocates the universal applicability of Taoism; he also amplifies its messages by furnishing his *Neidanxue* with modern scientific significance.[10] Taoism, according to Hu, seeks the common origins of the universe and the sources of natural reproduction, and it pursues enlightenment from insights into the essence of the universe. According to Hu's reading of Taoism, at the beginning there was only 'nothing' and 'being'. Being was created from nothing; then, there was a period of chaos, which comprised latent capacity and eternity. This became the Tao, the metaphysical principle of order in nature. The Tao gave birth to time and space, matter and spirit, movement and inertness, concrete existence and the natural world, human society and the individual. It links up the past with the present (Hu Fuchen 1993: 7). Hu bases this cosmology on the work of Lao Zi, who says: 'The Way gave birth to one, two gave birth to three, and three gave birth to the universe.'[11] 'One' here means the *qi* of chaos;[12] two, the dual nature of yin and yang; and, three, the three principles of the universe, in which *qi* plays a main role. *Neidanxue* distinguishes between *qi* before heaven and *qi* after heaven (*xiantianqi* and *houtianqi*). The latter refers to breath and the former to the original *qi* (*yuanqi*), or the function of the movement of fate. This *qi* is also called the Great Void (*tai yi zhengqi*).[13] It means the hidden order or 'vacuum' of chaos, which was the ontological state of existence before the universe came about, that is, before the big bang. It is a form of information that existed before the beginning. This *qi* (one) gave birth to yin and yang (two), of which the space in between constitutes an intermediate (three). This space is also defined as a clash between yin and yang (*chongqi*), providing empty space with qualitative features. Thus *neidanxue* regards these three basics also as *qi*, form (*xing*) and quality (*zhi*). These, again, are seen as corresponding to information (*xinxi*), energy (*nengli*), and matter (*wuzhi*) (Hu Fuchen 1993: 8–9).

Natural scientists, social scientists, philosophers, psychologists and biologists of the whole world will always be able to obtain enlightenment from the wisdom of Tao (especially *neidanxue*) (Hu Fuchen 1993: 9–10). Famous foreign authors, such as Needham, Yukawa Hideki and Fritjof Capra, Hu points out, all have acknowledged the value of Taoism for the present. Therefore Taoism must modernize soon by absorbing the quintessence of modern science and philosophy, and by correcting the defects of Western culture. Moreover, it is given the task of enriching Marxist philosophy, and to serve the modernization of Chinese spiritual and material civilization. And, finally, quoting the well-known Marxist scientist Qian Xuesen,[14] Hu concludes that the quintessence of Chinese traditional thought could enrich and develop Marxist philosophy, a great project of academic engineering (Hu Fuchen 1993: 23).

Hu does not only give Taoism a scientific foundation; he also gives the Tao a place in time before the emergence of gods in other religions. In this way Taoism can claim the most ancient tradition of them all. In the eyes of Chinese Confucians, says Hu, heaven is the source of values and

68 *Group categorization*

transcendental principles; in Western culture, by contrast, all that is unattainable by means of rationality is called God. Furthermore, according to Nietzsche, modern science and rationality have destroyed God. Nevertheless, Hu argues, God is not the ultimate limit of human rational thought. Instead, the Tao is, for it stems from before the birth of the universe. The Tao does not only pertain to the thought of Chinese philosophers, but also harbours every kind of the most superior thought of Eastern and Western culture. The Tao embodies the highest wisdom of human civilization; it is the greatest cultural resource of Chinese culture, and it must also be the point of the mutual assimilation of world civilizations.

Universal markers of betrayal and linguistic supremacy: Tsuda Yukio

The next example of culturalist categorization is built around the issue of linguistic supremacy. I discuss two cases, which clearly show that the structures of opposite arguments phrased in terms of binaries may be nearly identical. Li Yang, a (formerly) shy student, acquired wealth and fame by teaching English through the so-called 'Crazy English' method of screaming. Li advocates English as a source of emancipation and an indispensable means for strengthening China by conquering foreign markets. By contrast, Nagoya University professor Tsuda Yukio does his utmost to ban English conversation classes from Japan.[15] Whereas Li tries to make foreigners speak English in China, the latter tries to compel foreigners to speak Japanese. Still, both strategies are phrased in East–West dualities, and proceed from the principle of national self-strengthening, although the former focuses on economic growth and psychology and the latter on cultural tradition; both attitudes emphasize the need for self-assertion, overcoming an inferiority complex and fighting imperialism. Running through the parks, Li Yang and his pupils alternately scream in English and Chinese. They shout 'I never want to let my country down', and 'I'm the best', 'I enjoy losing face', 'I'm the strongest', 'I enjoy other people staring at me', 'Let the Chinese Voice be heard all over the world' and 'Which are the biggest markets in the world?' 'America, Japan and Europe!' 'What is the Chinese aim?' 'To conquer all three!'[16] By contrast, Tsuda advises the Chinese and Japanese against the use of English, regarding English as a small blessing that entails a huge vice. Learning the language of the strong, Tsuda claims, means being an accomplice in the historical crimes of the white English-speaking nations (Tsuda Yukio 1996: 160–5).

Tsuda Yukio's views express the application of characteristics on to the national unit that are ordinarily associated with the behaviour of individuals. Just as religious believers may imagine a (monotheistic) god to have a personality associated with almighty power, wisdom and perfection, holistically and nation-orientated academics assign similar character traits to the ideal picture of the nation. However, when the nation does not live up to the ideal, dramatic propaganda against those thought responsible for its failure may

Culturalist categorization 69

be mobilized to rectify the situation. To Tsuda Yukio, English is a treacherous language and its ubiquitous presence must be countered. Tsuda regrets the presence of the English disease on satellite television, in journals and shops, and the unhealthy consequences of its use, such as the 'pornographisation of language'.[17] Although Tsuda does not want to drop English from the school curriculum, he regrets its suppression and contamination of other languages. English as an international standard has created a new class structure of unequal relations in the world, and Japan should become aware of its role as an accomplice in crime. The main accomplices to this crime at home, judging from Tsuda's writings, includes nearly the entire Japanese population: the Ministry of Education (*Mombushō*), academics, the mass media, companies, teachers, film-makers, musicians, mothers and young people.[18]

Tsuda's *The Invasion of English. The Counter-Attack of Japanese. How to Protect a Beautiful Culture* (1996) is mainly concerned with the global rule of English and its inclination systematically to strengthen America (Tsuda 1996). To Tsuda the tendency to increase the use of English for joining processes of internationalization is a threat that should be met by resistance (Tsuda 1996: 24, 26). In academic life, Tsuda argues, great effort is required to write sophisticated English. Without English it is difficult to acquire academic credit in the anglophone world, and research themes and methods in English influence research all over the world. This, he argues, is also one of the reasons that the world lacks research on the hegemony of English (Tsuda 1996: 36–8). The privileged position of English in Europe and America (Ōbei),[19] Tsuda explains, is a result of the legacy of colonial control and imperialist invasion, that is, by wiping out great numbers of people and destroying their cultures and civilizations. The ideological basis of this cruel behaviour, Tsuda claims, lies in the first place in a sense of racial superiority felt by whites. In imperialist history the Christians, who regarded themselves as the children of God, felt they had to convert peoples of other belief by means of the Word, that is, the language of God: English (*sic!*). So-called primitives and wild peoples were made subject to colonial civilization because of the white man's burden (quoting Kipling) or at God's order. Similarly, English teachers subconsciously feel racially superior. And, when they say that Japanese teaching methods of English are inadequate, they adopt the attitude of the 'civilized' teaching the 'primitive' (Tsuda 1996: 51–4).

According to Tsuda, English has produced a new class structure. The English speakers and racially closely related Europeans form the top layer, the linguistic upper class; the second level constitutes the inhabitants of the English ex-colonies; the third level consists of other coloured English-speaking races; and, at the bottom level we find the non-English-speaking nations and peoples. This last category contains the misunderstood, silent class. The English speakers, according to Tsuda, are considered to be civilized, while the others are regarded as barbarians. Tsuda maintains that Ōbei people,

70　*Group categorization*

especially the English and the Americans, have structural power and control over the production of expressions of thought. Tsuda asserts, 'We (not the foreign reader), as a non-English speaking people, are defined and determined within their framework. The predominant rule of English affirms the racial superiority of English-speaking peoples and Ōbei people' (Tsuda 1996: 55–6). 'We Japanese have developed an inferiority complex because of English. Put in extreme terms, we have become colonized by means of English mind control. Whether we want it or not, we have to learn English in school for many years' (Tsuda 1996: 60–1). Even the government and Ministry of Education encourage the use of English, Tsuda charges, although many English loanwords cause confusion. Many people are excessively infatuated with the English language Tsuda laments. To make matters worse, commercials and television programmes show a preference for using white people (Tsuda 1996: 60–9).

Tsuda regards the education of English (*Eikaiwa*) as a tool for the colonization of the spirit: taking English conversation lessons, especially with a native English speaker, confronts the student with the victors of history, that is, the 'master-race'. Moreover, learners of English risk losing their identity in ideal images of the English speaker. It may even hamper the autonomous growth of the individual, society and the nation. The risk is especially great when the student becomes good at English. As Sapir and Whorf have shown, Tsuda argues, every language contains a specific cultural view.[20] Learning an additional language taints this view, for instance, when English values enter the head of the advanced student (Tsuda 1996: 70–2). Tsuda criticizes especially advertisements that use the 'foreign white English male' in combination with the 'Japanese female', propagating the 'independent American beauty' and, thus, making targets of Japanese females (Tsuda 1996: 83, 86). Compared with military and political control, Tsuda calls this kind of cultural influence 'soft control'. It is aimed at the more primitive needs of people, such as McDonald hamburgers, Disneyland and Michael Jackson.

The inferiority complex of the Japanese, according to Tsuda, is due to the dominance of Ōbei in the important fields of science, politics and culture, enabling it to perpetuate its control over Japan. Tsuda's view on the history of Japan's tragedy is that before Commander Perry and his black ships forced open Japan (in 1853), Japan had been like a child, playing innocently in the world. Invoking the view of the psychologist Kishida Shū,[21] Tsuda maintains that, until this crucial meeting, Japan had been closed and narcissistic. After it was forced open, however, it became traumatized and schizophrenic.[22] Japan never grew up and, instead, split into an outwardly and inwardly directed self. The outward self was expressed during the Meiji era (1868–1912) when Japan embarked on its modernization, and after World War II, when it started to orient itself internationally. The inward self appeared in periods of self-assertion: during the wars against Russia and China, and in the post-war period of explosive economic growth (Tsuda 1996: 97–100). Tsuda maintains that when America bombed Japan, scorched the Japanese earth and many lives were lost overseas, Japan had to admit defeat. Japan felt the same fear as when Commodore Perry's black ships had displayed Ōbei's strength. After the war these atrocities continued. Although Japan had become an economic power, the Americans were still violating Japanese territorial sovereignty (by its military bases stationed in Japan). Japan was targeted by trade friction, accompanied by incessant Japan-bashing. It caused 'internal' Japan to hate Americans, while many Japanese at the same time continued to be infatuated with America and internationalization (Tsuda 1996: 101–2). When the outward self comes to the fore, the Japanese can afford to love English conversation and Ōbei. But when the inward Japanese self is dominant, the English language and Ōbei evoke hatred. Specifying his theory of the Japanese self, Tsuda claims that girls prefer to learn English more than boys do. According to Tsuda, boys are 20 per cent less infatuated with America than are girls. This, again, is because losing the war grieves boys more than it does girls; after all, men have to fight wars. To illustrate its importance to national pride, Tsuda comments that even in a photograph of General MacArthur and the emperor, the former is shown as a winner and the latter as a loser. Because the women were disillusioned with the men, who could not protect them, they overdeveloped their outward Japaneseness and became attracted to Ōbei. Because Ōbei has become a part of the relationship between women and men, real love and trust between woman and man is no longer possible (Tsuda 1996: 108–9).

The simple dualities in which Tsuda divides the world affect the way he structures his academic views. His interpretations of the meaning of the use of language, images and behaviour are steeped in natural symbols that are projected on to his targets: the traitors of Japan. For example, he turns the images of the emperor and General MacArthur into a contemporary symbolic duality of victimhood and triumph. This he strings to a list of corresponding dualities such as those of loser and winner; Japan and America; man and women; inward and outward; Japanese and English; self-assertion and betrayal. Such thought associations, indeed, form the ingredients of acrimonious forms of academic nationalism. The deployment of natural symbols such as disease, pollution and schizophrenia are expressed in Tsuda's description of the colonization of the Japanese mind, mind control and its general suppression. Observing the weakening of the Japanese nation-state, especially its large number of potential traitors frustrates him. Although the language problem is a very real one, Tsuda seems to have lost his eye for proportion by applying negative personal markers to nations, races and parts of the world. He seems to have learnt how to regret this world deeply by rooting symbols of evil and disease into a configuration of archetypes that, in association with the English language, cause Japan's victimization.

72 *Group categorization*

Cultural categories

Umehara, Ye, Hu and Tsuda all insist on the cultural particularity of their nation and blame the West for the problems associated with modernity. They all frame their theories in terms of dualistic relations of East and West, although each searches his own 'national' solution to world problems. Despite their claims about cultural particularity, all four authors refer to universals derived from science or Jungian psychology in trying to convince their audience of the value of the culture they champion. Paradoxically, this kind of argument, in the near future, seems to offer no prospects for solving world problems as perceived by the authors. After all, how can the West learn how to bring its cerebral functions in equilibrium if thousands of years of cultural training are required for such change in their physiology? And how does the West return to forest life after it has become incapable of understanding or even having an adequate appreciation for it? And, how do English speakers avoid being cultural imperialists if political history has turned them into arch aggressors that victimize a schizophrenic nation such as Japan?

Umehara Takeshi and Ye Qiaojian make use of natural markers such as the brain, human instinct and the cultural gene to augment their cultural definition of national groups. Thus Umehara supports his ideology of returning to Jōmon forest culture with religious assertions about the continuity of Japanese culture and claims of support from modern evolution theory. To Umehara, the innocence of the Jōmon Japanese is preserved in their instinct and intuition. But his main message is cultural and ethical: the link between man and nature has been preserved in the Japanese religion, temples and customs. Instinct and intuition are mainly expedients. Racial and physical criteria are subordinated to spirituality and moral argument, implying that the world could emulate the 'Japanese' quest, a return to nature. And modern science is mobilized in support of Umehara's view. Nevertheless, it is the Japanese cultural carrier gene, in the form of the Jōmon inheritance, which makes possible this return to the forest.

Ye Qiaojian's study of the brain shows forms of direct and indirect cerebral determinism of the regional identities of East and West, and the way in which yin and yang elements are used interchangeably as an analytical tool and attribute of research objects. Ye, like other authors, hesitates to use dualities between East and West as absolute opposites and refrains from drawing extreme analogies between East and West and the right and left cerebral hemisphere. But in the way that yin–yang contrast relate to one another in East and West, respectively, Ye reads a vast difference between Eastern forms of equilibrium and Western leanings toward imbalance and self-assertion. Here we come full circle. We keep on returning to the departure point at which we ask questions that contain their own answers.

Hu Fuchen's example indicates that typologies of East and West are not necessarily intended to stimulate world dialogue but function to forward particular political and cultural views at home. Just like Umehara's Jōmon spirit, Hu's Taoism has been misused, neglected and forgotten by history. And both animistic Shinto and Taoism now are advocated as universal modes of thought. The authors do not even pretend that all nations have equal spiritual access to their 'universal' knowledge and principles for the saviour of mankind, as the instructions to them lie hidden in the nation's past and are retrievable only by the initiated.

The language of national self-assertion does not have to be the national one when the foreign language is regarded as a ticket to world markets and wealth. When wealth is achieved, however, fears of spiritual impoverishment may fester. Li Yang, for instance, advertises the skill of speaking English as essential to China's success in the modern world. In Li's view learning English brings joy, hope and power to China. In Tsuda Yukio's case, however, the English language evokes resentment and bitterness over its invasion of Japan. It is felt to be the historical carrier and legacy of imperialism and Western (especially white American) supremacy. Tsuda applies an enormous range of cultural disease markers to the English-speaking world, using natural symbolism to give expression to the perceived Western threat. Those at home who do not support his crusade by taking English conversation classes are classified as traitors and accomplices with the foreign imperialists. A causal link is forged between Western imperialism, Japanese foreign policy, Japanese language and the Japanese unconscious, whose archetypal symbolism and disease markers divide the world in simplistic dualities of male and female, aggressor and victim.

The dogmatic use of cultural categories generally implies that designated groups are capable of crossing natural boundaries, such as those created by racial markers. Although cultural attributes are employed to draw a clear distinction between cultural regions, the possibility of learning from other cultures and the exchange of at least practical skills and knowledge in most academic theory of this kind is in principle possible. When conflict occurs, however, the adoption of foreign knowledge and skills are questioned as some form of moral betrayal. Various groups of academics compress and mould the temporal dimensions of cultural tradition into static shapes, such as the cultural gene, the brain, historical sediment left at the bottom of the national character and national archetypes. They become mental weapons that aim to reverse processes of confrontation with the foreign Other, outsiders, dissenters and powers that are believed to intrude in the time-honoured tradition of insiders.

Despite the relativity of natural boundaries, in cultural zones seemingly small differences too can escalate into major conflicts, fuelled by disputes over language, socio-cultural belonging, sacred symbols, territorial rights and the infringement of sovereignty.[23] In culturalist approaches to the nation, the use of the family metaphor, historical roots and the collective mind contribute to the perception of cultural symbols as stable and everlasting. Quasi-kinship ties easily link the cultural with the natural, and therefore are perceived as

74 *Group categorization*

symbols of stability. Such stability is expressed in the great intimacy, mutual understanding and special knowledge of linguistic and behavioural codes attributed to those symbolic ties.[24]

The builder of cultural walls excludes people on the basis of disloyalty and a failure to adhere to accepted notions of linguistic and cultural behaviour. Nevertheless, when outsiders observe the 'correct' codes (linguistic, social, customarily) of behaviour, principle acceptance may take place. But when the academic reveals cross-cultural differences to be etched into the brain and the unconscious, or to be inherent to birth, the 'home' of the people, or to the 'cultural gene', the academic author indicates a political unwillingness to accept external cultural influences.

6 Global categorization

This chapter proceeds from the idea that the frameworks used for defining domestic culture and its place in the world presuppose one another. I argue, contrary to what is usually assumed, that apart from particularist and cultural categories, universalistic ones are central in theories of national uniqueness. I discuss these categories in the works of a group of Japanese academics that expound the concepts of civilization and culture, systems and complexity. First, I point out that academics engaged in advocating certain national models are quite aware of the friction between the cultural and the universal. This friction is an incentive for some authors to define societies in ideological terms of 'borderlessness' or in universalistic terms of economic theory, although, at the same time, they urge the world to emulate certain cultural models. The friction between the cultural and political, and the particular and the universal, in fact, is a condition for the successful cultivation of theories of national difference. In the examples of works by Īda Tsuneo, Kenichi Ohmae, Hamaguchi Eshun and Yoshida Kazuo, the universalistic guise of modern science serves this purpose very well. My discussion of theories borrowed from systems science, information theory and complexity reveals the ambiguous position of the author of Japanese systems. Ambiguous, because it leaves one wondering whether the Japanese author in such scientistic theories is merely an objectified cog in a complex organic system or whether she/he takes the position of its ambiguous systems manager.

The kind of nationalism prevalent in east Asia since the mid-1980s has been referred to as cultural nationalism, that is, a form of nationalism different from political nationalism. The concept of cultural nationalism seems to imply that the nationalism in this period finds its expression in terms of cultural and social categories that are used to articulate the particularity of the nation. But in fact, in nationalist theory both particularist and universalistic elements have a function to play in delineating the differences and similarities between nations. Particularist factors are associated with, for instance, cultural uniqueness, racial features, physical characteristics, the collective national sub/unconsciousness and the unique features of a language. Universalistic elements are associated with genetic transmission, the universal functions of human language and its general commensurability,

76 *Group categorization*

the formation of social systems and civilizations, the universal development of a similar human brain and other biological features that are regarded as human and the universal existence of the un/subconscious. But in fact it is the particular combination of universalistic and particularist features concealed in terms of a framework of nation-states that makes for ideological and obscure academic practice. In this sense, nationalist ideology or nation framing may well be widely prevalent in academic research in both east Asian countries and elsewhere in the world.

The concepts of cultural nationalism, political nationalism and racism can be very confusing. Sometimes a double distinction is made between racial and cultural nationalism, and a distinction between cultural and political nationalism. The first distinction is based on the attributes of nationalism, that is, whether the physical characteristics ascribed to a certain group of people are genetically transmitted or learnt. Yoshino Kosaku, for example, made a distinction between racism and racist thinking, and decided that the latter, not the former, formed the basis of the *nihonjin-ron* theories of Japaneseness. In other words, it was not a form of racism that would lead to a fascist form of nationalism, but it was a form of thinking associated with cultural and social forms of national identity that would lead to cultural nationalism (Yoshino 1995). The second distinction between cultural and political nationalism is based on the attributes of the carrier of nationalism. The question here is whether the state politically encourages nation-state nationalism or whether the general populace is the carrier of it. Thus, Caroline Rose makes an analytical distinction between state nationalism and cultural nationalism, implicitly equating state nationalism with official patriotism and popular nationalism with cultural nationalism (Rose 2000: 169–81). Even though 'to a certain extent there was a symbiotic relationship between state and cultural nationalism in China and Japan in the 1990s', and 'cultural nationalists were partially encouraged by their respective government', the presumption that cultural nationalism belongs to the domain of a general population remains (ibid.).

I signal confusion between the way in which notions of nationalism are conceptualized. I agree with Rose that in the nationalism in China and Japan of the 1990s a large part is reflective of discussions held on problems at home, and therefore cannot be regarded as a reliable barometer of Sino–Japanese relations. However, I would like to point out that especially in nation-centred theories the terms used for defining problems at home tend to also be the ones that serve as a framework for defining international ones. Hereby I wish to direct some attention away from the sensational aspects of nationalism and take a closer look at the way definitions of the nation-state and the role of the nation-state as a framework in academic research leads academic thought in certain directions, be it intentionally or not.

Academics are a major source of nationalistic formulations, and play an important role in, for as far as the distinction is valid, both state and popular nationalism. For this reason I believe that in academic research it is not

Global categorization 77

helpful to ascribe cultural and political nationalism to the state and the general populace, respectively. Nor, is it useful to make a distinction in the work of academics between racism and racial thinking, as racism is engendered through a misuse of the tools that empower people due to their position in society. In the case of academics it is only too obvious that the tools that empower the intellectual lies in his/her thought, making the tool by which racism is expressed the same one as that of racial modes of thought. In my view, the question is not just whether the nation-state is presented as unique, particular or superior in comparison to others. The problem of particularism versus universalistic criteria lies in the way a presentation is argued and legitimated by the nature of a particular research problem. For any mode of nationalism ascribes particularity to a nation only in reference to other nations and therefore presupposes, by definition, some universally shared features. The more important matter is whether the selection of the research population or unit, and the choice of criteria for identifying variables are adequate for solving the research problem under concern. Presumed universality and particularity always must be argued in the context of the problem at issue.

Thinking in terms of nation-states is a force of habit, and often very useful indeed. Comparing educational systems, law, election systems and so on, between various nation-states in order to explain specific problems may be very serviceable. However, we cannot equate a system ascribed to a nation-state with its population because the features and potentialities of the number of individuals ascribed to that population are always richer than a simulation or definition of the system. Definitions of systems and 'wholes' are, by definition, reductionist, for they only describe particular aspects of the domain they are meant to represent. In social science research the research population is chosen in correspondence with a research problem. And as research problems do not all automatically vary according to the nation-state in which they occur, research variables sometimes lead us to look for other units of research. Many research problems vary not according to national culture, but are determined by a variety of factors such as environmental circumstances, practices of labour exploitation and élite ideology. I believe that employing the boundaries between nation-state as a standard framework for academic research disregards that what research problematic we are dealing with, that is nation-framing, apart from being a source of nationalism, is a result of uncritical thinking or political ideology.

Borderless values

Global equality in the sense of not privileging any group is non-existent to the globalist nation-framer, even as an ideal. Here the term 'globalist' serves to describe academics that advertise themselves as believers in universal principles and values, but who also keep a spare set of standards to fit in with the situation of the nation they believe in. Ida Tsuneo's case exemplifies this

78 Group categorization

category. Īda is the former head of the Department of Japanese Studies of Nichibunken and one of the ten main advisors of the Institute for Peace, Happiness and Prosperity (PHP).[1] He is a renowned economist, and not very modest about Japan's economic success in the 1980s. This success has led him to draw conclusions about Japan's national superiority, measured by means of standards presented as Western universal ones:

> The nature of the Japanese economy is such that, in comparison with the United States and Europe, it observes the spirit embodied in modern economics better and it functions more effectively in accordance with the principles of neo-classical economic theory. In a broader perspective, one can say that the national characteristic of Japan, in comparison with the West, is to pursue more seriously such bourgeois democratic values as liberty, equality, and respect for the individual, and to realize these goals on a wider, more effective scale. In short, the basic character of Japan consists of purified strains (*junsui baiyō*) of the West.
>
> (Pyle 1988: 482)

> Generally speaking, then, in terms of achieving the ideals of democracy, egalitarianism, and individualism and in maintaining a competitive (economic) mechanism, Japan may appear to be an ordinary nation. But this 'ordinariness' is only in appearance. The fact of the matter is that what are 'principles' (*tatemae*) in the Western nations have become 'reality' (*honne*) in Japan.
>
> (Pyle 1988: 483)

Ohmae Kenichi, like Īda, is a fan of Matsushita Konosuke, the founder of and brain behind the PHP institute.[2] In his *The Borderless World*, he recommends Matsushita's 'mind that does not stick' (*torawarenai sunao-na kokoro*) as a tool for spotting opportunities, and for rethinking approaches from the ground up.[3] With the right mentality, Ohmae believes, it is possible for anyone to make it in the world. For example, Ohmae recommends 'the China mentality', or thinking that one is the centre of the world. It obliges people to take the trouble of thinking up ideas for enhancing the service and products the company can offer (Ohmae 1990: 79–81).

In the same vein, Ohmae argues that the role of government should be limited to providing education and information. Ohmae maintains that today's global corporations are nationalityless because consumers have become less nationalistic. Today's companies invest in a country's infrastructures, train staff and pay taxes. It is good business (Ohmae 1990: 194–5). Being consistent, Ohmae criticizes the nationalism of Japan's government too:

> The government continues to claim, for example, that Japanese blood is different enough from North American and European blood for all drugs

Global categorization 79

approved elsewhere in the Trust to go through five years of clinical tests to be re-approved in Japan. This is for the good of the people, they say. This is to protect them from drugs like thalidomide that wrecked such havoc elsewhere. But it is really only a way to protect their own turf and their own power. In fact, when Japanese consumers sued the government for having approved drugs that proved to have harmful side effects, the powers-that-be claimed that they were not legally responsible.

(Ohmae 1990: 184)

Ohmae claims also, however, that it has become increasingly difficult for governments to pretend that their national economic interests are identical to those of their people. Information flows in a borderless society express, instead, the variety of taste in the world: 'As the boundary lines on maps fade, the underlying clusters of value and preference become increasingly visible' (Ohmae 1990: 185). Therefore,

company branches abroad should not depend on (company/national) headquarters but go ahead themselves, adjusting to the 'soft-ware' or market conditions in other countries. At the same time the company must keep its identity by a universal value system, communicating information throughout the amoeba-like organization and tearing down the pyramid.

(Ohmae 1990: 99)

Moreover, Ohmae believes his universalism is in congruence with the environmental aim of planting for a global harvest. Furthermore, stage five of the process by which companies move to global business is the set of universally shared values that holds together the members of a genuinely amoeba-like, network-based, global organization (in stage five).[4] Each industry has its own characteristics (Research & Development, manufacturing methods, accountancy, investment, pay-off) which together form its identity. In different environments, the industry has different requirements because tax conditions, advertising laws, environmental laws, unions, market access, distribution systems and so on differ. It is therefore important to uphold company values and, also, allow different company cultures in different environments. 'Shared values are not at odds with these variations in soil' (Ohmae 1990: 101–13).

There is no arguing with Ohmae about whether his borderless world is accessible to all or not because his politics are clearly in favour of the application of the universal principles of competition and fair play. But, then, Ohmae is not an academic but a business advisor, who is not supposed to write about how things are but to advise on how things could and should be. Interestingly, Ohmae adopts a view of self-organization and network relations that has become quite common among sociologists and economically

80 Group categorization

oriented academics who attribute to Japanese society a holistic tendency for spontaneous self-organization. Such views do not take into account the political and ideological factors affecting the modes of organization of companies and other institutions, and take for granted or ignore relations between management and labour. They are centred on the cultural value of 'economics first' and consumerism. Moreover, Ohmae has no eye for skewed relations of economic power. Some countries clearly have a comparative advantage, if only for possessing full-grown infrastructures built with support of nation-state power.

Balancing scientistic arguments against Japanese uniqueness

In contrast to many other comparative studies of civilization that borrow concepts from culture to construct theories of national difference, Hamaguchi Eshun applies scientistic concepts, borrowed from systems-science and complexity theory. Hamaguchi defends the idea that Japanese systems are historically and socially in particular good shape as Japanese civilization and culture is in system phase. Being in phase is a concept borrowed from complexity theory. It is deftly applied to denote a dynamic form of balancing culture and civilization. The Japanese dynamic equilibrium is contrasted with the unpromising mechanistic ways in which transformation in the West, or Ōbei, take place.[5] To understand why culture and civilization have to be balanced, and why this means that Japan constitutes a unique and systems-model to other nations, I will introduce Hamaguchi's ideas on these concepts.

The distinction between civilization and culture as used by Hamaguchi entails a whole range of 'relative contrasts'. Because of the links between these converse typologies, the use of one concept affects the meaning of the entire list of contrasts. Understanding how clusters of contrasts are lumped together in the long lists of interconnected (dynamic) opposites is essential to understanding Hamaguchi's theoretical apparatus. Initially, Hamaguchi borrowed Umesao Tadao's distinction between civilization as equipment, systems and organizational models, and culture as value system. Civilization constitutes the material factors of systems of living, while the norms that are used to select a certain system are the values of culture. Whereas the civilizational artefacts are characterized with universal applicability, cultural values express the preferences inherent to a certain society. 'Civilization' therefore expresses universality and 'culture' particularity. In other words, civilization is the 'etic', external viewpoint and culture expresses the 'emic' internal point of view (Hamaguchi 1996a: 52). Hamaguchi regards the lack of a clear distinction between civilization and culture as one of the causes of trade friction. This, he believes, is because the internationalization of all aspects leads to 'egoistic competition' and protectionism: The coexistence of 'borderless economics' and fields that are difficult to internationalize, such

Global categorization 81

as politics, culture, habits and nationality, leads to trade friction (Hamaguchi 1996a: 53).[6]

Culture is associated with a certain 'country' and 'stability', while civilization, which comprises 'artefacts', may be seen as a value-free instrument.[7] By separating culture and civilization, the Sekotac report of the Masuda Foundation offers other societies the *superior aspects* of the Japanese system of 'civilization' as a *value-free* alternative.[8] But Hamaguchi creates confusion by pushing his argument on the value-free nature of 'artefacts', such as televisions, cars and MacDonald's hamburgers, are unrelated to ideology (Hamaguchi 1996a: 54). On the one hand, the dualities complement one another and 'civilization' at one point may share the characteristics of 'culture'; on the other hand, civilization is value free and thus exportable as a model for other societies. Nevertheless, Hamaguchi is aware of the ambivalence of this standpoint and shows how the definitions of, for instance, Umesao, Itō and Kumon cannot adequately establish a link between civilization and culture:[9] Umesao's definition lacks a link between culture and civilization. And, according to Itō's and Kumon's definitions, culture produces civilization: culture functions as the programme of civilization. According to Hamaguchi, the conversion from civilization to culture is lacking, that is, phase transition.[10] When the life system (civilization) becomes more efficient and is 'levelled up', then the design (culture) must adjust as well: values change and designs change. When civilization and culture are in tune, phase fusion occurs. This, in turn, results in the levelling up of civilization (Hamaguchi 1986: 22–30).

Hamaguchi uses the analogy of computer hardware (computer system) and software (design) to illustrate phase conversion. He compares Japanese civilization with the hardware of a computer and language, organization and control with software, belonging to the level of culture. In the case of the epoch-making invention of the character processor, the software for characters is an expression of Japanese culture (Hamaguchi 1988: 18–19). Fortunately, Japanese civilization, Hamaguchi maintains, is traditionally intimately connected to Japanese culture so that it can easily introduce aspects of the functionally superior foreign civilization and adapt well to them. Japanese civilization, which is based on small flexible group activity, can easily adopt Euro-American technology. There is no guarantee, however, that everything will go smoothly when foreigners adopt Japanese civilization (Hamaguchi 1996a: 59).

Hamaguchi applies the term mutual phase dynamics to describe the dialectical process of the interaction between culture and civilization, a process that expresses how culture and civilization determine and reflect one another. Depending on the circumstances, the two are sometimes well adjusted and hardly distinguishable from one another. Then it is possible to avoid the dangers that accompany (cultural) internationalization. Hamaguchi believes that the universality of civilization makes it possible for any society to flourish. Culture, however, is inherent to a specific ethnic group. Nevertheless, in the

82 *Group categorization*

context of (civilizational) globalization, the two phases are often at cross-purposes. As a result, there is a high chance of conflict between externally introduced civilization and culture. Because the dynamics of the correlative (mutual) change of culture and civilization are complex, Hamaguchi argues, there is a need for careful research into their interaction (Hamaguchi 1996a: 53).

Aidagara, kanjinshugi and autopoiesis

For Hamaguchi, three different approaches are associated with three types of human system. First, individualist systems that control individuals independently and equate the whole to the sum total of individuals (independent decentralized control). Second, collectivism, in which the whole controls individuals in a centralized manner, according to a given set of criteria (centralized control). And third, *aidagara*, in which individuals co-operate spontaneously in controlling their own behaviour so that the whole is in proper order (holonic decentralized control). The third form of control Hamaguchi regards as appropriate to non-linear open systems (Hamaguchi 1985: 320–1).

The concept of *aidagara* denotes that human relations are not mere temporary reciprocal interactions: preference is given to mutual favours among persons who are connected and transcends individual interests. *Aidagara* as the nexus among contextuals can be said to follow a holonic path oriented toward a harmonious relationship among persons and the higher order system to which they belong.[11] Maintaining stable relations among people is the greatest merit of *aidagara*, which is comparable to the bonding patterns of chemical substances. In contrast, Ōbei-an social relations are based on instrumental transactions in which individuals seek maximum profit (Hamaguchi 1985: 314).[12] Due to the selfishness of others, social relations collapse easily.[13] Individuals therefore take recourse to contracts and written law. Whereas *aidagara* has consummatory significance for contextuals, social relations are utilized instrumentally by individuals (Hamaguchi 1985: 317).[14] Hamaguchi uses the concept of *aidagara* as a holonic form of decentralized control to argue for the necessity of trust. While *kanjinshugi*, the counterpart of individualism, is conducive to trust because the *kanjin* places great value on relationships between people, *aidagara* is contrasted with other approaches for controlling systems.

Systems theory has come to regard society and the individual (*kojin*) as merely different co-ordinates of the social system's phase.[15] Furthermore, Hamaguchi draws a parallel between the Japanese social system and Koestler's 'holon'. The Japanese word for person, '*ningen*' and Hamaguchi's *kanjin* (the contextual), literally 'the space between persons', cover the concept of holonic society in the *kanjin* model. In it, the degree of people's common life-space is relatively high (Hamaguchi 1995: 391).[16] The *kanjin* model contrasts with the individual intensive model in which the autonomy of the individual and the distance between separate individual actor subjects is emphasized. From a systems theory point of view, these two models are called the 'individuum' and the 'relatum'. In the latter, people always take others into account in their (systems referential) behaviour. The concept of actor subject that Hamaguchi uses is also applicable to groups. Accordingly, human groups as actors can be redefined as self-organizing systems that intentionally plan variations in their own organization.[17]

A strong sense of community is vital for the stable continuation of the community in defence against disturbing external influences. For instance, Hamaguchi argues the ambivalence between individualism and community that makes American community systems vulnerable (Hamaguchi 1996a: 24–5). The problem then is caused by modern unilineary dichotomous thinking. It causes sharp swings between sentiments of extreme communalism and individualism: tradition and modernity exist along side one another. It is necessary to cause a breakthrough in this dualistic map.

This is where Niclas Luhmann's social systems theory comes in. Luhmann pointed out that the function of a system is to reduce the complexity of the environment through meaning while defining its borders (*Sinngrenzen*).[18] Within these limits, the system maintains its own subjectivity. The system preserves its subjectivity to the extent that it gives shape to its borders on the basis of selecting simplified forms of the complex environment. According to Hamaguchi, Luhmann made clear that his concept of 'system relatedness' is the basis for the system's subjectivity. The best way to deal with the extraordinary degree of the complexity of social systems is through mutual trust. Systems trust is formed through the generalized media of communication, including truthfulness, love, power, currency, and has the function of reducing the system's complexity. Hence, this trust goes beyond 'personal trust' and provides a stable response to the complex and, therefore, uncertain world, enhancing the process of social civilization (Hamaguchi 1996a: 59).

Hamaguchi believes that the most adequate formation principles of Luhmann's systems can be found in the 'autogenous compilation of social systems'. For a system to attain a goal, the relations between the members of such a system need only be managed in unison, functionally and efficiently; the system's process produces systems order spontaneously. This process corresponds to the autonomously distributed hierarchical system seen in life in general.[19] Here, the fermentation (maturing) of the goal of systems behaviour is based on the 'internal goal-setting' of Japanese systems, in contrast to Western systems whose transcendental goals are projected on to the system artificially.[20]

Hamaguchi also refers to Luhmann's concept of 'double contingency' to show the significance of trust.[21] People make decisions about their own behaviour by estimating that of others who, in turn, try to gauge theirs. In other words, their behaviour depends on the uncertainty factor in predicting the behaviour of others. In order to make correct estimations and to resolve insecurity, people need relations of trust. Trust, here, refers not to ethical

84　*Group categorization*

trust but to social trust, which has a social function across time (Hamaguchi 1996a: 9–11). Luhmann defines 'trust' as 'making other people's or societies' expectations one's own'. The social system reproduces itself by mediation of the relations between its constituent elements (autopoiesis). In order for the mechanism of the social system to reproduce itself on its own basis, trust in others and in social systems is indispensable for diminishing the complexity of the surrounding environment and finally preserves the subjectivity of the system. Regarding self-consciousness and cognition, which are paradoxically ultimately based on the differences in meaning and values *vis-à-vis* the external environment (which means self-referential closure), the system is open (Hamaguchi 1996a: 58).

The difference between culture and civilization echoes throughout this application of social systems theory. According to Luhmann, the boundaries of social systems are formed through meaning (*Sinn*). Even though the system is closed where differences in meaning and values *vis-à-vis* the external environment are concerned (culture), in terms of self-awareness or cognition (civilization) it is entirely open. In order to deal with the complexity of the environment and to diminish it, there is no other way than for individuals to trust others and the social system to share those same values (Hamaguchi 1996a: 58–9). Similarly, Francis Fukuyama has drawn attention to trust as social capital. This form of social capital is returned to the individual (Hamaguchi 1996a: 59). After all, co-operation and sharing common norms and values generate group advantage, satisfy the needs of the individual, and consequently generate great 'trust'. Trust, according to Hamaguchi, refers not to trust in the organizing principles of a bureaucracy but to trust in the autogenous compilation of social systems. In order to reach the systems target both members and the space between them (*aidagara*) have to be united and managed, both functionally and effectively. The system's order will then be produced autogenously.

The necessity of a shift from 'effect' to 'trust', according to Hamaguchi, has been demonstrated by the results of a questionnaire conducted in some twenty countries. The questionnaire compares the values given to 'individualism' (emphasizing self-reliance, egocentrism and the instrumental use of humans) and 'contextualism' (emphasizing co-operation, mutual trust, reliance and the stressing of interpersonal relations). The results show that the English are even more contextualist and less individualistic, than the Japanese. From the results, according to Hamaguchi, we may conclude the following:

1　The common-sense idea that Western European society is based on individualism and Japan on collectivism is of doubtful validity.
2　*Kanjinshugi* has universal value. Every country's social system is based on the dynamic dualism of individualism and contextualism.
3　The acknowledgement of interpersonal relations and models such as those of Fukuyama and Luhmann that express mutual trust are suitable

Global categorization 85

for the post-modern society to which they refer. More generally, this acknowledgement shows the need for a paradigmatic shift from the concept of 'utility' to 'trust' (Hamaguchi 1996b: 29).[22]

Key persons and national systems strategies: Mutual trust and uncertainty

Whereas Luhmann provided a tool for understanding social systems, Hamaguchi is concerned with providing the tool and advocating the model it generates. Thus, Hamaguchi provides us with concepts and distinctions for observing autopoietic systems and also with an image of what they look like. This raises the question of how to define the borders of systems. Niclas Luhmann argues that '*Sinn*' (meaning, intentionality) in general rather than trust in a specific society reduces world complexity and defines the borders of human autopoietic 'action systems'. *Sinn*, here, refers to *bringing order* in human experience to a level of complexity that people can handle (Strijbos 1988: 138), while trust is a *systems strategy* for reducing uncertainty. An additional problem concerns the way in which trust between people is achieved. According to Luhmann, it is not just a matter of feeling optimistic about conditions that may lead to safe estimations of behaviour. A crucial factor is the freedom of choice.[23] Luhmann's concept of trust does not mean 'personal trust' or 'ethical trust' as such, but in addition requires *contingency*: trust is not necessary and not impossible. The element of risk does not seem to be present in 'spontaneous co-operation' and some thought is required as to what extent social pressure and convention allow the development of trust in any society.

Hamaguchi seems to delineate the *Sinngrenzen* or boundaries of meaning of large systems implicitly by taking the 'nation' (country, society) as his point of departure, choosing all his examples in terms of 'Japanese' thinking, systems, behaviour and culture. The Other system usually is Ōbei. In either, as far as meaning and value are concerned, systems (nations, cultures and societies) are closed. The structure of the system is given and at the same time both constitutes and generates the actual changes that the structure undergoes functionally, that is, by means of distinctions. The closure of meaning is accompanied by intersystemic communication that, in Hamaguchi's theory, should involve the universal aspects of civilization. The import of civilization is, by definition, the equivalent of the structuring of meaning by the system itself, i.e. phase transition. Where there is a large gap between the universal and cultural aspects of the respective systems, fluctuations will occur and the danger stands in danger of becoming unstable. However, in Japan 'key persons' are capable of selecting culturally adequate civilization (inventing tradition); they know how the system constitutes the shared meanings embodied in the relatum and the ways in which people co-operate spontaneously.

Autopoietic systems have their own subjectivity and intentionality, transcending the logic of individual persons. In other words, their *Sinn* is

86 *Group categorization*

incomprehensible to ordinary observers; systems possess a supra-rationality that is also characteristic of *aidagara*. Rational behaviour is no longer a question of matching choices with an aim (either egotistical or altruistic) but has become inherent to the efficiency of a functional system equipped with mind and a capacity of self-reproduction (autopoiesis). But if social scientists belong to a social system, one wonders how members of the individualistic social scientific community system can cause the desired hypothetical paradigm shift merely by being persuaded by arguments. Or is the paradigm responsible for its own revolution? Will scientists be persuaded or replaced by other scientists who have become enlightened as a result of *kanjinshugi*? How can Hamaguchi know the consequences of altering 'the system' by means of persuasion, if the system itself is its own maintainer? Do we still have a 'knowing subject'?

It is relatively easy to put into perspective the absolute 'Cartesian' duality between subject and object, by becoming aware of the circumstances and methods of observation. However, it is very difficult to abolish the observing subject altogether, since most people cannot help but build their theories on observations on their own experience and find it impossible to conjure themselves into nothingness. Attempts up to now have succeeded in doing so only by referring to superhuman entities such as god, the emperor and systems. Systems theory seems to achieve the same effect by taking the 'system' as the mastermind behind the structural change of its constituent components. However, the problem is how does the individual systems theorist observe a system that transcends his own logic.[24] The trouble is that systems do not observe. For that very reason, Jürgen Habermas suspected that the Cartesian dualism between knowing subject and object has been replaced by one of 'system' and 'environment' (Strijbos 1988: 144). The system here has become the medium by which the scientist author makes observations without the apparent need of a signature. The system as a mediator gives us the illusion of the ultimate form of self-relativization.

So how is structural change produced by the system on the basis of *Sinn*? If we take a look at the book *Japanese Systems*, compiled by the Sekotac Research Project Team for Japanese Systems, of which Hamaguchi is the representative,[25] we gain some insight into how knowledge 'from the outside' is treated by mysterious 'key persons' in Japanese systems:

> The Japanese have always incorporated foreign ideas and institutions in such a way that they are compatible with their own objectives and views and have made 'invented traditions' whenever they have needed to. In other words, they have interpreted even foreign ideologies and paradigms in the way best suited to the pursuit of their own practical and utilitarian ends and have often put them to skilful use as a means of attaining their own objectives. Thought and ideologies in Japan have never been thoroughly examined with the idea of plumbing their depths, but rather they are seen more as 'slogans' for the realization of policy and tend to

Global categorization 87

be put to use by political and administrative leaders in policy guidance and by the mass media to manipulate public opinion.

(Sekotac 1992: 63)

Apparently, it is possible for individual 'leaders' to induce change by means of manipulation. This fact tells us a great deal about how to interpret the 'spontaneous co-operation' characteristic of *aidagara*. Furthermore, the system has a clear division of labour between 'key persons' and 'ordinary people'. The former surely employ a rather relativistic concept of 'tradition':

Japanese society has responded to the international environment of the day, introducing what was needed as civilization, creating overlapping, multi-layered cultural and social structures in the same way that we put on layers of clothing according to the weather and our physical condition. Even from the perspective of the working features of Japanese systems, it takes time and effort to work out measures to deal with strong external pressure. Even so, key persons have promptly implemented reforms of the system. In such cases, 'invented tradition' is the device used to synchronise the 'endogenous evolution' of ordinary people and the 'exogenous revolution' carried out by key persons. The mechanism that operates here is one of <selection – invention/rediscovery – integration>. Tradition is not simply the repetition of ancestral patterns, but is created as necessary. Here attention is on 'the politics of interpretation' among the actor subjects involved. In this sense, invented tradition is 'negotiated tradition'.

(Sekotac 1992: 35–6)

Despite the autopoietic nature of systems, which precludes the possibility of monitoring them at will, it seems that a limited group of 'key persons' in Japan's case has the technology for and is capable of steering societal change. And as the system itself changes and embodies the emergent will of all its social constituents, intellectuals need not worry about possessing a disproportionate amount of influence due to their position as 'key persons'. After all, the system itself makes the crucial non-choice of 'key persons' by the selection of the fittest.

A final issue pertains to decision-making and consensus. Striving for consensus is thought to be an important factor in Japanese communication and decisions are to be obtained through the natural inclination of Japanese *kanjinshugi*. According to Habermas's concept of action, however, all communication aims at consensus, even if only ostensibly so. Luhmann, by contrast, disagrees with Habermas's concept of consensus-oriented 'communicative action' (Knodt 1995: xxix). He explains his disagreement as follows. First, consensus can never be more than local and temporal, for communication requires dissent to continue its operations. If universal consensus were to be reached, it would terminate the system's autopoiesis.

88 *Group categorization*

Second, the concept of action cannot provide the grounds for a social theory because it is an *effect* rather than a precondition of the social dimension (Knodt 1995: xxix). Both reasons are framed from the point of view of the system: a consensual meaning can exist only if it concerns congruence in meanings generated by the system itself, including the relatum. Again, it should be pointed out that only in the absence of consensus does trust makes sense: trust needs choice freely given. To the extent that action is produced by a static system, it is limited. In a dynamic system, however, scope for action is contingent. Action is not regulated, as Parsons believed, by referring to a priori social consensus regarding cultural norms and rules of conduct.[26] The concept of action is framed from the point of view of the observer, and is therefore part of the dynamic process of autopoiesis. The tension between the recursive process of self-reference and change is absorbed by autopoietic systems. In other words, processes of change and structure are part and parcel of autopoiesis.

Hamaguchi seems to give priority to trust in *social systems* above trust in the kind of humans that make up such systems. Methodological relatum-ism shows that Japanese social systems are *especially* conducive to autopoiesis without the regressive fluctuations that result from communication failure in other societies. The main reasons for this conductivity are the high value placed on the relationship between people, trust in systems as social capital, their autogenous compilation and the internal goal setting of Japanese systems. Those factors are supposed to help to strengthen the relations between social sub-systems and the whole, and facilitate the process of reducing the complexity of imported information and energy according to the contours of the system. *Kanjinshugi* is, as it were, the lubrication that keeps the system in shape and running.

Japan, then, is an open, dynamic system, corresponding to both the cultural ideology of Japan, i.e. *kanjinshugi*, and to the rising world paradigm of *kanjinshugi*. *Kanjinshugi* is at the same time a cultural and social phenomenon, a cultural design for civilization and a paradigm. As long as the Japanese remain *kanjinshugi* and do not become Ōbei-style individualists, Japanese civilizational systems will remain relatively in tune with culture. Foreigners and international values (based on Ōbei) thus form a threat to Japanese systems if they fail to adjust. After all, Japanese culture produces the system's identity, lubricates it, and is recursively reproduced by the system. If foreign elements fail to adjust to the organizational principles of the system, their effects may trickle down to the realm of culture. Here, I think, lies the cause of Hamaguchi's anxiety about the so-called universal values of individualism, revisionism and fairness.

According to Luhmann, however, autopoiesis is no normative concept that tells people how to behave. Behaviour incongruent with systems principles or, that criticizes them does not necessitate *advocating* a paradigm shift. Even though Luhmann accords communication (information, utterance, understanding) a central role as the basic unit of the social system and sees communication as used by the system as a particular mode of autopoietic reproduction, he remains at the level of objective theory. There is a very good reason for him to do so. As soon as scientists start to advocate their theories as a prerequisite for solving world issues and at the same time draw attention to the superiority of the system of which they are a part, they become interested campaigners.

Even Koestler, who coined the concept of 'holon', had strong misgivings about closed systems of meaning. Under the heading 'The Comforts of Double-Think', Koestler expressed this worry in his description of the inner consistency and uncanny persuasiveness of 'delusional systems'. Such systems are closed: 'a cognitive matrix, governed by a canon'. Here 'closed' means that such systems direct all incoming information into a process of producing new elements that maintain its existence and refuel its capacity to reproduce its internal goal. He then sums up the peculiarities of the closed system of thought:

> Firstly, it claims to represent a truth of universal validity, capable of explaining all phenomena, and has a cure for all that ails man. In the second place, it is a system which cannot be refuted by evidence, because all potentially damaging data are automatically processed and reinterpreted to make them fit the expected pattern. The processing is done by sophisticated methods of casuistry, centred on axioms of great emotive power, and indifferent to the rules of common logic. In the third place, it is a system which invalidates criticism by shifting the argument to the subjective motivation of the critic, and deducing his motivation from the axioms of the system itself.
>
> (Koestler 1989: 262–3)

Rigid analogous processors and adaptive parallel processors

Yoshida Kazuo, a colleague of Hamaguchi and professor of economics at Kyoto University, interprets Japanese-style social systems by means of the neural network model. This metaphor of the brain functions ideologically similar to *aidagara*, and focuses on the complex activity between different parts of the brain.[27] The relevance of Yoshida's example lies in the magic attributed to the co-operative capabilities of systems and, in particular, those of Japan.

Yoshida has come to the conclusion that complexity and self-organization are important features of organizational forms in economic life all over the world. Fortunately for Japan, Japan is endowed naturally with a spontaneous form of self-organization, very similar to that of the holistic principles on which the neural networks of the brain are based. Here, it is parallel processing that plays an important role.[28] The brain is a complex combination of synapses and neurones that enables this organ to perform actions, such

90 *Group categorization*

as learning, remembering and making judgements and thought associations. In order to do this the whole must have one main integral function only. The neural system is generated, in analogy to the brain. This neurological structure, according to Yoshida, describes Japanese social systems quite adequately. For instance, in the Japanese company, information processing takes place at the workplace, where the workers share and deal with information together. Because all the workers jointly participate in the process of dealing with information, it brings about a holographic structure.[29] The judgement of participants with a low working capacity passes through this holographic structure. From the point of view of the process as a whole, the holographic structure can never be wrong, even when mistakes occur as a result of a low working capacity. This is because all participants together form the 'integrative memory' of the system: the memories of the parts contain a copy of the whole. Thus, workers automatically adjust themselves within the system so that the production process runs smoothly and jobs get completed on time (Yoshida 1998: 78–90).

Japanese-style social systems, according to Yoshida, comprise multiple networks of which the elements are controlled by decision-making at the workplace: because all members have a holographic memory, they can make correct decisions without the need for instructions from a leader. By contrast, if a leader is assigned all information dealings, as is the case in Ōbei, his powers become strained. If the leader then fails to feed the right input (of information/instructions) into the system, the whole system will be affected and may collapse. Even though the Japanese system uses manual information input, mistakes, Yoshida argues, are automatically corrected by the system. Ōbei systems, which depend on the leader as a central processing unit (CPU), process all information centrally. The leader must have great capacity to deal with the entire system and therefore receives a high salary. The efficiency of Ōbei systems, according to Yoshida, can easily be understood as a methodological result of providing incentives and applying sanctions to individuals. This system is efficient within the bounds of hierarchical structures that are not 'complex' (in the systems theoretical sense, simple tree-structured hierarchies). An additional disadvantage is that the costs of producing a leader are high. Moreover, as the quantity of information used in management increases rapidly as a result of the information revolution, leaders are bound to make mistakes eventually. Mistakes, then, are likely to extend in arithmetic progression over entire systems. By contrast, a Japanese system does not need to spend financial resources on a leader, and if the complexity of the shared-information system increases, it has no trouble in dealing with it adequately.

Scientism and the unit of the nation

Ironically, it was the dissatisfaction with modernization theory in particular which arose from views of the Japanese as undemocratic, feudal, uncreative, that gave an incentive to social scientists to apply scientistic concepts in an

Global categorization 91

alternative fashion. The Japanese systems model is largely supported by and follows developments of modern science. This can be seen in the changing ways in which the scientistic proof (autopoietic systems and complexity) of Hamaguchi's main theoretical concept, *kanjin*, has been defined from the 1970s to the 1990s. The conceptual framework Hamaguchi used in this period evolved from simple networks to system theory and from systems theory to complexity, which he bolstered by rooting it in Buddhist ontology. The main theme is that developments in particle physics, and particularly in quantum mechanics, have led to the collapse of the mechanistic view of nature. In the classical Newtonian world view nature was regarded as a machine, the whole was treated as the sum of its parts, and the inter-relatedness of the whole was overlooked. Ideas on rationality and unilineary causality were re-evaluated, and some academics put their belief in a paradigm shift from atomism, individualism and Cartesian dualism to holism, interrelatedness and spontaneous self-organization. Some believe that it is a global trend that will favour oriental cultures, and especially Japan.

A major problem with this shift, however, is the definition of the territorial and political boundaries of the Japanese nation-state as a cultural system, and its equation with the intellectual traditions of the Japanese élite. In the first place, the notion that a system has clear boundaries is hard to maintain outside scientific experiment, as the assumption of isolability is very much in doubt. Furthermore, the system is usually treated as a (logically) closed system (mental black box), closed by the very act of conducting thought experiments in social science research. Thus, in dealing with an open empirical system, the system is assumed rather than proven. In a nation-centred paradigm, the relations between nations are treated as relations between isolated individuals. For example, Hamaguchi regards the 'inequality between nations', competition between nations, and the national character of Japan and Ōbei of major importance. At home, however, in Japan, people do not have personalities but are in the first place appendages of organ-izations, which are the product of a system that reproduces itself. Another example shows how Hamaguchi emphasizes the link between nation and culture. He maintains that capitalist development is taken as a standard way of development, thus leading to the ethnocentric application of values. If all nations were to internationalize and do away with the cultural gap between systems, all would end up in international egotistical competition. Why, one wonders, does he not apply the '*kanjin*' concept to relations among nations?

Apparently, there are some problems in the trend of conflating systems with society, or, the nation. Whenever system boundaries are equated with those of the nation, the experimental notion of clear boundaries is projected on to those of the nation and takes on the assumption of isolability. Systems, even open ones, must be closed logically by the very act of constructing an experiment; in dealing with an open empirical system, the system is assumed rather than proven. Therefore even theories that regard nations, organizations and parts of the world as open systems, tend not to justify

92 *Group categorization*

the construction of assumed boundaries, enclosing the system logically. For example, the frequently used notion of Ōbei, short for America and Europe, is a strongly generalizing, historical concept, hardly conducive to systems analysis as a logically isolable unit.

In nation-centred approaches, errors are taken to represent deviation from a conceptually pure system or model that values co-operation, coherence and harmony. In turn, harmony and co-operation are important conceptual sources in constructing mechanical and organismic models of thought and perception, transforming the relation between knowing subject and object into a dualism between 'system' and 'environment,' or 'nation' and 'world'. The observer identifies himself with the system, which is the source of supra-human knowledge. By organismizing subjectivity, the nation-centred observer has become the transcendental subject. In Hamaguchi's work, for example, ordinary observers become the authoritative speakers of the 'autopoietic system', a system that replicates itself. Systems exist only *vis-à-vis* their environment. In Hamaguchi's work the dualism between object and subject has become one of Japan versus what he calls the West.

The societal conditions that favoured the emergence of systems theory after 1945 are easily forgotten. Among them of particular importance were the growth of the role of government in the economy, the bureaucratization of society and the rise of new industries based upon technology and automation and an increase in administrative and technical occupations. These trends were accompanied by an intellectual tradition of optimism, a belief in progress through scientific rationality and in an increase of faith in expertise. Formerly, the relatively small number of intellectuals had been seen as a guarantee of their relatively independent (from class interest) position that enabled them to develop and criticize ideas from a great variety of perspectives and interests (cf. Mannheim 1929). But with the rise of a large class of intellectuals, intellectuals could well develop an ideology appropriate to their 'collective interests'. Theories that privilege the intellectual as cognitive engineer of societal views in all societies that include a growing class of academics and highly educated members have an increasingly influential role in the formulation of policy-making by the administration of modern nation-states. Here, systems theory can be regarded as one particular attempt to formulate the ideology of the administrative intellectual among others.

The problem with attempts to relate science and technology, in specific, to Japanese culture is that it is based on a misreading of science as something transcendental and value free, and evolving according to its own internal laws. Ironically, these laws are projected back into a static view of 'traditional culture', hidden among the relics of societal systems today. But science and technology are the products of society, which is more than a holistic product of tradition. It is shaped and reshaped from generation to generation by social structures and conflicts, economic needs, political pressures, including the science politics of each administration. An intellectual framework that

Global categorization 93

emphasizes harmony, self-organization and 'in-betweenness' is not just a result of ancient Japanese views of nature or Buddhist ontology at the heart of the Japanese unconscious. It is also the product of more recent domestic ideologies and social experiences that combine the foreign and the threatening into a framework of thought. Although it structures thought around the unit of the nation, the sentiment that could accompany nationalism need not be there at all. Nevertheless, its mobilization is facilitated by the fact that discursive tradition does not explore possible remedies for solving or understanding problems, but seeks to define perceived threats in terms of intruding factors and outside others.

Any academic view presupposed the use of particulars and universals. Depending on the ways in which problems are identified, and the way in which they are defined in terms of research populations, and on the basis of research materials, the researcher argues his or her case. Similarly, any theory of uniqueness ascribes particularity to a nation in reference to other nations, and, in order to make possible comparison, presupposes some form of shared, universal, features too. The crucial matter is whether the selection of the research population or unit, and the choice of criteria for identifying variables are adequate for solving the research problem under concern. If universality and particularity are presumed in the definition of a study it must be argued in the context of the problem at issue. Many research problems vary not according to national culture, but are determined by various factors such as environmental circumstances, practices of labour exploitation and élite ideology.

The notion of the universal availability of resources is problematic because cultural and financial sales techniques make them scarce: not everyone has access to basic resources, let alone luxury products. If we ask why conditions for economic growth are not universal in the first place, cultural abnormality markers are mobilized effortlessly to explain the particular 'shortcomings' of certain societies, diagnosing the mistaken insights these cultures have into their own, deplorable, conditions. The tricky aspect about globalist theories is that universal pretence is kept up. Thus, while everyone advertises property and happiness as attainable, resources that are essential to all may be monopolized by some, or are accessible to only a few privileged or qualified groups. In itself, this can be explained by principles from economics, biology and psychology, and so on, but in scientistic nationalism, the success of prospering groups in employing universal principles is explained by reference to the cultural resources they rely upon.

Behind the universalistic claims of academic globalism nationalist ulterior motives are hidden. Although cultural products are advertised as universal necessities, essential hardware for building civilization, and universally exportable and applicable, there is a catch in the end. Globalists employ concepts such as civilization, modernization, universal struggle, class, field, universal religion, science, universal wisdom and art, to show the relevance of their theories by means of globalist categories and universal principles,

94 *Group categorization*

but ultimately root those theories in Our national tradition. Furthermore, underlying globalist notions is the presumption that all sources needed for attaining happiness and prosperity are potentially available to all peoples under the right conditions and by applying the right methods. In scientistic nationalism, the right conditions are found in Our nation, and the right methods in Our tradition.

Part III

Group-framing habits and strategies

7   Grouping

In Part II, I made a distinction between three kinds of markers used by academics for delineating national identities: natural, cultural and globalist markers. Although it is often thought that national identity is composed of factors that emphasize culture, I have shown that in nation-centric research cultural, natural and globalist categories are all deployed in the course of advocating various forms of national identity. The use of one category in characterizing society shapes the space and scope of discussion in a certain way, though it does not determine it. Thus, cultural markers leave space for negotiation between different cultural and political groups although the national identity markers of culture employed by the establishment may dominate public debate. The use of two markers, e.g. cultural and natural group markers, generates other effects. Physiological categories, such as race and the brain, turn out to add extra force to cultural theories of national particularism, and are usually presented as expressions of nature, obeying the laws of nature, and therefore 'scientific'. When these natural markers are used to reinforce the boundaries of the nation, isolationist forces and discrimination obtain a politically free hand, especially in the case of cultural markers that take ancient tradition and collective spiritual purity as their base. And, finally, the categories class, middle-mass, modern civilization, science and liberalism are easily viewed as universal but are also deployed as globalist criteria in ascribing particularity to nation-states.

I emphasize here that the three ways of identity creation as such occur in all academic descriptions of national identity, simply because any distinction is based on criteria that derive from discriminative perceptions of nature, culture or the universal. The argument, however, revolves around the ways in which *patterns of markers* are used in definitions and theories of the nation. For in nation-centric and regionalist research it is the creation of boundary markers, whether natural, cultural or global, which in certain political designs always coincide with national borders. The exclusive use of specific boundary markers, the way nations and regions are staged in the world, and the roles given to natural, cultural and/or universal categories in debate all form clues to the politics of identity creation and its consequences.

Important to an understanding of the socio-political dimension of nation-centric approaches are the ways in which intellectuals at home use the various

98 *Group-framing habits and strategies*

category markers to delineate themselves from their opponents. The circumstances in which factions stress the importance of certain criteria rather than other ones are crucial. An example in which all three modes of identity creation can be found is Maoist propaganda during the Cultural Revolution (±1966–76). The markers for class background, norms and values and blood relations were all three considered as criteria for belonging to 'the people', albeit by three different factions.[1] Although human malleability (*culturalist* categories), associated with socialist emancipation, was stressed in official propaganda (Munro 1971, 1977), in factional struggles all three markers were used, depending on the particular political background of the faction under concern. Often, national identity was defined using *universalistic* criteria of socialism: universal socialist emancipation, the laws of proletarian revolution and the leadership of the communist party. However, *natural* markers were used to denote hereditary qualities of socialism through blood ties. According to the first view one could learn how to be socialist through emancipation; the second view regarded socialist identity as a matter of historical determination, while the third made socialism inheritable.

A further distinction should be made between the level at which debates take place and the situation in which they are held. Debaters at an international level, for example, use different arguments and pursue different goals than they do at lower levels of organization, such as on a national or institutional level. Thus, a 'pro-Western' liberal may be in favour of open international markets at an international level, but appears to be a staunch socialist moralist or Confucian neo-authoritarian when it comes to domestic issues.[2] Moreover, a Chinese academic who identifies him/herself with both the Chinese nation and democracy may use a different set of arguments in discussion with a foreigner than with a domestic socialist or democrat. Foreign socialism to this academic may appear not as 'true' as Chinese socialism, and foreign democracy less humanitarian compared with Chinese democracy.[3] Furthermore, attitudes toward academic theory are also related to the different ways in which scholars relate to their nation. Umehara Takeshi, for example, identifies not with a bureaucratic or parliamentary but with a communitarian Japan (Umehara Takeshi and Inamori Kazuo 1995); Nichibunken's former director, Kawai Hayao (1995–2001), identifies with Japanese narrative and a traditional mentality, not with a rationalist and scientist modern nation-state (cf. Kawai Hayao 1993). Both were radically against the modernizing influence of science, which they associated with the industrialized West, and in favour of academic research that takes as its basis a humane, that is Japanese or Eastern, approach, perhaps in combination with a selection of 'Western feats of civilization'.

Thus, to understand the constellation of markers used in nation-centric research it is necessary to take account of the academic 'faction' to which intellectuals belong, the 'level of interlocution' and the 'nature of the bond with the nation'. These factors contribute to a deeper insight into the ways academic theories are framed and constructed regionally and politically.

Group architecture

The examples are not representative of, but a selection from, the construction of group identity in academic debate in China and Japan. They serve to illustrate the ways in which groups are built and shaped in space and time.

Family metaphors

One clue to the group construction of nation-centric and regionalist research lies in the use of the family metaphor. The 'natural closeness' of blood-ties and the shared social experiences of family members yield a strong symbolic image. Its ambivalence facilitates group application. The family metaphor resounds in the manner in which the term *We* is used in academic argument, and in analogy to the family concept includes references, as explained below, to a network of associates, adversaries and absentees.[4] The We and They groups are contrasted discursively to influence the views of the audience by emotional or political means, and acquire their meaning from a biased context. The family metaphor indicates that the groups defined share a certain identity, or family resemblance. Criteria of in- and exclusion need not be explicit and are context dependent. For instance, We can be used as an abbreviation for 'We Japanese', 'We of this company', and 'We friends' in Japan, and for 'We Chinese', 'We members of this work unit' and 'We from this village' in China.[5]

'They' denotes reference groups that are used as units of contrast, for instance, 'the West', 'the Orient' and 'the capitalists'. I use the concept of They to refer to the practice of They-ing, in the same way as the practice of constructing the Other is referred to as Othering. The Other is the object of observation and research, and is recreated by the powerful, knowing subject through the creation of a temporal distance between 'the primitive' Other and the Self.[6] A distinction between They and the Other may be useful as They refers to the image of a powerful bully, or a group personalized as a big brother or menace. The presence of They is felt as a threat and constantly nags at the pride of the us-group, as They remind Us that We need Them to be Our unique selves. Examples of such They-groups are the USA, capitalism and the West, perceived by scholars who identify themselves with powerless countries that are victimized and discriminated by Them.

The existence of groups of absentees is felt by virtue of their absence. Absentees, such as political dissidents, outcasts and dropouts, when ignored or forgotten are absent from academic theory. They may be the poor, ethnic minorities, the unemployed, or other groups that do not fit the current notion of 'the people'. The absentees of hostile nations, however, are spotted easily and analysed by Our academics. Thus, academic research dedicates much space to the victims of Their abuse of human rights, denying the existence of such practices at home. More specifically, the influence of absentees forms a clue to understanding the selection of research problems, such as why the

100 *Group-framing habits and strategies*

success of Chinese overseas migrants is a rewarding topic at home, while the topic of successful overseas dissidents is not;[7] why resistance fighters are the heroes of the Chinese revolution, but resistance against oppression in Tibet is invisible to the broad academic audience; why the affiliation of a Christian believer to the Chinese Christian Church is acknowledged, but the existence of Roman Catholics is not; and, why the reverence for the word of the party chairman is condoned but the muffled support for Li Hongzhi, the leader of Falungong, is deemed too loud for academic theorizing.[8]

Not only establishment academics use their group vocabulary uncritically and politically. Establishment opposition, to a certain extent, must too bow to the ideological grammar of mainstream discourse, and takes care not to invoke the politically sensitive absentees. Sometimes establishment strategists, by uncovering a select choice of absentees, may gain the sympathy of the public, and employ this redress against the opposition. For example, the victims of official corruption in pollution scandals, drug trafficking and trade in humans, are occasionally resurrected in calls for rectification campaigns. No matter how much sympathy there may be around for absentees, if the law does not protect free expression of dissent and if it entails negative sanctioning, sympathetic words are likely to remain unpronounced. Although the inactivity of students, the poverty of peasants, the views of political prisoners, the angry consumer, the corrupt official, the depressed schoolchild may be discussed, it is done only sporadically in carefully defined contexts. Absentees have no place in nation-centric ideology for they are not an integral part of a functional, national whole, the smooth running system, socialist unity or the civilizational feats that academics may boast about.

In nation-centric and regionalist research, the composition of a particular constellation of friendly and hostile neighbours and other referent groups is flexible and varies in time and context. Adherence to several groups at the same time requires identification with various groups, sometimes according to different or even contradictory criteria. The abundance of ways in which group identities are created facilitates reference switching: by varying the use of group markers one can delineate new groups and create new identities for Us, Them/the Other and absentees. However, patterns of referencing are not random or changeable at will. They are constrained by the pressures of political legitimacy, discursive credibility and academic debate, which require reasoned (not necessarily logical) arguments and, at least outwardly, loyalty to established conventions. Scholars may also feel pressure to change their position and produce new group combinations and categories when others do. A common example of Us/They switching is when Chinese and Japanese scholars come together and talk about a common (Our) Asian/Confucian background. The same Chinese scholars may switch from the Us code (Japan and China) to the Us (the Chinese) and *They* (Japan) code at home, and immediately switch modes of associations made with that country.[9]

Framing group differences

Whether and how academics frame and contrast the nation (Us) with Others (Them) but leave out some (absentees) depends on the academic's discursive context and on the ways s/he perceives that context. Thus, the way in which an academic construes an image of different nations also depends on his/her institutional context relative to the way s/he perceives the context of Other nations (and They) in relation to Us. There are several methods by which the relative position of the Other and They are envisaged. Here I mention three general approaches that are used in combination: horizontal polarization (lateral juxtaposition), vertical stratification and temporalization. These strategies of contrast can be applied alongside one another, though usually only one prevails.

A theory that does not make a distinction between groups, hierarchy and temporalization does not even exist. For this reason, grouping is essential to any theory of society. I am concerned, however, not with whether group distinctions are made but with the way in which methods of grouping occur in certain patterns with certain modes of identity construction and boundary markers. Such patters may tell us about existing trends in nation-centred research. My concern lies with the pattern in the nation-centric and regionalist application of these methods. Its relevance is that in nation-centric research, marking group by means of set frames of construction carries more weight than does the acquisition of knowledge on the basis of problem-solving. By observing changes in the application of these methods of group construction in academic discourse over a period of time and in several places, it should be possible to perceive and acquire some understanding of the taxonomic usage of nation-framing.

A discussion of this understanding follows an elaboration of the three methodological approaches of horizontal polarization (lateral juxtaposition), vertical stratification and temporalization (Table 2).

Table 2 Three methods of group division

Means of group construction	Sub-division of forms
Horizontal polarization	Antagonistic, continuum, multipolar
Vertical stratification	Duality, multilayered, absence
Temporalization	Progressive, regressive, cyclical

Horizontal polarization

In *horizontal polarization* (juxtaposition) academics create opposites by polarizing the characteristics of and relations between adversaries. Thus, We and They (the Other) are constructed as bipolar opposites. Between the two poles relations of various quality figure, varying from antagonistic to friendly. If antagonistic, the relationship between We and They/the Other is put in

102 *Group-framing habits and strategies*

absolute terms of good and bad, right and wrong, and is characterized by a clash of interests. During the Cold War, the US and the SU were related as such; in communist China, the proletariat and the bourgeoisie; and, in some strands of Orientalism, East and West.

By contrast, less antagonistic relations between the two poles means that the two are ascribed a less extrapolated relationship, imaginable as a bipolar continuum. However, even when bipolar opposites are presented as relative and gradual, the latent friction thought to exist between the poles can still be of crucial importance to the tenure of the debate in which it is couched. For, discourse constructed in terms of opposite identities and in an atmosphere of political overture is more ambiguous and complex than is discourse couched in antagonistic terms of good and evil. Examples are characterizations of East and West as relatively peaceful versus relatively aggressive, relatively feminine versus relatively male, relatively natural versus relatively artificial (cultural) and relatively groupist versus relatively individualistic.

A third method of presenting the relationship between groups is its definition in terms of multipolar configurations. Examples are characterizations of the world as 'multicultural',' and 'multiethnic'. By implication, multi-culturality negates the possibility of coming to a value judgement by comparing cultures. In other words, all cultures are respected by virtue of their culture inherent criteria. Especially academics that take a stance against a perceived threat of a homogenizing, globalized world tend to call for multiculturality. Nevertheless, such calls often equate culture with the entity of the nation-state, while oppressed cultures at home remain Absentees in the so-called multicultural debates.

Hierarchy

Various forms of *hierarchy* are ascribed to national modes of organization. They divide societies into so-called dual- and multilayered societies, and societies without stratification. In a *dual society* a simple hierarchy between the leadership and the people (positive) and rulers and ruled (negative) makes for a division common to democracies, communist regimes and dictatorships. Further distinctions include soft and hard stratification (depending on the presence of upward and downward mobility) and the extent to which one or two directional flows of communication between the top and lower layer of society are effective.

The academics who praise dual-societal hierarchies usually perceive only a soft separation between the vertical layers of the hierarchy and a two-way (albeit unequal) communication system of consultation and remonstrance by the lower stratum, and a just form of election of the leading top. In the 1933 Maoist conceptualization of the mass-line, for example, the simple hierarchy between leaders and masses included the education of both the leadership and the people, the consultation of the masses by the communist leadership,

Grouping 103

and the just implementation of the mass-line in the interest of the people. Thus, in point four of 'Some questions concerning methods of leadership', Mao defined all correct leadership as 'from the masses, to the masses'.[10]

Another example is Nichibunken professor Kasaya Kazuhiko, who uses systems theory in his articulation of rulers and subjects.[11] Kasaya studied the Edo meritocracy (*nōryokushugi*) in Japanese-style organizational systems. The power of the 'lord' (*kugi*) is usually imaged to be absolute, while the samurai (*bushi*) had lost their freedom and independence. But the samurai, in fact, Kasaya argues, functioned as a correction to an otherwise absolute form of political rule. Especially in times of rioting, the vassals would admonish the lord. Here, according to Kasaya, lies the prototype of Japanese-style organization in which both the meaning of 'vertical society' (*tate-shakai*) and individualism are upheld. Kasaya insists that groupism did not suppress individualism. Besides, the Western concept of 'the individual', he argues, is different from the Japanese Bushi-type of individual, which is expressed in *Hagakure*, a Samurai manual (1716).[12] Accordingly, it should be read as a code of honour and correct behaviour. However, despite the general references to honourable behaviour and etiquette, referred to by Kasaya, the book begins with 'The Way of the Samurai (*Bushidō*) is found in death' (Yamamoto Tsunetomo 2000: 17). It does thoroughly discuss the behaviour of the Samurai separate from what it regards as loyalty and honourable death.[13]

Nowadays, Kasaya maintains, criticism of modern Japanese-style organization is growing stronger. In companies there is a call for 'capability' and for 'restoration'. The prevailing seniority system used to be based on work experience and credentials as well as on age. It was also a meritocracy, as people from any background were eligible for promotion. Therefore modern managers, in Kasaya's view, could learn much from the Japanese-style modern system. It used to uphold both hierarchic organizations in which capable managers would advise the leader and the Japanese conception of individual freedom, which grounds initiative and capacity in the freedom of self-sacrifice by transcending the individual self and the system.[14]

Compared with simple dual societal divisions, approaches that analyse vertical hierarchies are more complex, comprising multiple layers, tiers or segments of hierarchical organization. Positive evaluations of such hierarchic organizations include Dumont's analysis of Indian caste systems,[15] and Nakane Chie's description of Japan as a vertical society.[16] In such analyses, vertical or hierarchical power structures are not associated with dictatorship, but rather with orderly rule, unity and harmony. Opponents of hierarchical structures reject attempts at legitimizing national identities that are ideologically rooted in such hierarchical structures. They do not acknowledge their 'autocracy', 'discrimination' and 'dictatorship'.

Complex hierarchic identities are found especially in regimes that are based on religious, socialist and state bureaucracies. Communitarian critics of the bureaucratic state apparatus establishment try to unite the bureaucratic

104 *Group-framing habits and strategies*

hierarchy with communitarian notions of equity. Complaints usually address the low speed and impersonal nature of communication between different levels, and the numerous heads of divisions and branches one must pass before decisions are made. By contrast, those who identify with the hierarchy take pride in the wisdom and fairness of the hierarchic process and the body of moral, legal and political considerations taken into account in the interest of fair treatment for 'the people'.

In some cases an *absence of stratification* is ascribed to nations that are represented as homogeneous or egalitarian. For example, in Murakami Yasusuke's analysis of Japanese attitudes toward class, the Japanese population is ascribed homogeneity: a majority of the Japanese identifies with the middle class. Murakami therefore regards Japan as a 'middle-mass society'.[17] Similarly, communist societies, in principle, formally do not allow for socioeconomic stratification. At the same time, however, the organization of party and administrative grade systems is positively elaborate. Hierarchies seem to attract legitimization by nationalist ideologies that stress the homogeneity of the national character and the fairness of the system.

Temporal projection of Us and Them/the Other

The ways in which time is used to construct the Other in anthropology has been the subject of Johannes Fabian's *Time and the Other*.[18] The book relates how faith in salvation was replaced by faith in reason with which the Other's present was denounced as primitive or savage, and relegated to the past (Fabian 1983: 10–11).[19] If we extend this form of temporal projection of the Other to Them, further distinctions can be made between different dimensions of time. The projection of Us, Them and the Other into the past, the present and future yield various scenarios in which time politically shapes the meaning of cultural value:

- Placing the Other into Our past by comparing the Other to Us when We were primitive (e.g. 'American Indians are primitive').
- Placing Us in Their past by designing a course of development that places Them into modernity or postmodernity (e.g. 'We Chinese have to catch up with the modern West'; 'We Europeans must catch up with postmodern Japan').
- Appropriating Them into Our future by envisaging a future in which We rule and They has to follow and learn from Us (e.g. 'the East will rule the world in the twenty-first century'). In other words, They will become the Other.
- Transplanting Our past into Our and Their future by projecting Our lost paradise into the future (e.g. the future of the world lies in reviving the ancient Japanese form of forest life of the Jōmon (*c.* 10,000–300 BC)).[20]
- Emphasizing the ancient Other's influence on Our past (e.g. only focusing

on the influence of Arabic and Chinese science on the development of knowledge in Europe).

- Forgetting Their modern influence on Our society (advocating anti-modern ideology without acknowledging the conditions it creates for continuing traditions).
- Absorbing the Other into Our present (They must follow the same path of progress for Their own good, and therefore should use Our medicine, method of schooling and manners).
- Combining Our past with Their present (advocating Our Eastern ancient values merged with Their Western modern knowledge).

The various temporal projections of Us, Them and the Other are part and parcel of the process of national identity creation and reflect political intention. The demarcation of the temporal dimension of this relationship indicates an imbalance, which serves to steer and control the relative position of Us in relation to Them (the Other). Notions of civilization, evolution, and development in such national frameworks all stress this temporal dimension.

The way in which the nation develops through time can take on various shapes: theories of evolution 'add' something to the past, depending on the criteria the author assigns to the path evolution is claimed to follow. In most views of evolution time goes upward, a conception embodied in notions, such as the progress of science and technology, economic growth, social differentiation, modernization, education, self-control. Other points of view shape evolutionary time differently, shaping it in the forms of a wave (as in rise and fall theories of civilization), a cycle (in dynastic histories – *wangchao xunhuan*) or a spiral (general systems theory). Again other theories envisage evolutionary change as the switching of gears, in which many bottle-necks (inefficiency, injustice, exploitation) lead to periods of fast transformation (modernization, protest and boycott, emancipation) and then to chaos (collapse, civil war, revolution). From this chaos new forms of organization emerge (reorganization, order, liberation), after which change may slow down again to a speed at which adjustments of society are thought to be an adequate form of governing. Examples of such views of evolutionary time are theories of revolution, transcendental change, chaos, dissipative structures, positive feedback mechanisms and punctuated evolution, all of which have been borrowed by the social sciences. Pessimistically inclined estimations of global and societal change reverse time, envisaging it as a slope (gradual or steep) or an abyss (e.g. the decline of the West; the fall of capitalism; the fall of communism; the end of time; and the millennium). Similarly, the backward direction of time is given inevitability by its definition as an environmental process of dying, due to the squandering of natural resources and pollution in the modern world (entropy; heat death; moral sin; environmental movements).

In short, in nation-centric and regionalist ideology the tactical manipulation of time is expedient to saving the nation, or making it powerful. Thus

106 *Group-framing habits and strategies*

nation-centric modernization efforts are an attempt to acquire what They have by speeding up time, going back to nature is a nostalgic attempt to revive an idyllic past. And, finally, revolution and national emancipation are meant to make possible leaps over evolutionary stages, helping Us to survive the natural selection of nations.

Grouping in short

I argued for the merits of making a distinction between the Other and Them. Although both concepts tend to be embedded in dualities of the central we-group and its referent (the Other/Them), the structure in which these concepts are embedded is of a different nature. In the first case (We versus the Other), the we-group tends to perceive itself as powerful and condescendingly endeavours to help the weak Other. In the second case (We versus Them), the we-group perceives itself self-righteously as an underdog, and systematically defines itself (and the rest of the world) as a victim, exploited by Them. In both cases, however, the we-group believes in the superiority of its views, its mission to save the world, and the fairness of the views proposed. Although the underdog we-group is full of indignation about Them, groups of suppressed absentees populate their own theoretical Us-unit. Their absence seems to be correlated with the academically over-represented Them-bully, in relation to whom the absentees relate themselves, and whose positive feature They sometimes borrow in constructing their arguments against the Us-under-dog at home.

In my discussion of methods for constructing groups, I made a distinction between horizontal polarization, vertical stratification and temporalization. I described three forms of horizontal division: antagonistic bipolar polarization, the creation of a bipolar continuum, and the multipolar configuration. All three methods lend themselves to political manipulation in ideological fights between nations, world parts or groups of countries if the framework and units of research are taken for granted. A systematic conflation of units of research with nations invariably leads to a confusion of method with observations: nations become poles when they are treated as such systematically without critical reflection. And groups that do not fit into the current frame of thought become neglected absentees.

The *hierarchy* ascribed to national identities divide into dual- and multi-layered societies, and societies characterized by an absence of stratification. Hierarchies seem to attract legitimization by nationalist ideologies that stress the homogeneity of the national character and the fairness of the system. The verticality of such hierarchies means to express a measure of co-operation between the layers of the hierarchy, ranging from the symbiosis of class and mutual consult between leaders and followers to the upward and downward mobility of free agents along the societal hierarchy. But, in fact, nation-centric images of such societies indicate that any discontent, dissent and protest are suppressed or channelled into specially devised institutions for problem-solving, while the interests of establishment rulers and authors are protected.

In the *temporal projection* of Us and Them/the Other nations are reconstructed in time, shaped into various patterns and manipulated in politics. The projection of Us and Them in the past, the present and the future is part of the process of national identity creation and reflects political intention. In nation-centric and regionalist ideology the tactical manipulation of time, its direction (forward, backward, round), form (wave, spiral, cycle) and speed serve discursive strategies of saving the nation, recovering its essential being or strengthening it. Thus nation-centred approaches to modernization are part of an attempt to acquire what They have by acceleration, going back to nature is a nostalgic attempt to revive an idyllic past, and 'isolation' from the world promises the realization of the nation's real potential. And, finally, in nation-centred and regionalist research revolution and national emancipation are meant to make possible leaps over evolutionary stages, helping Us to survive the natural selection of nations.

Although much effort is being exerted by scholars to avoid nationalist discourse, an uncritical and unreflective use of the regional unit of analysis and the habit of creating discourse by forging dualities between the Other's opinion and My knowledge hampers other self-reflective exertions. Much work remains to be done in mapping the ways in which the nation and world parts have been personalized, systemized and given a variety of temporal dimensions and forces, for the link between national frame and politics annihilates its academic credibility.

8 Framing the nation in the short history of the International Research Centre for Japanese Studies (Nichibunken, 1987–)

In this chapter I argue how initial conditions of the establishment of Nichibunken (1987), a national academic research institute, set the stage for an altered, nation-centric development of its curriculum and research agenda. The 1995 discussion on its controversial inception, between former Premier Nakasone (1982–7) and the founding director of Nichibunken, Umehara Takeshi, illustrates the intertwining interests of Nakasone's views on international politics and the self-styled 'apolitical' philosophy of Umehara.

Nichibunken began as a producer of plain nationalist ideology, but changed its tune as criticism of the institute increased and as its members became increasingly involved in international discussion. Under Nichibunken director, Kawai Hayao (1995–2001), the institute's nation-centred rhetoric altered and its political hue mellowed. However, despite its universalistic pretence, the production of nation-centred research and debate has become a structural feature of the production of knowledge at the research centre.

Finally, I discuss this nation-centred form of knowledge production with references to the organization of academic debate and group research at Nichibunken. I illustrate my argument on the bias of nation-framing with the examples of director Kawai's research on the Japanese psyche and the organization of research on a comparative research project on chess (*shōgi*).

Institutionalized nation-framing and its failure as social science

What makes Japan a Japanese civilization? The answer to this question in theories of Japanese cultural uniqueness (*nihonbunka-ron*) is sought in a wide range of academic concepts, ranging from bio-cultural, linguistic and cerebral studies to the study of concepts such as culture gene and group evolution. Such approaches tend to equate the Japanese nation with the Japanese nation-state, and have in common the presumption that the meaning of Japanese society and civilization lies 'in between people', that is, the special nature of the relationship between Japanese people (*kanjin*).[1] The Japanese would share features and tools, such as language, a common genetic origin, intuition,

History of Nichibunken 109

cultural elements, religious concepts and a collective unconscious, enabling them to communicate by means of other media than those available to what is pictured as the modern West. I believe, however, that the most menacing feature of the *nihonbunka-ron* in academic debate is not so much the nationalist ideology it is associated with but its less salient feature of categorically focusing on the nation as a framework of research. Although the feature has a long history (cf. Harootunian 1988; Wakabayashi 1986; Morris-Suzuki 1998), in this chapter I want to concentrate on the structural effects of institutionalizing the nation as a unit of analysis in the organization of academic research done at Nichibunken. Nevertheless, it is a feature shared with academic theory in many academic communities, directing attention away from processes that occur at transnational levels. In order to go beyond the *nihonbunka-ron*, that is discussions of Japanese uniqueness, it is necessary for both academics in general and critics in particular to examine the role of the analytical unit of the nation-state and the nation in their own work as a unit of research or comparison.[2] For the *nihonbunka-ron* thrives exactly because it is spurned and rejected, unaccompanied by attempts to explicate why the works of *others* belong to the *nihonbunka-ron* and not that of our own.

Nations do not develop according to set laws, and not all social problems and cultural clashes can be explained by reference to nation-state characteristics. Problems in human group formation and communication, depending on the issue, may be better understood by reference to processes that transcend the framework of the nation-state. On a basic level, principles of group formation may be located in and influenced by but not determined by the shapes and structures of nation-states. In fact, important social and cultural interest groups form across the borders of nation-states. Transnational group formation results both from national limitations placed on the development of communities, causing migration, and from activities only indirectly related to nation-state policies, such as home-making, brain drain, population growth, adventure, ethnic war, natural disasters and policies carried out by NGO's and other global organizations. Although these phenomena are related to nation-state politics and administration, the complexity of the factors related to each of these examples results in relatively independent clusters of links and processual regularities, rather than in exclusive national products.

For this reason it is important for the humanities and social science research to take into account initially the influence of the nation-state as one among many factors when defining research problems, depending (of course) on the problem area under concern. Studies that omit to do this, and automatically proceed from the framework of the nation-state, I call nation-centric. One of the difficulties in acquiring an understanding of the function and consequences of nation-centrism in academic work is that it moves at various levels of abstraction. It is produced by people of flesh and blood, who lead an existence at the micro-level of research, while their product is conditioned,

110 *Group-framing habits and strategies*

affected and steered by processes that take place at a macro-level. Research institutes reside in both of these levels at once. Because they are the main link at which communication takes place between academics and academic policy-makers, they constitute the location at which research facilities are provided, status is conferred and regulations (formal and informal) are laid down.

Academic debate, then, does not take place in a vacuum but is held by people with various needs, under various pressures and with various ambitions. The local socio-political circumstances in which academic debates are held and the prospects of financial remuneration are of great importance as a pre-selection mechanism for the selection of a population eligible as academic crew. Furthermore, academic debates are part of an ever-changing but ongoing intellectual tradition. Usually these factors have developed in relation to, although are not determined by, processes of the emergence, shaping, reshaping and replacement of nation-states, i.e. a framework of emerging nation-states. Social science, then, came to function as a means of explaining and designing phenomena related to the development of nation-states, including itself, but was never fully determined by the nation-state or fully designed by its own administrators. Social science is not part of a pre-designed project.

Academic policies, however, in some countries are more closely related to state policies than in others. In the example of the International Research Centre for Japanese Studies (Kyoto, Japan), however, patterns are discernible that indicate concerted efforts of academic steering while focusing pre-dominantly on the nation as a unit of analysis. This is expressed in a tendency to direct research targets (certain topics, disciplines and projects), encourage certain academic approaches (applied or academic, quantitative, qualitative, interdisciplinary and international), set specific research aims (nationalist, economic, political, academic), and define academic procedures (selection mechanisms, teaching requirements and evaluation standards).

Nichibunken

The International Research Centre for Japanese Studies (*Ninhon Bunka Kenkyū Sentā* or Nichibunken for short) is a research institute founded in 1987 by the Ministry of Education, Science and Culture, and its establishment was made possible by the enthusiastic support of former prime minister Nakasone Yasuhiro (1982–7).[3] The Centre's founding director, Umehara Takeshi, defined the aim of the centre's research programmes as 'to identify the uniqueness of Japanese culture and pass this on to the rest of humanity' (Dale 1993: 124). The ideas of the so-called new Kyoto school nationalists, such as Umehara Takeshi, Kawai Hayao, Kuwahara Takeo and Imanishi Kinji, for establishing the research centre of Japanese studies in 1987 were reportedly in agreement with the views of the then prime minister, Nakasone Yasuhiro. The Kyoto school (*Kyōto-ha*), as a pre-war school of thought, is associated with its founder, Nishida Kitarō (1870–1945) and other graduates

History of Nichibunken 111

and professors of Kyoto (Imperial) University, such as Tanabe Hajime (1885–1962), Kōsaka Masaaki (1900–96), Kōyama Iwao (1905–) and Nishitani Keiji (1900–90). Nishida's work has been criticized for its ambivalent stance taken during the war, and Tanabe Hajime, in particular his 'Logic of the Species', has been marked as ultra-nationalist especially by Chinese critics (cf. Bian Chongdao and Suzuki Tadashi 1987: 7–8). The other members of the Kyoto school, too, are regarded as nationalist ideologues. Thus Kōsaka, Kōyama and Nishitani had to retire during the post-war purges but, nevertheless, still count as leading philosophers today. Partly as a result of its intimate ties with the new Kyoto school and former Prime Minister Nakasone Yasuhiro, and because of the political considerations that played a role in its establishment, Nichibunken has been criticized as a nationalist organ of propaganda. What this means and whether this accusation holds is arguable. However, the important role of the nation in academic debate held at the institute, played and continues to play a main part in Nichibunken's academic performance.

A summary of discussion on the inception of Nichibunken between former premier Nakasone Yasuhiro and the founding director of Nichibunken, Umehara Takeshi (1995), illustrates the intertwining interests of Nakasone's views on international politics and the self-styled 'apolitical' philosophy of Umehara (Nakasone and Umehara 1996).

Founding Nichibunken

Before he founded Nichibunken, Umehara Takeshi observed in the 1980s that the much closer relations between politics and science in the US justified the establishment of a research centre such as Nichibunken in Japan. Although he had an extreme dislike for bureaucracy and politics, it did not keep him from consulting Premier Nakasone. The new Kyoto school intellectuals, Umehara believed, had to grab the chance of organizing a cordial conversation with Nakasone when the premier was to visit Kyoto. And they did.

On this occasion, Premier Nakasone showed his interest in the writings of new Kyoto school authors. He proved familiar with the works of Imanishi Kinji, Umesao Tadao, Ueyama Shumpei and Umehara, and showed he shared with them a deep concern about the question of Japanese identity. He decided that the founding of an independent school of Japanese thought was feasible by 'leaving behind the categories of the past' (Nakasone and Umehara 1996: 66). Plans were made promptly, and financial negotiations were dealt with in a near-nonchalant manner. When at the end of their friendly meeting at Kuwahara's home the host spoke of their plan for the research centre, Nakasone asked, 'how much do you need?' Kuwahara answered, 'thirty million yen'. Nakasone suggested, 'let's make it fifty million' (Nakasone and Umehara 1996: 66–70).

Nakasone explained that science, international relations and a fresh approach to Japanese studies were his main intellectual concern, and believed

112 Group-framing habits and strategies

a research institute centred on the Kyoto school would fulfil a need. The institute was to include the students of famous thinkers such as Nishida Kitarō, Tanabe Hajime and Watsuji Tetsurō. Furthermore, Nakasone wanted a research centre that would dare to face the world. His aim was to build a scientific research centre and set up a fresh centre for Japanese studies: one that would not be encapsulated in a historical view of the Japanese empire. The institute was to study the position of Japan in the world, just as did his World Peace Research Institute. However, Nakasone's pleading failed to sufficiently persuade the Ministry of Culture under the Liberal Democratic Party (LDP): the amount of fifty million yen was lowered back down to thirty million yen. Nevertheless, Nakasone was not unnerved, for 'My resolution, in fact, derived from the idea that philosophy is the spill of politics, and politics is the (resource) material of philosophy' (Nakasone and Umehara 1996: 71). Thus, at the Fifth Karuizawa seminar in 1985, initiated by the LDP, Premier Nakasone advocated to establish Nichibunken in order to 'make another go of Peace and Prosperity this time, at the occasion of the sixtieth anniversary of the emperor' (Iwasaki 1989: 20).

Umehara spotted a similar need. Although the Japanese academic world harboured Japanese history and literature, he argued,

> we had virtually no curricula on Japanese thought, ethnology and politics; there were no scholars who could answer the question of why the economy of post-war Japan had been so successful. Neither was there a location available for foreign and Japanese scholars to exchange views.
> (Nakasone and Umehara 1996: 72)

This was so, Umehara complained, despite the fact that scholars of the Kyoto school were all outstanding and courageous:

> Someone like Imanishi Kinji, who forces the choice between 'Darwin or Imanishi', is rare among Tokyoite scholars. . . . I am really grateful for the thirty million Yen we ended up with. If Nakasone had not been Prime Minister at the time, we could not have pulled it off. I know quite a few politicians but no one but he can combine vision with power (influence). For great accomplishments you need strong politicians.
> (Nakasone and Umehara 1996: 73)

It is clear therefore that Umehara was fully aware of the political issues around and implications of founding Nichibunken.

Umehara also knew about the international role planned for Nichibunken, as Umehara defended the wish for a new academic research centre by alluding to the need for enriching Japanese international diplomacy:

> Nakasone told me that even before the start of (an international) summit the game has already begun. So when Thatcher and Mitterand take

History of Nichibunken   113

a break, they talk about Greek mythology and about Goethe and Shakespeare. It is imperative that our Japanese politicians talk about Japanese myths and thought, such as those written about in *Genji Monogatari* (The Tale of Genji) and in the works of Bashō. A need exists for a research institute that can teach politicians and foreign diplomats to do so. However, Japanese politicians regard this kind of feeling (thing) as distasteful, but in Europe it is only natural.

(Nakasone and Umehara 1996: 73–4)

In agreement with Umehara's view on the importance of culture in politics, Nakasone tells us a story illustrative of the peace-loving nature of the Japanese, in contrast with that of the instrumentalist attitude of the West:

When I was having lunch with Mitterand at the Elysée, we spoke about culture, monotheism and pantheism for two hours. I told Mitterand a story from my childhood. Even though at home we were not particularly Buddhist, when a mosquito flew at me one day, I did not kill it, but carefully caught it and put it out of the window. Mitterand commented that the mosquito would fly over to the neighbours and sting them instead.

(Nakasone and Umehara 1996: 75)

Furthermore, Nakasone illustrates the unique character of the Japanese by means of an anecdote that aims to show how solidarity is intuitive to the Japanese. In London, when Thatcher, Reagan and Nakasone were talking about stimulating economic growth, Thatcher asked them to explain to her how economic growth was achieved in America and Japan. First, Reagan told her that he did it by stimulating tertiary industry, information industry and the service industry. Nakasone, in his turn, explained that the Japanese source of sudden economic growth lies in robotics. He asserted that Japan uses 70 thousand of the 100 thousand robots in operation in the world, a fact related to the attitude of the Japanese to robots:

You all think that robots are some kind of strange beings, monsters, or some kind of Frankensteins, but the Japanese think that robots are mates who work for them and, like they themselves, toil hard. This is why at commemoration days and festivals, the workers, when drinking beer, pour some for the robots and say to them 'Oi, brothers, let's drink'. This is when Thatcher said, 'can't you offer them Scotch?'

(Nakasone and Umehara 1996: 75–6)

Meeting and talking like this, Nakasone believes, makes 'them' realize that 'Nakasone is a real politician', that is, they feel that 'they meet an incarnation of Japanese culture'. 'I think this is the work of a Prime Minister. In this sense, I think inquiring into Japanese identity is of great help' (Nakasone and Umehara 1996: 75–6).

114 *Group-framing habits and strategies*

Nakasone was impressed by the people who were related to the founding of Nichibunken, and praised Umehara's Buddhist philosophy, Yamaori Tetsuo's 'The Suicide of Religion', Inamori Kazuo's 'The Return to Philosophy', Hanihara Kazuro's 'The Origins of the Japanese' and Kawai Hayao's 'Jungian Psychology and Buddhism' (Nakasone and Umehara 1996: 78). He also managed to persuade himself that Japan's collective unconscious is linked to molecular biology and particle mechanics:

> Kawai says that the memory of knowledge and experience of individuals and ancestors is entirely stored up in the world of the unconscious. It settles there, but at some moments it suddenly rises to the surface. I am not sure whether this works the same as Yukawa Hideki's mesons.[4] The DNA of (our) ancestors is probably among these sediments, too. I think that intuition derives from such an unconscious.
>
> (Nakasone and Umehara 1996: 78–9)

Umehara agrees and turns the conversation to the reputation of Nichibunken:

> Leftist journalists called Nakasone an ultra-nationalist and therefore, Umehara (referring to himself), who set up Nichibunken, was an ultra-nationalist as well, and Nichibunken an organ of nationalist propaganda . . . The New York Times Weekly carried an article that compared Nakasone to Hitler, and Umehara to the Jew-torturing Nazi, Rosenberg.[5] They defiled the name of Nichibunken entirely. This happened at the time that Japan-bashing was in full swing.
>
> (Nakasone and Umehara 1996: 80)

> In Japan I am rather well-known, so it was not so bad here. But internationally this bad name was upheld for seven or eight years. From the start, I have been aware of this slander. Nevertheless, I was determined to go on, because I did it for Japan and for the world. So I ignored it. But I also received ghost (anonymous) telephone calls, so in Japan it must have had an effect as well. Ueyama Shumpei advised me to be patient.
>
> (Nakasone and Umehara 1996: 81)

Umehara makes a point of showing that staff recruitment is unrelated to the opinions of politicians:

> I have another thing to be grateful for to Nakasone. He left the organization (and recruitment of staff) of Nichibunken entirely up to me. He did not want his own acquaintances to come (to Nichibunken to fill jobs). He has been very kind, and said that he would like Murakami Yasusuke to join. Murakami is a very well-known economist and his knowledge is outstanding, so I wanted to add him (to the staff of Nichibunken), but it is not due to Nakasone's recommendation.
>
> (Nakasone and Umehara 1996: 81)

History of Nichibunken 115

Despite Umehara's claim to autonomy in matters of personnel assignment, the Ministry of Education has a final say. Finally, Umehara shows his concern about making visitors feel at home at Nichibunken, especially worrying about the image of Nichibunken as a representative of Japanese courtesy:

> Researchers can stay at Nichibunken for one year. They have hardly any duties, receive boarding and a rather good salary, and may research whatever they are interested in. In this way they will grow a sense of trust in Japan.
>
> (Nakasone and Umehara 1996: 82)

> The building is magnificent, good architecture. When his Majesty the Emperor was visiting, he said, 'This place looks much like the palace at home.' The designer was Uchii Shōzō. He made use of the design for the palace. Many universities and research institutes do not pay much attention to architecture. But the building is a symbol, and researchers from all over the world visit to conduct joint-research, so the building has to look beautiful.
>
> (Nakasone and Umehara 1996: 83–4)

Umehara and Nakasone do not hesitate in arguing the merits of Nichibunken. They weave together ideas from science (DNA, mesons), religion (the Buddhist treatment of mosquitoes), psychology (a Jungian Japanese unconscious), intuitive solidarity (with robots) national symbols (the emperor), narrative (e.g. *Tale of Genji*), international diplomacy, economics, money and political power in seemingly innocuous conversation. But in their friendly chat the political and so-called apolitical become one in their common wish for firmly establishing Japan's national identity and its symbolic significance.

Ten years later

Although Umehara, as the founding director of an international research centre, naturally took care not to scare off potential visitors by advertising the institute as nationalistic, the second director of Nichibunken, Kawai Hayao, shows even more sensitivity about the issue of nationalism. However, his prudence should be seen in the light of changing international relations and an increase in the awareness of intellectuals working at the centre about the political sensitivity of various cultural and historical issues. This is partly due to their participation in an academic discourse, which increasingly moves on a global scale.

An interview with Umehara Takeshi and Kawai Hayao indicates a slight increase in the awareness of the importance of conducting research that is not centred around Japanese particularity alone. The interview was held on the occasion of the celebration of the decennial of Nichibunken and published in *Kyoto Shinbun*, the local newspaper of Kyoto. Therefore claims made by

116 *Group-framing habits and strategies*

Umehara and Kawai should not merely be taken at face value but also as a sign of how Nichibunken likes to be perceived by the local public. Umehara's stress on Nichibunken's search for universals should be seen in this light:

> When Nichibunken had just been set up with the help of former Premier Nakasone, the institute was called a propaganda organ of Nakasone-nationalism, and I was accused of being a Rosenberg of Japan. On the surface, I conduct Japanese research but, in reality, I have come to think of it as global research. On the basis of Japanese research, I think, we can elucidate things with universal meaning for the future world. In the world culture of the twenty-first century, not only European thought, or Asian and Japanese research will be of use: the important thoughts of all the various cultures (of the world) will be part of it. This is the point of view of our centre. We always see Japan as being among universals, and we certainly do not universalise particular things. We always take the attitude of becoming aware of the pluses and minuses of Japanese culture in universals.
>
> (*Yomiuri Shinbun*, 3 January 1997)

Kawai affirms: 'I agree. In the beginning, there were cases of bad propaganda about the "Nakasone institute". Now, this view has changed enormously. In this connection, the Kyoto conference of 1994 was terribly important (*Kyoto Shinbun*, 3 January 1997). To emphasize that it was not a one-sided gathering of nationalist, rightwing buddies, Kawai, laughingly, points out that Nobel Prize winner Oe Kenzaburo had given a presentation at the conference too, implying that his co-operation made Nichibunken a politically okay institution of higher learning. Thus, Oe seems to have been a great catch for Nichibunken,[6] although Oe's work expresses an insistence on local, not national, identities.

Signs indicating that Nichibunken is trying to change its nationalist reputation are many. The propensity to centre research on the frame of the nation, however, is not something that can be changed at will. Kawai Hayao, a very popular and captivating television star and public speaker, seems to welcome diversity of thought more so than Umehara. Kawai studied in the US and Switzerland, and managed to adapt Jungian psychology to a special kind of psychology based on the Japanese mind. A closer look at his work shows that the new head of Nichibunken has added a new field of psychoanalytical nationalism, rather than rejected the naturalist categories central to Umehara's project of returning to the Ainu forests of the Jōmon era.[7]

Archetypal analogies and the analysis of the national unconscious

Kawai Hayao's views concern the Jungian psychoanalysis of the unconscious of peoples.[8] Problematic is that it is not always clear from Kawai's work

History of Nichibunken 117

whether his notions of the Japanese mind refer to the minds of individuals, the 'average Japanese', or the Japanese nation in general. Kawai, in a report to the late Prime Minister Ohira's study group on economic management in 1979 explained the 'three-dimensional structure' of the Japanese mind. He used the analogy of a three-dimensional object. The core of this object consists of emptiness, or nothingness (*mu*) and the centre of the unconscious mind.[9] A number of ideologies, such as nationalism, Confucianism, etc. are randomly affixed to the surface of this sphere. Sometimes, as a result of external pressure, this sphere rotates. If one could take a photograph, nothing but a two-dimensional picture would emerge, showing only one of these ideologies. Every time a picture is taken, another ideology appears. This does not mean, Kawai explains, that the mind of the Japanese people has transformed entirely: the essentially three-dimensional structure has not changed at all; the people have remained Japanese throughout (Kawai Hayao cited in Kumon Shumpei 1982: 17). It is unclear where the mind of the Japanese individual begins and that of the collective ends.

In 1986, Kawai expressed his concern about Japanese society, whose crisis had resulted from both the influence of modernity and the emasculation of Japan:

> One violent youth ordered his father to get into the bathtub with his clothes on, and to apologize by bowing to the ground a hundred times. When investigating this case, the writer (Kawai) was reminded of the now defunct Japanese Imperial Army in the period after Japan's surrender, and how the Allied Forces disarmed the army.
>
> (Kawai Hayao 1986: 306)

In Kawai's view the West is governed by the male principle, that is, it tends to differentiate everything into good and bad, subjective and objective, up and down, and inclines to individualism and independence. By contrast, Japan obeys the maternal principle, that is, it tends to contain everything, permits and forgives, puts feeling first, restrains self-assertiveness, and does not disturb the condition of equilibrium in which every person has his or her given space. According to Kawai, Japan has become subject to the unrestricted rein of the maternal principle, and this happened for several reasons. First, the US took away the paternal rights of Japan, i.e. the Imperial Army. And, second, 'affluent society' has made it unnecessary for children to do chores at home. Moreover, the mother spends her energy almost entirely on 'creating a good child'. In Kawai's opinion, the absence of close ties between community and nature, and an imbalance in paternal and maternal supervision is a tragedy for the whole of Japan. The child's appeal to 'strength' in the form of brutal force reflects the lack of the masculine strength of thinking and judgement.

Clearly, in Kawai's work, Japan is assigned personality traits used for drawing conclusions on international political and cultural relations, but also

118 *Group-framing habits and strategies*

on individuals. The principles that make the nation turn, in this case a sphere, guarantee the eternal sameness of the Japanese essence (only their external forms change). The national principle overrules both explanations on the individual level and on the transnational level. Thus Kawai has no problem in applying internationally his female and male principles so as to diagnose a Japanese case involving the unconscious level of the mind of an individual boy who is very angry with his father.[10]

On the occasion of the ninth international conference on transpersonality in 1985, Kawai spoke on the 'similarities of religion and science' (Kawai Hayao 1986a). Kawai argued that it is necessary to overcome the limitations of the individual, stressed by Westerners until now: the transpersonal and the feelings people commonly employ in mysticism should be explored further. Kawai does not comply with the Freudian interpretation, which regards the *Es* as the abstract location of suppressed urges, the libido, of the individual.[11] Instead, Kawai prefers Jung's notion of the unconscious, which refers to a collective unconscious identity, and is tied to culture.[12] From this collective pool of unconsciousness, the individual draws vital energies that are expressed in creativity.

Kawai regards Jung's concept of the unconscious world as awe-inspiring and fascinating. This irrational world, he believes, should be analysed with irrational methods using the concept of the transpersonal. Kawai regards the unconscious as a collective in which he distinguishes between the unconscious of the family and the cultural unconscious (Iwasaki 1989: 128–31). The individual builds a self-image on the basis of archetypes drawn from the collective unconscious. The images are acausal constellations, and the associations are meaningful coincidences (synchronicity). For example, the archetype for trickster (an association of 'grand-mother' and 'anima') is a potential, transcendental expression of the unconscious. It never surfaces as such, but exists in the depth of the collective mind. Dreams express the mutual effects of the conscious and unconscious in the form of symbols used by the individual to imagine and comprehend the self. Fairy-tales and stories play an important role as ethnic motives in universal archetypes. People need fairy-tales to survive, Kawai maintains, even though they do not always surface in our day-to-day consciousness. These fairy-tales have come about as a result of primitive man's attempts at explaining his experiences of fear, joy and anguish. This way of rooting experience into the heart is a way people have at their disposal of attaining a sense of security (Iwasaki 1989: 132–4).

The unconscious, Kawai believes, is more important than is intelligence. Kawai speaks of supernormal experiences, such as the after-death and near-death experience, and of the communication with all sorts of spirits of ancestors and spiteful demons. Although it is true that bookshops contain ample occult publications, Kawai publishes as an officially recognized academic. He also describes his object of research, the unconscious, as independent from human purpose, motivation, socio-political circumstances and

History of Nichibunken 119

societal change. Jung and Kawai ascribe a collective unconscious to insects and cells, while so-called primitives are found to have no signs of having developed a conscious at all in many ways. While the conscious is the upper layer and is severed from the unconscious in the case of the minds of modern Western people, the unconscious of the Japanese is defined as closely linked with the conscious (Kawai 1997: 144–53). Since the unconscious cannot be comprehended rationally, argues Kawai, explanations of the consciously experienced present by the Japanese mind are necessarily irrational and contain some mysticism.

Kawai in his *The Similarities between Religion and Science* regards rationalist science as unhelpful in explaining the similarities between dreams and external events. He therefore advocates 'synchronicity' and the logic of the soul (*tamashi*).[13] He criticizes the Western 'ego' which is separated from other people and regards the Western 'ego' as having been an important condition for science to have become autonomous. It also caused the loss of the 'whole self'. The West was left with 'ego', the centre of the consciousness, which is nothing but a surface layer of a hierarchical structure.[14] Although *tamashi* cannot be defined in rational terms, it is deployed to make manifest the fundamental attitude of the patient towards the world with the assistance of Jung's concept of 'individuation'. The patient is meant to retrieve his connection with the world that is lost to modern man. In Kawai's work, the Western ego is essentially masculine, and the Japanese ego necessarily feminine. The Japanese in the modern era are so blinded by the Western ego of industrialism that they can no longer even recognize their own true Japanese feminine conscious: 'The patriarchal social system that prevailed in Japan until the end of World War Two obscured our eyes' (Kawai Hayao 1988: 26).

At a symposium on *monogatari* (the story of things) in March 1997, Kawai told the audience that the essence of a story, in contrast with science, lies in its capacity to link the world to oneself. 'Modern science is sheer ideology. It seems theoretically very sound. Ideologists ask for everyday work and everyone getting the same salary. Ideological people have forgotten life. . . . Communism has caused people to become seriously ill. We need a view in which the self is included'.[15] In his quest for a healthy identity, Kawai cites the well-known philosopher Nakamura Yūjirō to the effect that ideology is a cosmology in which one has to include oneself. Then, dealing with science is problematic, as it does not include the self. Kawai explains what has gone wrong:

> Western influence brought science to Japan. The story has disappeared in the East because of science. This is why sects such as Ohm (*shinrikyō*) have come about. Belief has gone. Engineering, science, physics: no story. They think that stories are for kindergarten. We must create stories. Such persons wonder about the purpose of living. Such persons get into Ohm (*shinrikyō*): terrible people. A story can be very powerful. We have to

120 *Group-framing habits and strategies*

create stories to prevent such things (from happening): traditional old things have meaning for the present.

(Kawai Hayao 1997)[16]

Despite his position as director of the International Research Centre for Japanese Studies, Kawai has a fundamental disdain for science: Kawai blames science for robbing people of precious stories. The Japanese, who still have them, became its victim in particular. Somehow Kawai constructs his story in such a way that science seems to cause people to become terrorists, as science has stolen the story away from innocent Japanese children who, as a result have also lost touch with their unconscious. Not only does it seem that just Japan is in possession of the art of communicating with the unconscious, Kawai seems to think that Japan owns it, too. In *Kyoto Shinbun* (15 January 1997), Kawai cites Columbus's discovery of America as a parable for explaining the Buddhist discovery of the unconscious: both Columbus and Buddhism discovered something that was there and known by others before their discovery took place. In the process of comparing the two, Kawai assumes that no non-Buddhist culture has ever possessed the concept of unconscious, and that its discovery is a political issue between nations. Kawai concludes: 'a pity Ōbei may pick out some of the best of Buddhism'.[17] It leaves one wondering if Kawai has a Japanese patent on the unconscious.

Structural aspects of knowledge production

With founding director Umehara Takeshi, Nichibunken was in danger of becoming alienated from other academic institutions by some of its radical members, even though nation-centric theories are common in Japanese academic discourse. His successful television appearances embarrass some scholars who do not take the *nihonbunka-ron* seriously. Nevertheless, Umehara was awarded the forty-fourth *Chunichi-Bunka-Sho* (Chunichi Cultural Award) 'for the foundation of the International Research Centre for Japanese Studies and for his extensive and unique studies on Japanese Culture', one of the five recipients of this annual award for contributions to the understanding of Japanese culture (*Nichibunken Newsletter* no. 9, May 1991, p. 22). Furthermore, in 1992, Umehara received the forty-third NHK *Hōsō-Bunka-Sho* (Broadcasting Cultural Award) for his continued contribution to broadcasting and cultural activities (*Nichibunken Newsletter* no. 12, May 1992, p. 21).

The appointment of Kawai Hayao as the new director of Nichibunken may have shown a preference for someone with international experience and a wider horizon of knowledge.[18] However, Kawai made no secret of his stance against science. He stresses his belief that the world now needs beautiful stories, instead of science, which he regards responsible for the 1994 *sarin* poison scandals in Tokyo's underground metro. In a similar vein, Umehara's assertions of Nichibunken's concern with universals should be approached

History of Nichibunken 121

with great caution. The universals found in stories, debates on Japanese civilization, and social and natural science are given an ambiguous cultural twist that facilitate the continuation of the enterprise of maintaining and recreating conceptions of a unique Japan. This effect is achieved, largely, by the structural organization of disciplines and research groups.

Much effort at Nichibunken is put into the *kyōdō kenkyūkai* or joint-research meetings on Japanese culture (see Appendix I). Every professor has the duty to organize at least one general research a year, averaging five meetings, and attended by colleagues from Nichibunken and universities from all over Japan. In the academic year of 1996–7 (the academic year runs from April to March) five research fields were associated with fourteen professors and their research themes, and in total counted 266 outside members (and 396 members if Nichibunken staff are included) (see Appendix II). Each meeting lasts 2 days (12 hours on average, excluding dinner in the evening and lunch). The five fields covered various academic perspectives on Japan and its development: dynamics (contemporary, basic and traditional dynamics); structure (nature, people, society); comparative culture (cultural system, cultural thought); cultural exchange (ancient relations and new relations of exchange); and cultural information (Japanese studies in relation to other countries, Japanese studies in relation to the Japanese). The stated aim of research is the accumulation of research results in these fields and, at the same time, the transgression of research fields by researchers from different disciplines. This undertaking is facilitated through the provision of ample financial support for meetings, opportunities for publication and publicity.

Apart from these general research meetings, compulsory basic research meetings (*kisō kenkyūkai*) are organized and presided over by the main instructors of Nichibunken, its professors (see Appendix III). The purpose of basic research is formally defined as:

> apart from conducting general research on Japanese culture, co-operation with specialists in other fields would enhance its meaning. Furthermore, in order to study the deep structure/stratum of Japanese culture (*Nihon bunka no shinsō*) historical research plays an important role. This hermeneutic activity and ordering is not limited to literary materials but also includes the analysis, understanding and ordering of visual materials such as photographs, maps, pictures, prints, and empirical research, such as using surveys and statistics. Meetings are held every week or every fortnight and are usually held over a period of several years (on average three). The period of basic research is not stipulated and continues until the research aim has been reached. After each meeting a discussion and a general evaluation takes place. There are many cases in which specialized staff offers advise and lead the discussion. The centre's staff, researchers from other research organs (professors and associate professors) and research assistants (lecturers, assistant

122 *Group-framing habits and strategies*

professors) from other research organs (universities, etc.), Ph.D. students, foreign researchers may also participate as members (members average from ten to fifteen). Other meetings that are organized and may be attended by post-graduate students are symposia (open to the public), public lectures (in the lecture hall) and the 'Thursday Evening Seminars' (in English) and forums (organized in co-operation with the Japan Foundation and held at the Japan Foundation).

Nichibunken's preoccupation with searching the features of Japanese identity and its production of theories of Japanese uniqueness has undoubtedly contributed to this fiercely disputed nationalist image. Although it is the initial dedication to defining Japanese culture that became central to defining Nichibunken's internal labour division and organizational structure, its fields of research and its range of perspectives, nationalist sentiment is not the main force behind the distribution of theories of Japanese uniqueness. It is rather the combination of a dogmatic concentration of research on Japan as a unit of research and comparison and the high quantity and versatility of research meetings that encourage an obsessive discussion of Japaneseness and its delineation from what is defined as the West.

The versatility of research meetings is important as a staunch disagreement between the proponents of different perspectives and approaches encourages debate. For example, Hamaguchi Eshun's concept of *kanjin*, which derives from the notion of *aidagara*, describes the space between people rather than individuals and their relations (cf. Hamaguchi Eshun 1995, 1996). Although both concepts are used by other academics in institutions of research and higher education, many of his colleagues take a critical stance toward his scientist notions of society, such as can be found in his *Japanese systems* (Sekotac/Matsuda Foundation 1992). However, rather than leading to a rejection of these concepts, the widespread and frequently held discussions by a variety of academic approaches to Japan as a unit of research and comparison have contributed to the popularization of those concepts, which are embedded in the *nihonbunka-ron* more sturdily than ever. As a research centre that provides researchers with the opportunity to contrast Japan with the West and other parts of the world, Nichibunken does not just focus ideologically on the uniqueness of Japan. Rather it treats Japan systematically as a whole: as a system, an organ, a culture, a climate, a gene pool and as an individual. Research based on the presumption that nation-states are interrelated wholes, without any justifying argument, is bound to lead to national ideal-types and theories of uniqueness, that is *nihonbunka-ron*.

The mass production of symbolic knowledge: Shōgi

It is surprising how easily nation-centred research frames a subject on to the unit of the nation-state and exploits its envisaged differences with other nations by symbolic analogy. A striking illustration of the ease with which

History of Nichibunken 123

a new subject of social science research comes into being is provided by the physical anthropologist, Omoto Kei'ichi, who in 1996–7, as part of his duties, was required to organize research on a cultural topic by his employer, Nichibunken. As he was interested in Japanese chess (*shōgi*), he decided to organize a research series on that topic. The 'cultural debate of *shōgi*' (*shōgi bunkaron*) was to represent the unique Japanese way of symbolizing 'information fights between organizations'. Once Omoto had found his topic (chess), his research frame (Japan), units of comparison (the West, India, China), the topic was expanded by the application of analogies by Omoto, his network of colleagues and fellow researchers. The example shows how the recruitment of other researchers that take the nation as their main research unit for granted can increase the number of fields engaged in framing the nation exponentially.

In this example, thought associations and mental leaps were made between chess and other academic fields exploring the Japanese national character. Omoto wanted his joint-research group to think about Japanese culture by focusing on human behaviour in *shōgi* (Japanese chess) and human relations in competition (games). Omoto explains:

> We are not just doing this for fun. *Shōgi* is entirely different from chess. Though both originate from the Indian game, *chatoranga*, each has very different rules. *Shōgi* is very different from Chinese chess, too. It is a very complex game and requires large amounts of information to play it well.

Omoto then wondered about the possibility of playing *shōgi* with a computer, like chess, because *shōgi* is much more complex than chess. To find out, Omoto decided to invite famous *shōgi* players who could explain the game professionally. Omoto associates chess with cultural themes that concern Japan and with comparative culture. He expects that many scholars will show an interest because chess pertains to management, diplomatic negotiation and the philosophy of life.

At Nichibunken Omoto invited researchers from a wide range of academic backgrounds. For instance, there is Professor Kimura Hiroshi, a specialist on international politics. Kimura was interested in chess strategies, as from the point of view of games one can observe the way in which cultures shape their diplomatic negotiation. Then there is Kasaya Kazuhiko, who takes an interest in the close link between *Bushi* (Samurai) and *shōgi*. He believes it may illustrate ways in which Japan organizes state administration. Next, there is Inami Ritsuko, who wished to join the group in connection with her research on the Three Kingdoms, believing it may be possible to compare game strategy in China and Japan. Then there is Mitsuta Kazunobu, a specialist in Japanese literature, who wanted to join because the Tokugawa historical world of *renga* (a form of poetry) is related to the *iemoto* system (the Japanese household system), an organizational form said to characterize Japanese

124 *Group-framing habits and strategies*

systems; and, finally, there is Kurose Hitomi. Her interest in *kendō* (Japanese sword-fighting) requires martial strategy and may be related to that of *shōgi*. Furthermore, a symposium and public lectures were planned, and 'interesting people' were to be invited, such as the famous symbolical anthropologist Yamaguchi Masao, who was to lecture on 'winners and losers in Japanese culture'. As Omoto says, his joint research pertains to Japan, and is of an international and comprehensive nature. But Japanese particularity remains central, because the main purpose of this joint research involves demarcating Japanese chess (and negotiation, state organization, the history of strategic thought, life philosophy) from chess in other nation-states and in particular 'the West'. No one seemed to question the validity of generalizing the rules and strategies of *shōgi* to Japanese national culture and the nation-state, or those of chess to Indian, Chinese and Western culture. On the contrary, the institutional organization of researchers into nation-oriented knowledge production groups made it possible.

The unit of the nation

In order to go beyond the *nihonbunka-ron*, it is necessary for critics of the *nihonbunka-ron* to examine the conceptual role of the nation-state in their own work as a unit of research or comparison. For the *nihonbunka-ron* thrives exactly because it is spurned and rejected without a precise explication of why the works of *others* belong to the *nihonbunka-ron* and not to *our* genre. Any academic work that formulates research problems categorically in terms of the nation-state assumes that they vary according to national differences. They also automatically conflate a people and its problems with the administrative boundaries of a national system or essentialist definitions of national tradition likely to add to ideologies of national uniqueness.

Nichibunken is a special case in that fierce dispute took place over the justification of its founding in 1987, regarding its historical links with the Kyoto school and continuing ultra-nationalist forces in society. Ten years hence, the institute cannot be accused of a lack of self-awareness of its precarious position in international debates on trends and ideologies of globalization and nationalism. But the avoidance of nationalist rhetoric and the continuous scrutinizing of Nichibunken for signs of nationalist pronouncements have created a subtler, but no less inadequate, genre of framing nations and, in particular, an obsession with the Japanese nation, thus becoming part and parcel of the *nihonbunka-ron*. In fact, most of Nichibunken's research meetings are concerned with checking whether Japan is unique from a particular perspective, or not. This led to a collective pre-occupation with how Japanese phenomena differ from, say, China and the West and, alternatively, to debates on how 'typically Japanese' concepts could be regarded as universal tools for studying other countries.[19]

Not despite, but because the application of academic perspectives and approaches of Japan are manifold and because researchers share the research matter of Japan as a unit that is set off against the West, concepts of Japanese uniqueness flourish, also in the academic world. Thus, the scientistic approach of Hamaguchi Eshun was not supported by many of his colleagues at Nichibunken and even rejected disdainfully by some. However, some of his concepts, such as *kanjin*, the notion of *aidagara* and his Buddhist ontology were at least partly shared by his colleagues, who take other, literary, mystic and historical approaches to Japan as a unit of research and comparison.

Disregarding of whether it be in the field of religion, language, the unconscious, social organization, climate or scientific approach, in the *nihonbunka-ron* Japan remains special. More importantly, also in cases in which academic nation-framers depict Japan as inferior, a victim, mystical, an aggressor, bureaucratic, feminine, simple or primitive, Japan either violates or creates universality by privileging the nation-state as the unit of analysis beforehand, thereby pre-empting the meaning of international comparison in principle.

9 Nation-centred political strategies in academic thought
Examples from China and Japan

In this chapter I briefly discuss political strategies of development in social science research that automatically proceed from a national framework and use the nation as comparative unit of research. National efforts at employing development and modernization strategies in China and Japan have been based on the presumption that certain formulas and models exist that can be applied not only in national policy-making but also in social science research. Thus, China's strategic concentration on Japan's modernization experience is based on the presumption that the two nation-states share features crucial to the modernization effort. At the same time the adoption of such models engenders worries about possible concomitant degenerate influences. Thus, much Chinese academic research tends to focus on how to pick out the 'useful' from foreign cultures and the 'excellent' from the national past. Debates separate the excellent from the dregs in newly imported theories and tag, mould and reshape them to suit the particular views of academics and policy-makers on the home nation and progress.

A distinction should be made between intentional strategic planning of nation-state policies around the unit of the nation-state, and the unintentional and habitual deployment of the nation-state as the focus and unit of research. If in social science research we unquestioningly accept the nation-state as the overall planner of the lives of its people, we neglect the influence of the cultures and politics of local communities, transnational movements, the unintended consequences of government policies and developments in the natural environment. Although there is a fundamental difference between development strategies based on presumed cultural similarities of nations in 'cultural regions' and strategies based on universal laws of development, both approaches skip factors influential at a local level by neglecting the specific, the situational and the contingent. Additionally, it is not always clear whose welfare and prosperity is at stake when the welfare of the nation and the nature of a nation's identity are being defined and discussed.

Social science approaches that mean to facilitate the design and formulation of development strategies do not proceed from straightforward concepts of the nation concerned. The categories used to describe the home nation can vary as much as those used for others nation-states. Thus, materialistically inclined academics tend to regard the nation as a product of evolutionary mingling, geographical features and genetic development. Academic racists argue for the superiority of one or the other race. Again others, such as Chen Liankai (1992) and Li Shaolian (1990), argue that China's racial origins have made the country extremely fit, not because of its pure racial roots, but because of its advantageous racial mix. Various socio-cultural approaches present China as a product of psychological and cultural development. According to such views, the essence of Chineseness can be found in the residue of the national psyche, inherited over many generations.[1] Again, other views hold that the Chinese nation is a product of socio-political relations, organized on the basis of family principles and anchored in the lineage (bloodline).[2] Finally, some statist and Marxist views presume the Chinese nation to be a product of administrative politics, characterized by the universal applicability of the dialectics of struggle and unification.[3]

According to official advocates of using social science in the service of modernization at the Chinese Academy of Social Sciences, nationalism (or patriotism) in the academic world is required to join efforts in building a modern nation-state and attaining higher levels of prosperity and welfare.[4] It is presumed that without the nation as a main framework of research planning would be hampered, while intelligence directed at national order and stability in a developing country such as China requires nation-centred research policies. In order to formulate such policies, it is assumed that we need to understand national identity, the national economic, social and cultural situation and the history of the nation. Besides, instilling national pride could stimulate national development. Moreover, if a country wants to design a strategy to work itself up in the world it has to know which countries are its natural allies and which stand in the way of its aspirations.

In the following I argue that these presumptions should be treated with utmost scrutiny or, even, abandoned. Taking the nation-state as an unproblematic framework of applied research implies that national behaviour and identity can be treated as controllable units, assuming that strategies of development for nation-states have predictable outcomes. Such nation-centred strategies of acquiring (applied) knowledge affect the social sciences in various ways. They incline, first, to neglect the local and specific; second, to subordinate the universal to the national; third, to represent the views of certain interest groups and not those of others; and, fourth, to proceed from the illusion of the controllability of the 'national organism' and the 'system'.

A neglect of the local and the specific

The nation as an exclusive unit of research directs the attention of the researcher to the boundaries between nations, thus keeping him/her from appreciating the diversity of local circumstances relevant to the formulation of research problems. Consequently, local problems tend to become an issue only when they are meaningful to the national question. Action gets directed

128 *Group-framing habits and strategies*

into finding methods to increasing the GNP and not, for instance, to search for ways of mobilizing local and international resources in order to optimize the distribution of wealth, governance, working conditions and the quality of life according to local standards. When local targets of research, i.e. the environment for the implementation of national planning, are regarded as a mere function of overall state-planning, the regional and specific character of the local community and potential resources for local planning and implementation remain unused.

Thus nation-centred approaches to policy-making social planning and design tend to be severed from the interests, creativity, imagination, sense organs and practical needs of the locals. In some cases the exploration of the talents, imagination and histories of the local community are mobilized seemingly only in the service of the creative development of the local community, and serve a hidden state-centred agenda for national purposes. In such cases, local communities dig up local folklore in order to fortify national cultural boundaries, erecting a defence against homogenizing forces from abroad. For instance, in Japan a trend of recreating the old local communities (*furusato-zukuri*) has been going strong since the late 1970s. According to Robertson, it is planned and orchestrated through the national government. In her *Native and Newcomer* (1994), Robertson argues that:

> the 'new' culture – the 'authentic' community – appears as a state-regulated project in which the nostalgia for nostalgia is manipulated, on the one hand, to mask human responsibility for socio-ecological change and, on the other, to create a collectivist mythopoeia predicated on the reification of the 'old village'.
>
> (Robertson 1994: 29)

In *furusato-zukuri* literature, the genre of literature concerned with recreating the old village community,[5] changes for the worse in the local community are described as precipitated by external agents. Changes for the better, on the other hand, are presented as a wholly Japanese undertaking, a rallying against intrusive foreign agents (Robertson 1994: 29–30). In stressing the local, one can make a distinction between the business of 'designing' the local community and its actual running. In the latter case, propagated images confirm that the value of the local community lies in its Japaneseness, forming a protective zone against foreign agents. The local community business is run by people who embody and discuss these ideas, and live the 'game' of make-belief, just as elsewhere in the tourist industry. But even under the extreme reaches of state influence in Robertson's account, the people who are running the local business of recreating old Japan are not just puppets manipulated by the state. They, too, are but vulnerable humans who integrate their beliefs, needs and circumstances with the ideologies they harbour and invest their talents with the business they run. Although the decisions on how to deal with local past and future prospects are redirected into nation-wide

Political strategies in academic thought 129

campaigns of nostalgia, brushing them off as nostalgic kitsch misses the opportunity of exploring how these, often, Meiji era- (1868–1912) derived images are part of other dreams realized by contemporary locals. These dreams are specific to their communities and to new generations of human beings, not by-products of state planning. Nationalist ideologies that stress the holistic thesis of 'the whole (nation) is more than the sum of its parts' easily lend themselves to functionalist academic applications that throw light only on those aspects of humans that reflect the results of state planning.

To avoid this kind of holistic reductionism, I take as point of departure that 'the sum of the parts is greater than the whole'. A whole as reflected in a metaphor can never encapsulate all dimensions of the thing the metaphor reflects. In other words, in nation-centred approaches the researcher's scope is limited to the various angles from which one can observe the nation: from an outsider perspective, from another nation-state (comparatively) and from the various hierarchic sub-strata. In each case research objects acquire their meaning through the mediation of the logically closed whole of the national framework. Moreover, the national unit tempts researchers into asking questions that treat history like a series of succeeding pictures, based on rigid periodization, and designed to answer questions that envisage the national unit within the contours of a contemporary national historical frame. Whereas the national framework is limited, perspectives for observing phenomena found across national borders can generate innumerable new insights into functions, and historical relations between the parts of con-stellations of social facts. Thus, insight could be obtained into processes that are not totally dependent on, or even independent of, the particular state in which the nation is conventionally framed.

Nation-framers, however, choose to follow established national boundaries of socio-cultural identity, and help to renew and elaborate them. In approaches that try to picture the nation-state by contrasting national units, internal differences are minimized. Masamura Toshiyuki in his *Himitsu to Haji* (Secret and Shame) (1996) criticized this practice. Masamura's work is critical of nationalist ideology, but the strength of his critique is limited by the extremity of his approach. His radical criticism of the negligence of Japan's internal differences by, it seems all, Japanese thinkers leads Masamura to generalize the effect of nationalist ideology over the entire Japanese popula-tion. Besides national identity, he leaves no space for other factors relevant to the ways in which nationalist ideology forms and lives on. In Masamura's reading of so-called discussions of Japanese uniqueness (*nihonjin-ron*), general variables (such as gender and social class) and local variables (such as religious practice, local conditions of labour and the local natural environ-ment) seem to have no effect whatsoever on the capacity of the Japanese to transcend their ethnocentrism.

According to Masamura, the *nihonjin-ron* and its emphasis on Japanese homogeneity, serves to contrast the foreign with the Japanese and to keep the difference between the Japanese and Oubei (Europe and America) vague

130 *Group-framing habits and strategies*

so as to stimulate the unity of Japan. He calls it the technique of secrecy.[6] The Japanese, Masamura maintains, have covered up their internal and regional differences. Vague boundaries were created and a secret social language was applied to communication. In contrast to Europe, the Japanese could not express their internal differences. Instead of admitting the existence of internal difference, the Japanese insisted on emphasizing invisible boundaries so that vague lines demarcated various groups of people. Examples of such boundary markers are the notions of *amae* (coaxing) and *giri* (sense of obligation and duty), which are read as uniquely Japanese forms of coaxing and obligation.[7] Vague and ambiguous boundary markers facilitate the development of shame as the possibility of the divulging of 'secrets' (*himitsu*), that is the revelation of internal discord, in itself is sufficient to incur feelings of shame (*haji*). It could even cause well-balanced boundaries to crumble, endangering the Japanese 'national identity'.

Where boundaries are clearly defined, this kind of fear is not present. Powers of building and removing boundaries are at work both at the same time. In order to avoid confusion and prevent a monopoly of these powers, in many societies efforts are put into clearly dividing and defining those powers. However, in Japan, Masamura argues, it is possible to refrain from using legally defined powers by ascribing a major organizational role to tradition in political matters. Thus, by evoking the powers of tradition and custom, political organs try to pre-empt attempts to organize resistance and protest. Therefore, in order to settle conflict, efforts are made to create cosy relationships between interest groups at the costs of formal powers that tend to dissipate. Masamura contrasts this way of dealing with power with western European societies, where people are ideologically encouraged to make use of rights and laws, which are defined explicitly. According to Masamura, establishment theories of Japaneseness hide the will of individuals and unacknowledged groups and categories. They focus on the passive notion of 'becoming' (*naru*), whereas in the ideal typical West 'acting according to one's will in agreement with the law' is behaviour expected from people by political, juridical and educational organs. In the Japanese *Nihonjinron* human will is taken out of the picture and behaviour is modelled on standard patterns of so-called tradition; deviance from this model of behaviour is sanctioned by means of shaming.

Mercy (*nasake*) and selflessness (*mushi*) are two other concepts Masumura believes are central in theories of Japanese national identity. The two terms stem from the egalitarian ideal of the villagers (merchants and farmers) and the hierarchical relationships of obligation that maintained Bushi order, respectively (cf. Ikegami 1997). The terms also correspond to the domains of western and eastern Japan: the eastern emperor supporters and the eastern shogun supporters. During the Meiji period, it was said that the gods united these contrasts. This unison constituted an attempt to cover up interregional differences by means of the symbolical integration of 'mercy' and 'selflessness' in the system of emperor worship. As a result of this ideological mechanism,

Political strategies in academic thought 131

divergence had become a measure of social deviance. This technique had made it difficult for members of a Japanese community to co-operate with people that are regarded as outsiders, without incurring the displeasure of the insider community. By contrast, in a situation in which differences between persons are expressed, according to Masamura, it is possible to develop a concept of co-operation on equal terms.

In many societies, Masamura maintains, future uncertainties are dealt with by making laws that, ideally, are based upon the will of its peoples. Facing problems and a great diversity of views, democratic societies establish 'laws' created by means of a technique for expressing difference; solutions are tried out on the basis of the 'common will' of the people and humanitarian decision-making. The difference between self and others is extrapolated and brought out into the open. It is an instrument for solving opposition. In Japan, however, establishment ideologies support the organizational principles of order; difference is covered up by reshaping it in terms of accepted categories, based on notions of obligation (*giri*), coaxing (*amae*), selflessness (*mushi*) and mercy (*nasake*). The rare violator against the social codes loses face and is isolated in order to prevent repetition and a spreading of unrest.

Although critical of theories that cover up internal differences, Masamura's theory has a severe drawback in that he, in turn, homogenizes the theoretical insights of Japanese theorists by giving the impressing that they can all be defined in terms of secrecy and shame. He does not show us how 'the expressions of difference in the West' and the 'concealment of difference in Japan' relate local variations and conflicts that are expressed in conflict not mentioned in or defined as Nihonjinron. He does not tell us anything about the variety that exists in attitudes towards local differences in, for example, the city, villages, mountain hamlets and industrial areas, and he does not explain the political factors that play a role in, for instance, gender-related requirements of role affirmative behaviour. Although Masamura claims that the cover-up techniques in Japan are no longer effective, he does not specify the local, global and transregional factors responsible for this development. In other words, Masamura remains stuck in the framework of the nation.

Subordination of the universal to the national

Researchers that apply *universalist* principles to perceived changes in the development of nation-states fail to discern universal patterns that explain problems in various local contexts and that may have broad consequences for the ways in which human groups are formed and behave anywhere. As explained below, the academic users of such universalist principles frequently draw upon the modern sciences to create systems models and neurobiological models or psychology to create personified models of national character. This practice may have severe drawbacks. For instance, creating a scientific or mass psychological model by using the idealized experience of

132 *Group-framing habits and strategies*

one nation-state in order to find solutions for region-specific problems could have hazardous consequences. Thus, China's strategic concentration on Japan's modernization experience is based on the presumed crucial features the two nation-states share, ranging from being east Asian, Confucian and sharing a similar script, to belonging to the same race and having a similar Eastern character (Jackson 1996). Holding such views is only possible, however, by ignoring historical, circumstantial and socio-cultural differences.[8] This development strategy has a long history, stemming from the time after China's defeat in the Sino-Japanese War, in 1895, when Chinese exchange students decided to import Japanese ideas and Western knowledge in order to strengthen and 'save China' from evolutionary extinction.[9]

Some theories in international relations (IR) tend to apply realist ideology to nation-state behaviour in general, but make an exception of the ethically correct home nation, creating a situation of self-victimization. Declaring the world a hostile place, they use Hobbesian language and international systems principles to capture the behaviour of rival states as predicated on the principle of survival of the fittest in a world of competing national interests. At the same time, the motherland is presented as an exception, and, hence, the home nation is placed uniquely above selfish international behaviour, with the added reservation that history teaches us to join the world or perish.

Dominant views of *realpolitik* in Chinese IR theory follow this mode of theorizing. As a consequence, diplomats that hold such views find little goodwill and, consequently, little space for manoeuvring to protect national interests (Yong Deng 1998: 308–29). Thus, the practice of framing the nation can have debilitating effects on negotiating behaviour with foreigners. The academic and political harm of setting up one's own nation against others in framing the nation can be found in the sweeping generalizations and naïve essentializations employed in the categorization of nation-states in strategic designs. The prejudice built up against (self-) composed rivals creates an atmosphere of, possibly, one-sided hostility and a negative attitude towards opportunities for the improvement of international relations. Academically, a dominant attitude of *realpolitik* hampers research as it encourages rigid ways of thinking, restricted to pre-structured politically correct alternatives.[10]

Similarly, social science paradigms based on theories of the evolution and revolution of nations introduce a nation-state bias, which serves the political views of scholars at home rather than the understanding of processes of nation-state transformation. Thus, in Chinese social science, since its inception at the beginning of the twentieth century, the concept of evolutionary change of society has been associated with bourgeois liberalism (read: Western capitalism) and the violation of socialist laws of revolution.[11] Until the late 1980s/early 1990s, advocating 'peaceful evolution' (*heping jianhua*) in theories of social science was viewed by the academic establishment as a denial of the scientific nature of Chinese socialism;[12] it was equated with committing an act of national betrayal.

Political strategies in academic thought 133

Perhaps the most destructive influence on social science derives from debates of national uniqueness which, when obtaining a strong influence in the social science community at large, blinds researchers to the similarities of problematic situations elsewhere in the world. Crucial opportunities of comparing and discussing politico-economic phenomena on the basis of other units than that of the nation may be missed. For example, the organization of labour into unions and methods of management cannot be explained objectively in the limited framework of national culture, race or state power. They are understood more fully and concretely by focusing on and including references to other factors, such as political ideologies, the configurations of various interest groups, the role of the labour market and local circumstances. The same is true for issues of language change and second (third)-language acquisition that we cannot understand fully by defining them as static entities subject to centralized control. Rather, they need to be seen in the light of the relationship between global and local changes, the various state policies on language education, the practices of linguistic choice and behaviour in the economy, the mass media, art, the interference between local dialects and the creativity of young people (cf. Manabe Kazufumi 1994: 35–44, 1996: 6–11). The understanding of many important issues of language usage does not primarily hinge on the effectiveness of state policies between nation-state borders. In other words, nation-centred approaches are predicated on the fallacious presumption that comparative research, in the first place, is about comparing nation-states. Such approaches do not tell us why particular topics are suitably put in national research frames, and do not discuss national identity and nation-state policies as a dimension of and relative to the research question. Often it is forgotten that other forms of identity, such as an identification with the local community, religion, trade, gender, ethnic group, peer group, depending on the research question, may serve as framework and units of comparison more relevant to the particular research problem conserved than does the nation-state.

The nation and its various interest groups

Academic writings that claim to represent 'the people's' interest in the construction of policies on economic growth and national identity favour certain interest groups above others by virtue of the way they represent. Especially when a monopoly on communication and information systematically distorts information flows, academic knowledge about politics, economy and society becomes obfuscated. Ironically, among the factors that inhibit long-term economic growth and social science research, most damaging are forms of government that attempt to restrict and manipulate communication and information flows (through media restrictions and censorship) in order to control the opposition. These controls discourage investors and the circulation of new ideas. Restrictions on the freedom of thought, in the long run, are likely to constrain the potential for growth (cf. Lingle 1997: 69–102). In an

134 *Group-framing habits and strategies*

authoritarian political system decisions are formulated, made and implemented from above, even though 'the people' are formally consulted or represented. For example, all Chinese policy-making and academic research is done, formally, with the aim of serving 'the people'. Here, 'the people' are represented by the socialist leadership, who claim to protect national interests. The words of Lin Ganquan, head of the History Department of the Chinese Academy for Social Sciences (CASS), aptly illustrates China's neo-socialist transformation from a dictatorship to authoritarian nationalist rule by his assertion that 'at the service of politics' (*Wei zhengzhi fuwu*) has become 'at the service of the people' (*Wei renmin fuwu*) (Lin Ganquan 1998: 75). Usually, a distinction is made between the ruling class and the nation, although they are assumed to be compatible without explanation. For Chinese scholars and officials alike, national interests are the embodiment of the nation (Yong Deng 1998: 312–14). According to Deng Xiaoping, national rights (*guoquan*) are more important than 'human rights' and the latter should not be allowed to undermine the former (Deng Xiaoping 1984: 347–8). In the academic world the official leading ideologies of socialism with Chinese characteristics, Marxism–Leninism–Mao Zedong thought, the propaganda network, and rule by regulation through documents ('documentocracy') make for a limited frame of thought construed around the unit of the nation-state.[13]

In the long run, academic organizations and economic systems built upon the exchange of favours for party–nation loyalty produce a distorted incentive structure and an inadequate framework for understanding phenomena that fall outside the official list of problems. The nation-centred etiquette of academic and administrative bureaucracies enhances the likelihood of political corruption stemming from the trade in political favours between patriots of the 'right' hue. But providing for patriotic nation-framers for political purposes works only when it pays off, rendering the maintenance of theories of 'patriotic unity' increasingly expensive as they increasingly lose their ability to solve problems.

Moreover, national consensus-building has the unintended consequence of strengthening solid hierarchical structures by limiting open debate about whose interests are represented and embodied in the national project and its symbolism. Short-term gains from building national consensus may be weighed against related long-run costs arising from social injustice and economic inefficiency.

Controlling the 'national organism' and the 'system'

Metaphors allow us to grasp one thing by means of a vivid or lucid, figurative representation. Understanding the metaphor can help us to feel in control of the thing represented. Thus, understanding the nation-state through an organic metaphor, such as that of the dragon, the family or the open feedback system, may create the illusion of the controllability of the nation's 'character', its 'order' or 'operation'.

Political strategies in academic thought 135

When personal metaphors are employed to understand national behaviour, individuals are used as micro-mirrors of the national character. A simple example is that of the advice offered to the nation by social scientist Fan Hao (1992). Fan believes that the different concepts of 'self' in East and West are a clue to making Chinese modernization a success. His advice to China is to preserve the Chinese social self and ethics, absorb the Western emphasis on an independent self and respect for individual initiative (but discard its egotism), and to adopt the Japanese emphasis on the whole self (but dispel its emptiness). Fan argues that the Japanese since ancient times have regarded the individual as a part of the group, so their national coherence is great (although the individual is weak) (Fan Hao 1992: 110–11). This confidence in the capacity of constructing a nation may derive from the fact that the metaphor can turn the nation-state into an object 'out there', amenable to the mass psychoanalysis of 'national selves' and experimentation with the 'open door' (policies). Intellectuals that have appointed themselves to look after the needs of 'the people' and those who have appointed themselves as advisers to the state are faced with a difficult task. From their viewpoint, academic research is perceived as a matter of looking after the interests of the nation. Their task is to diminish uncertainty, instability and increase national advantage, leading them to view the nation as a unit in a controlled experiment.

Nevertheless, the decisions academics make on how to construe their version of the nation and its aims depends on various factors, such as their own political views, who they represent, their academic discipline, ambitions and other more mundane factors, such as their circumstances of living and status. What the various framers of the nation have in common, however, is that they turn the nation-state into an object of study severed from the world. The national unit is logically isolated from the world on which existence it is premised and surrounded by the static boundaries of the nation-state. Transnational phenomena are complex and hard to define in terms that do justice to the fact that national boundaries do not define all aspects of life and traffic, apart from in our heads. If transnational phenomena are mentioned, say, ethnic minorities or multinational companies, they are more easily defined by reference to the unit of the nation-state.

Thus, some overseas Chinese have never set a foot in China, but are defined in terms of a nation-state that did not even exist when their ancestors migrated. Furthermore, we speak about Ford of the USA and Toyota of Japan, even though we do not know where the products they make come from. We talk about cars as if they are manufactured by nation-states and not by people, and if we think about how the cars arrive to where we are, we try to imagine the borders they cross. In this sense, nation-states are closed unless we open them by 'adding' a marker that indicates 'movement' to show that something 'entered'. Similarly, the policy of opening 'national doors' is premised upon the (logically) isolated 'home' unit of the nation. The doors are safety valves that allow communication and exchanges to be planned,

136 *Group-framing habits and strategies*

regulated and stopped. Doors make possible the requirement of permission for exit and entrance; the idea of a bounded nation is a condition for the notions of national tolerance, national banning, and national taboo.

Analogous to territorial state borders, socio-cultural boundaries are erected, marked, protected, researched and planned, fit into systems and equipped with forefathers and a soul. Some academics control the system and others protect the motherland and tame the enemy, while again others aim to keep the nation in good health, safe from foreign contamination. Despite the difference in jargon employed by the various kinds of mechanical, cultural and organicistic approaches, they regard 'chance' with suspicion where the foreign is concerned, exactly because the outside is crucial to the recognition of its existence. Although the foreign takes on a different shape to the various framers of the nation, all aim to channel the required but dreaded flows of exchange under national control.

Problems that sprout from such worries in Chinese academic research tend to focus on how to pick out the 'useful' from foreign cultures and the 'excellent' from the national past. This leads to a forced mode of inquiry, such as when Hu Fuchen, a scholar of Taoism at CASS, asked the famous Marxian historian of philosophy, Ren Jiyu, 'how can we pick out the cream and discard the dregs?' 'How can we pick out the excellent parts of Western culture?' and, 'how can we mobilize tradition so as to become strong?' Such questions promise the possibility of future control by combining the ancient past and the modern West. Note that the image of traditional China here is that of a logically isolated unit, from which treasures you can make a choice. You just combine your selection with a choice of foreign valuables and integrate them with the treasures from the past. The belief in such optimistic explanation is augmented by generations of Japanese nationalist ideologues that ascribed Japan's success to its unique and innate dispositions in the field of socio-cultural organization. They claim that it enabled the Japanese to select and absorb foreign elements of civilization into the dialectical change of its own ancient tradition.[14]

Of course, it is possible for academics to avoid the trap-questions raised above. In this particular example, the socialist historian Ren Jiyu (1916–) seems to be well aware of the dangers of the essentializing force of nation-framing, probably because he has experienced the ideological extremes of the Cultural Revolution.[15] In his attempt at answering Hu's queries, he nimbly dances around the fallacies invited by questions such as 'how can we pick out the cream and discard the dregs?'

> This is very difficult, since they are all mixed up. It requires much research in addition to putting into order our feudal legacy. The issue bears similarities to the question of how to view children's performance at kindergarten: the children seem all very well behaved, intelligent, loveable and clean. But we do not see them while they are at home: naughty, crying loudly, wilful and unhygienic. Traditional culture is

Political strategies in academic thought 137

similar to this. Visiting foreigners merely catch a glimpse of China and return home. They marvel about Confucianism talking about benevolence and love. But *we*, as Chinese people, cannot be selective about traditional culture. We live and die here. Therefore we must be particularly cautious about national culture and not listen to foreigners praising us, thinking that all is good.

(Ren Jiyu in Hu Fuchen 1988: 52)

In this interview, foreigners and children seem to appear out of the blue. The former group serves to represent outsiders who are incapable of understanding China, its facades and the true nature of Chinese tradition (performing children and children at home). Ren's criticism of Chinese tradition, therefore, is made possible by means of introducing visiting foreigners who praise China for the wrong reasons. Ren further uses the idolization of Mao to criticize this autocratic feature in both communism and tradition. 'Even when we choose the cream', Ren argues, 'it may turn out to be dregs'. Advocating the spirit of self-sacrifice for the revolution is the communist spirit of the revolutionary. However, if it only consists of loyalty to one individual, or dying for a leader, then this spirit is also entangled with the concept of 'loyalty to the monarch' (*zhong qun*) and thus belongs to traditional culture and violates the *true communist spirit*. This time Ren uses the backwardness of traditional culture to recommend a true communist spirit. Worshipping Mao is not a feature of communism, but of tradition (Hu Fuchen 1988: 52–3). To Ren tradition is phoney if it is understood through metaphors of the family. He argues that traditional culture stresses correct interhuman relations by wishing people to be like one big family with peaceful, neighbourly relations. However, the traditional view that the emperor is the son of heaven Ren looks upon with scrutiny. After all, the emperor was also made the monarchic father of the entire people, and the empress the mother of the nation. Traditional culture advocates that all levels of the bureaucracy love the people like children; all members of the family should display fatherly kindness, filial children, obedient wives and mutually respecting and loving brothers. These features, Ren asserts, belong to feudal and patriarchal tradition. Whether all this is good or bad, we must earnestly try to illuminate it, Ren argues. In the last analysis, however, Ren subordinates the revolutionary spirit to the national spirit. For Ren argues that

> the spirit of suffering and simplicity (as part of the socialist cause) must always have free reign, but if ugliness maintains simplicity and cruelty preserves defect, it will break any spirit of creativity and renewal, leading to an *inert national spirit* (MS) that obstructs social progress.
>
> (Ren Jiyu in Hu Fuchen 1988: 54–5)

Ren's views indicate that academic work is biased not only by the nationalism of some traditionalist work but also by privileging the unit of the nation in multicultural views. Nation-centred approaches penetrate sophisticated

138 *Group-framing habits and strategies*

debates characterized by a variety of views on culture, socialism and international relations. They provide an axis of dualities between tradition and modernity, outside and inside, open and closed. This limits research to a few perspectives such as culturalist, scientistic and organicistic views of the nation, not allowing for a free exchange of argued propositions applied to the variables and units of research appropriate to the argument. Moreover, nation-centred approaches appropriate the national unit as a mediator between various political ideals. Finally, academic problem-solvers handle the nation as if it is a test tube, subject to operations applied to it in a laboratory situation.

Many approaches ascribe features of scientific and psychological metaphors to the nation without discussing their suitability to the problem at hand. For instance,

- the forces of push and pull allow scientific knowledge to push the nation-state forward, while superstition pulls it backward;
- the principle of 'action is reaction' forms the justification for *our home nation* to retaliate against *foreign* (their) action;
- the mechanism of 'stimulus and response' serves to control 'the people' by rewarding 'the people' for their loyalty;
- applying input–output analyses to the nation serves the belief that the GNP output will rise proportionally to the net information flow running into China;
- cybernetic principles of positive and negative feedback allow for a strategic theory of giving positive feedback by a policy of learning from the West and applying negative feedback regulation in order to bring a halt to 'spiritual pollution' from the West by, for instance, rectification campaigns (cf. Pang Yuanzheng 1986; Wei Hongsen 1985);
- yin–yang analysis makes possible, for instance, the ascription of national gender to parts of the world, such as the feminine to the East and the masculine to the West.

Social science approaches that automatically use the nation as a framework of research and as a unit of comparison encourage the inappropriate application of terms not meant as standard characterizations of large regional units of research such as East and West. Thus, the conceptual pairs of capitalism and socialism, feudal and (socialist) modern spaces and (Confucian) tradition and modernity are very imprecise when treated as characterizations of large spatial units, such as nation-states, East and West and Europe and Asia. Moreover, this practice facilitates the assignment of non-territorial 'boundaries' and 'doors' to the nation, which can be opened and closed, and channel communication between 'inside' and 'outside'. Social science disciplines far to easily focus research on the unit of the nation-state, its health, quality, wealth, victories and powers, without questioning its presumptions and consequences.

Political strategies in academic thought 139

In nation-centred approaches, various tactics and practices are to avoid drawing attention to cultural debt owed to rival outsiders for borrowed knowledge by attributing to modern scientific achievements new origins and precursors rooted in works of national tradition. If fear or criticism follows the importation of things *recognized* as foreign, the process of adaptation of the alien may be scrutinized by academic theory in order to create a sense of 'control', which is augmented by attaching to foreign products and practices labels of approval. Thus, so-called sinification is a form of unofficial permission underwritten by academic factions for the indigenization of certain trends from abroad.

According to Fang Keli, the key issue is whether Western philosophical trends conform to Chinese needs, and whether circumstances allow integration with Chinese traditional thinking.[16] At least communication and dialogue between the two must occur, argues Fang. In the case of the sinification (*Zhongguohua*) of foreign thought, the foreign must always be integrated with Chinese traditional culture. If not, and a Western school of thought is introduced purely as it is, it cannot be considered as Chinese philosophy (even though it has knowledge value in itself and may form a contribution to the development of Chinese philosophy). Western philosophical schools in themselves cannot be categorized as Chinese philosophy. Fang's argument seems to be obvious: his tenacity expresses great worry about the unheeded adoption of foreign things without having a chance to scrutinize them properly first.

Therefore, as long as the border patrol of foreign ideas checks everything thoroughly, Fang has no problem with giving imported products a place in Chinese tradition. Although Buddhism and the schools of Tiandai, Huayan and Chan (Zen) in the Sui and Tang dynasties were part of Chinese philosophy, Fang argues, they were forms of sinified Buddhism. Similarly, Roman Catholicism in Taiwan and Marxism in mainland China are also indigenized (*bentuhua*) (Fang Keli 1994: 2). On the other hand, the advocacy of Chinese traditional philosophy, Fang believes, includes the absorption of Western philosophical concepts and methods. For example, He Lin in the 1940s advocated 'A Confucianist spirit for essence, and Western culture for utility' (*yi rujia jingshen wei ti, yi xiyang wenhua wei yong*). This form of 'China for its Essence and the West for its use' (*Zhongti Xiyong*), according to Fang, is an important characteristic of modern neo-Confucianism. Fang also considers the modernization of other ancient philosophies and religions so as to create a modern neo-Taoism, modern neo-Buddhism, modern neo-Mohism, and modern neo-legalism. To Fang, they have in common a propensity to absorb Western science, democratic thought, and assimilate China and the West (Fang Keli 1994: 3–5).

Fang's views illustrate an anxiety about foreign thought entering China uninhibited, especially 'Western thought'. It is as if every thought coming into the country needs to be tagged, registered, quarantined and treated until it is properly indigenized. In fact, one of the main tasks of academics in the

140 *Group-framing habits and strategies*

Chinese humanities is the introduction of foreign writings, their translation and provision of critical comments from the 'Chinese' viewpoint.

Habitual nation-framing and its consequences

Social science approaches that proceed from framing arguments around the nation have various debilitating influences on academic research:

- It leads to a neglect of the local and specific. It tends to homogenize all within the framework of the nation and ignore local variety. Thus, the specific in China can only be a generalized specific such as in socialism with Chinese characteristics, the characteristics that have been acknowledged and given a place within the national framework of China. The contingent and unexpected have no place in this framework, apart from as an affirmation of what is known in the light of national stereotypes. Such approach is incapable of making discoveries as it assumes everything on its path to be part of a complete jigsaw puzzle.
- Consequently, it misses the opportunity to discover the general. Universals in nation-centred approaches are only acknowledged as essential in as far as they are applicable to the behaviour of the national unit. At the same time, the home-nation is easily made into an exception as only the unique status of the home-nation can explain why national efforts have to be channelled into certain policies. Other possible universal variables, such as class, gender and age, become subservient to the specific nature ascribed to them in the particular context of the nation. Thus in the Hobbesian world of international relations, in which quite a few Chinese researchers place so-called Chinese ethics, only *realpolitik* is conducive to her survival.
- A close link between national policy-making and the national framework in which academic policies are embedded forces academics to express their views in terms of the national unit. As a result the national unit becomes an arena in which the political and academic projections of various academic groups struggle about international and home policies. In such an atmosphere patriotic phrases such as 'at the service of the people' hampers precise wording and encourages academic shadow-boxing. Such practice is not likely to represent the interests of those who place the nation-state in a disadvantageous light.
- Scientistic metaphors of the nation-state provide nation-centred thought with a scientific aura and allow the academic to feel comfortable with thought experiments that involve the nation as a giant project of systems engineering, and the application of cybernetics on the information exchange flows between nations. Personalized metaphors of the nation allow the naïve psychoanalysis of the national past, its decomposition into character traits and a recombination of elements with ideal traits from other nations.

Political strategies in academic thought 141

Nation-framing limits academic research, and does not allow for a free exchange of argued propositions applied to the variables and units of research appropriate to the argument. And, finally, it violates the ideal of independent academic enquiry, and, consequently robs the nation of the capacity to check its policies by objective means.

10 Nation-framing as an academic strategy in the PRC

In this chapter I discuss consequences of using nation-centred approaches in academic work, and probe into the presumption that nation-centred research in the PRC is conducive to nation-state building. I argue that instead of aiding national policy-making, nation-centred approaches in the social sciences diminish the capacity of checking its effectiveness and evaluate its results, thereby diminishing the possibility of reliable knowledge of the workings of nation-state policies.

By treating China as a giant project of systems engineering with Chinese characteristics, academics can neither understand the universal regularities of development nor the particular conditions to which they apply. On the one hand, a systematic nation-centred perspective in the social sciences hinders the reach of a useful estimation of what is specific to local social life. After all, generalized national particularity is its point of departure. On the other hand, nation-centric social science cannot live up to the methodological demands of systematic research, as the tendency to concentrate on definitions of group behaviour in the context of the motto of socialism with Chinese characteristics tends not to pay attention to universal aspects.

Observations of research in the CASS show that if nation-centred formulations, regulations and documents are the authoritative guidelines for scientific conduct, allowing 'free debate' makes a mockery of social science, as it tends to take refuge in rehearsed and rigidly structured politically correct alternatives. In this chapter I discuss the inherent handicap of nation-centric social science in attaining national self-knowledge, its tendency to conservatism, its failure to imagine alternative views of the nation and its political predictability.

Social science and state building in the PRC

After the establishment of the PRC, party efforts at state building were fuelled by socialist nationalism. In the process, its conscious expression of patriotic symbolism was used in strengthening Chinese socialism. National strength, power and unity were measured in terms of racial features, shared historical origins and unique revolutionary tradition. Nationalism and socialism translated national aims of grandeur and victory into concrete political measures for uniting scattered populations by a combination of administrative means, patriotic appeal and military force (of liberation). In science debates, too, socialism and nationalism were translated into abstract philosophical debates that produced guidelines for doing science in practice. Such debates legitimized and deduced national policy guidelines from abstract principles on the nature of the universe. Thus, more than half a century of philosophical debate on issues concerning, for instance, the beginning of the universe, quantum mechanics and evolution, have attempted to formulate, legitimize and influence political decisions concerning the ways in which society was or had to be organized (Miller 1996; Brugger and Kelly 1990).

Although it was only after Mao's death in 1976 that official policies stressed the importance of independent knowledge and social science, the social sciences had played an official role in Chinese society and social policy-making since 1949. The social sciences were, however, mainly confined to the fields of history, archaeology, ethnology and literature. They performed important administrative tasks, such as conducting population surveys, the regulation of trade and economic planning, the organization of the military, the adaptation of a communist education system, the grooming of an educated élite and the standardization of the national language. Furthermore, in the field of political culture, social science engaged in research on, for instance, the comparative quality of the national character, the nation's history of military prowess, the creation of a 'people's literature' and writing socialist history (China Handbook Editorial Committee 1983).

The post-1978 reforms gradually changed the orientation of social science research. It began to include the design of a legal system and the renewal of the constitution, the formal legitimization of political power, the study of the quality of the people (culture, tradition, health and hygiene, education), the roots of the Chinese nation and the study of diplomacy and international relations.[1] At the same time, the major role national planning played in China left its imprint on the academic community in the shape of the systematic emphasis placed on the national unit in social science research. The framework of the politico-administrative nation-state has been used nearly interchangeably with the unit of the cultural, historical and social nation. Consequently, it encouraged the practice of tailoring research problems to items fit for national policy design, defining research problems in terms of *Our nation*, set off against Other nations. Solutions to, now, politically defined problems were phrased in terms of antagonistic and objective differences that stood out in the international relations between national units (such as the US and China) and regional units (such as East and West).

Although nationalist approaches have been subject to criticism for their tendency to lead to prejudice and inaccuracy, even in the work of critics of nationalism, the nation is often automatically used as the framework of research and as the main unit of comparison without explicit justification.[2]

144 *Group-framing habits and strategies*

Nation-centred research is both an outcome of political ideology and an unintended result of habit, that is, a lack of methodological and epistemological reflection. In this chapter I concentrate on the former: the consequences of taking a nation-centred social science approach as a political strategy. For instance, according to official academic policy guidelines, intellectuals at the CASS are expected to deliver patriotically inclined research, or, at least, have a patriotic attitude towards research tasks.

National loyalty, then, becomes a political burden to the academic ideals of pursuing objective and independent research. The question arises therefore whether academics can provide the knowledge needed for checking the results of policies implemented by the government. In other words, to what extent is a nation-centric approach conducive to nation-state building? In the academic world patriotism has the function of structuring political guidelines and communicating them to the world of the academic public. Not only does it influence the contents of research policies, but it also shapes concrete organizational functions, such as the way disciplines are structured around certain research themes, leadership structures, the distribution of financial resources, research regulations, research exchange, rules and guidelines for academic organization and award structures. This is especially the case in state-dependent academic institutions with a political 'think-tank' function. In CASS, for instance, co-operation between politicians, bureaucrats and scholars serves the realization of the national project of reforming the Chinese economy and legal and social structures, to control the process of foreign knowledge entering the country and its channelling into organs of national policy-making.[3] To a certain extent, it is a premature attempt at regulating unfamiliar foreign technologies, knowledge and political strategies, and a futile effort to manage the unintended consequences of opening up and policy-making for domestic social and political relations.

By direct and indirect means, CASS influences the leadership of academic institutes and steers the entire hierarchy of personnel. One method is to fill strategically the important positions at the top and middle of the academic hierarchy. Another method is making the heads of the levels below accountable to parallel-organized party committees and to the leaders of organizations one level above. CASS is embedded in a structure of political party and state institutions, such as the Ministry of Education, the Department of Propaganda, the CCP and other academic institutes it competes with for projects and financial and material support. This arrangement has consequences for the kinds of research stimulated in CASS, but also for the distribution of financial and material research means.

Appraising national policies

Academic institutes of social science in the PRC, to a certain extent, can expect their personnel to provide politically correct interpretations and provide academic legitimacy for the regime's policies of national self-

Nation-framing as academic strategy in PRC   145

strengthening. Open dissenters are not usually kept on. All academics, in one way or another, have to deal with the overwhelming influence of nation-centred thought in- and outside the establishment: through officially planned projects, libraries, discussions at academic and party meetings and so on. Although only a few academics are directly involved in the actual creation of propaganda materials in the form of texts, documents and speeches for various ideologies and policies of leaders, its pressures are continually present in the background. The opposition, too, couches its arguments in patriotic terms; not only to retain a place in academic dispute, but also because national self-strengthening is a generally accepted goal cherished by tradition-alists and liberals alike. It also influences academic life in general; many scholars couch their arguments in terms of the nation, partly because thinking in terms of the nation is a habit hard to lose.

Nation-centric approaches favour an atmosphere in which debates are centred on issues such as national progress, welfare, growth, backwardness, ancient traditions and national character. The irrational optimism of patriotic socialist propaganda and politics is contagious and affects scholars of every academic hue. It leads scholars to employ a measure of optimism so as to keep up their belief in the positive effects their projects promise for the future of the nation. The influence of framing research around the nation is expressed also in characterizations of other nations, for example, in the way they are staged as 'opponents', 'losers' and 'allies' on the world platform of international relations. Some scholars stress that the under-dog position of *Our nation* is only of a temporary nature, and try to attract the attention of other scholars to signs in international relations that announce a global turning point. Others foresee the demise of the *Other* imperialist nations written in the laws of the rise and fall of nation-states, predicting an era in which *Our nation* will triumph and create the conditions for a better and more prosperous world. In Chinese nation-framing, strategic game theory in international relations enables victims of the wrath of other nations to raise high, emotional support for the common nationalist aim.[4] A belief in the dialectical advantage of being evolutionary backward and in a brilliant future that can be hurried along by making the (politically) correct predictions to that effect raises expectations unrealistically high, encourages miscalculation and results in inaccurate estimations of the behaviour of 'the enemy'.

If, for the sake of argument, academics under an autocratic leadership were compelled to prove that patriotic optimism is expedient to the control of the population and order and stability in a self-strengthening nation-state more so than is objective analysis, social science could operate as a national ideology. But, would it justify using the nation as the main unit or frame-work of analysis?[5] In fact, such a nation would not cease to have a need for an independent science of society as optimal control is achieved only under a maximal understanding of the information decision-making is based on. In other words, nation-centric approaches limit the understanding

146 *Group-framing habits and strategies*

of leaders with regards to their own policies, situation and motives. For framing the nation cannot generate the information for the realization of such understanding of the nation.

In the 1980s, leaders attempted to run Chinese society with the help of nation-centric theories that linked the social sciences together into a system of cybernetic control operations. In the 1990s the concept of China as a giant project of systems engineering became part and parcel of official policies, which presumed the system to recreate itself and grow in an orderly manner. But such national focus in the academic world can understand neither the universal nor the particular of the society it studies. It is incapable of making a rational distinction between universal factors at work in human group behaviour and the way group behaviour is determined by its local environment, because the specific features of the nation carry the greatest weight in all of its explanations. Its *us*-centred orientation makes it quite impossible to clarify to what extent it is the 'uniqueness' of national characteristics that determines the way social life is organized at a local level, because the point of departure of nation-centric approaches is the collective, *national* self. As it focuses mainly on the national unit, the scope of nation-framing is narrow and the range of its perspectives limited.

In order to check the effectiveness of the nation-centric, one needs to investigate at least two possibilities. First, whether a current situation is the planned outcome of nation-centric strategies or whether other factors are responsible. In order to check, one has to observe the universal aspects of group behaviour and compare them with the effects of policies recommended by nation-framers. Second, one has to find out if the ideosyncracies of groups occurring at a local level thrive as an expression of rebellion against the Chinese nation-state or as the expression of exceptional ethnic/local characteristics. Neither of the two forms of checking is on the research agenda of the nation-framer. This is not surprising for, after all, nation-centred approaches cannot generate accurate information on nation. The value of nation-centric knowledge is dubious, especially as it is meant to facilitate national control and generate political stability, for it cannot be said to be either political or objective in nature and intent.

In nation-centric debate views tend not to be carried beyond the point of the politically acceptable. In a context in which the contention between nation-centric schools is encouraged, a stalemate 'competition' between ideologies runs the show, hampering a relatively unrestrained sort of academic freedom, ideally only limited by the constraints it sets itself. When the rule of nation-centred formulations, regulations and documents as authoritative guidelines for scientific conduct also *allows* 'free debate', it makes a mockery of social science, as it is limited to rehearsed and rigidly structured politically correct alternatives (Schoenhals 1992; Su Shaozhi 1994, 1995).[6]

National prescription and conservatism

In an environment that emphasizes the centrality of the nation considerable research time is wasted on proving how the nation should be and therefore is and vice versa. Decades of debate in China on the nature of the universe, quantum mechanics and genetic evolution have been aimed at legitimizing and influencing political decisions on organizing society. Such debates proceed from the following logic, 'because the universe works like this, society should work like this, therefore this measure is correct'. Thus, conflicting views on the nature of the universe make for heated debate on the nature of the society, but actually are concerned with national policy-making.[7] In other words, is means ought. A relatively simple example of the conflation between 'is' and 'ought' is Li Shangkai's view on the urgency of studying national psychology. The example shows that description and prescription are easily confused. Furthermore, it shows the futility of the so-called scientific politics of the motto of the 'unity of opposites' (Li Shangkai 1991).[8]

Referring to Stalin's definition of the nation,[9] Li Shangkai (as many others before him) points out the importance of the study of national psychology. Its significance lies in the knowledge of national psychological elements. It can be employed in the task of realizing the Four Modernizations;[10] it can be used to stimulate national unity, solidarity and getting rich, all at the same time; and, finally, it contributes to the enrichment of ethnological studies. Li concedes that European and American nations (Oumei)[11] have produced much more psychological theory than has China. But as their national spirit and circumstances are different from those of China, it reflects different features of the moods and character of nations. Lee concludes, 'As the Chinese population represents one fourth of the world's population', Li concludes, 'without studies on China national psychology cannot be regarded as truly universalistic'.

It is interesting how Li relates the universal validity of the discipline of 'national psychology' to China's population size, i.e. one feature of a rich research region. Li wants his discipline of national psychology to be both a descriptive science and a prescriptive recipe for creating an ideal nation. In a nation, Li argues, all classes share common national characteristics. At the same time, different classes may leave a class imprint on their national character. A second characteristic of the behaviour of nations, argues Li, is that they express themselves in national culture through features such as language, art, ethics and religion, making a contribution to the objective conditions of the nation. A third feature is the great coherent power (*ningjuli*) and driving force of the nation, expressed in a sense of self-identity and self-respect, pride and self-confidence; thus, the *Zhonghua Minzu* character has been formed over thousands of years. And lastly, Li characterizes the nation's state as stable and its history as one of 'the unity of continuity and transformation' (Li Shangkai 1991: 27–8).

Li's definition gives no clue as to whether he refers to the nation in general or about China, where class begins and where national character ends, which

148 *Group-framing habits and strategies*

is belief and which are objective conditions and, lastly, what he means by stability and the unity of continuity and transformation. In this case, the attempt to use science in support of a certain view of the nation (instead of the other way around) is a clumsy one. If science, ideally, is about compressing observations into scientific laws or regularities, nation-centrism tries to control these patterns or at least steer them into a desired direction, blessing them with the label of academic insight.[12]

A main reason for the ineffectiveness of nation-framing as a source of support for reform policies and the insights they require is its inclination toward conservatism. The expectation for academics to express their patriotism in their work results in research formulations that not only are dressed in patriotic vocabulary, but also, as both Jiang Zemin and the then CASS president, Hu Sheng, complained, are phoney or made to suit establishment views on patriotism.[13] When researchers feel forced to adhere to views on the nation that are acceptable to the establishment, they will tend to discard other, possibly politically unacceptable, conceptions of the nation. Furthermore, research projects formulated from a deviating perspective are not easily accepted by planning officials, nor does it attract the attention of researchers who do not share the same (implicit) assumptions on which they base their views of national problematic. As a result, 'incorrect' views tend to be published abroad, in the province (far from the centre), or, tragically end up in a waste-paper bin.[14] In short, independent research is structurally discouraged, though possibly unintentionally, as long as it depends on the support, or is under supervision of the government administration and party organs.[15]

The failure to imagine other views of the nation

Nation-centrism gives social science research an establishment bias when research tasks are formulated under the influence of government policies and the bureaucracy. It encourages prejudice about the formulations of nationhood among established rival groups, but ostracizes alternatives to establishment formulations. For the establishment frame of academic reference may disadvantage dissident groups. Thus, in June 2000 the members of the World Bank's board approved a controversial US $40 million loan to China for the relocation of 58,000 impoverished Chinese farmers to Qinghai province on the Tibetan plateau. As the area is known as Qinghai, that is, not belonging to administrative Tibet, the ethnic Tibetan inhabitants of the region, which is claimed by ethnic Tibetans, were not consulted.[16] Defining a social science research problem therefore requires a careful consideration and argumentation of which geographical, administrative, political and cultural units of analysis are justified in particular circumstances. More generally, the analysis of problems such as poverty and unemployment are intertwined with the cultural politics outlined by officials and thought out through nation-centred research.

Nation-framing as academic strategy in PRC   149

Tibet is regarded as an inseparable part of China. At a symposium on 'the History of Chinese Minority Relations' in 1981,[17] it was formally decided in what way China's border areas were to be viewed from an historical perspective. It was argued that the meaning of the concept of 'China' (*Zhongguo*) changes over time and corresponds to an 'era' of development. This is why, as the argument goes, it is impossible to define the meaning of China on the basis of ancient Chinese history. The 1991 symposium entitled 'The History and Current Situation of Tibet' illuminates how eminent scholars, who share a similar institutional history, spend their time and effort thinking about strategic arguments to legitimize national boundaries and policies. They decide on which are the appropriate markers of the historical era, and define the is and ought of relations between the main referent (the West), *us* (PRC (*Zhonghua Minzu*)) and the subreferent, Tibet (Meng Xianfan 1991).[18] They 'objectively' include both *us* (the Han Chinese) and the Tibetans in their concept of China (*Zhonghua Minzu*), defining China as a 'united multi-nationality Nation'.[19]

The following account of the symposium describes the various views of participants discussing thorny problems with relation to the 'historical' status of Tibet and the proper formulation of research problems. Famous national minority scholar, Weng Dujian,[20] observed that present-day China is the China common to all Chinese peoples. From the point of view of history, Weng argues, the notion of China does not only include the original dynasties, but also the kingdoms and political power established by other national minorities. Therefore one must not use the original Han dynasty or feudal dynasties as the source for defining China's borders. Instead, the borders of *Our* motherland and its national minorities were established in the Qing dynasty (1644–1912). Weng concludes his argument with the final discourse killer, 'We are a united multi-nationality nation' (Weng Dujian 1991: 170).

As for the status of Tibet, Wang Furen, professor at the Central Committee Academy of Nationalities (*Zhongyang Minzu Xueyuan*), strategically points out that to use the phrase 'during the Yuan dynasty the Central government established an official administration in Tibet (*Yuanchao zhongyang zhengfu zai xizang zhengshi shezheng*)' can prevent several problems. This way of defining the relationship between Tibet and the motherland avoids the confusion between the concepts of 'Chinese territory' and 'administrative region'.[21] Wang clearly expresses the political sensitivity of the issue by warning that the phrase 'Tibet is added Chinese territory' could provoke negative sentiments from Tibetans.

Zu Qiyuan, from the CASS Institute of National Minorities, stresses the family metaphor of the Chinese nation, by drawing attention to the continuity and stability of the brotherly relations between Tibet and the other nationalities. Even though there were tensions from the ninth until the thirteenth century, Zu argues, Tibet did not sever its ties with the Central Plains (*Zhongyuan*) (Zu Qiyuan in Meng Xianfan 1991: 173).[22] Yao Zhaolin, from

150 *Group-framing habits and strategies*

the Institute for Nationality Studies at CASS, provides us with an official family metaphor version of Tibetan liberation history, and asserts that, in the course of time, the adherence of Tibet to the motherland has become increasingly strong. The Central dynasty (*Zhongyang Wangchao*) never sent soldiers to Tibet, Yao maintains, and at the end of the Qing dynasty, when imperialism attempted to divide up China, the patriotic part of the higher classes in Tibet and the Tibetan masses always tried to maintain the unity of the motherland. Even when the thirteenth Dalai Lama fled to Darjeeling, his heart was still with the motherland. In 1959, Yao maintains, Tibet implemented democratic reforms, smashed the politico-religious totalitarian and feudal regime, and abolished the feudal slavery system. For the first time people were free and gained democratic rights. It underwent a complete transformation. Under the leadership of the CCP and the government of the people, the Tibetan economy experienced great development (Yao Zhaolin in Meng Xianfan 1991: 173).

Song Yue, a law lecturer at Beijing University, employs the East–West duality in support of the liberation of Tibet theory. The West, Song asserts, must not use human rights as an excuse to intervene with home affairs. International law does not talk about the right of segregation or independence of national minorities that have autonomy, Song argues, it only deals with colonized peoples and those that have no self-government. Furthermore, China has acted in accordance with the 1956 Geneva Convention that forbids slavery: in Tibet the population's 5 per cent slave owners owned all territory. Only under the leadership of the CCP could the Tibetans be freed from the fetters of the agricultural slavery system. In spite of this, Song maintains, some Western scholars say that during the Cultural Revolution (1965–75) Tibetan culture was destroyed and the human rights of the Tibetans were trampled on. But the Panchen Lama has already pointed out,[23] the Cultural Revolution, explains Song, was a question of China as a whole, and *not* of the Han annihilation of Tibetan culture. Again, the Han Chinese seem to hide behind the metaphor of the national family, and the notion of 'united multi-national nation' (Song Yue in Meng Xianfan 1991: 176).

The political predictability of framing the nation

Nation-centrism structures academic work to such an extent that it renders it nearly as predictable as the political guidelines it is expected to respect, produce and follow. There is no room for paradigmatic confrontations: the grammar of nation-framing allows confrontation only within the *us*-grouping, i.e. when the correct use of formulations is upheld and the proper hierarchy of relations respected. Thus the contours of official definitions of '*Zhonghua Minzu*' is respected; the formulation of Tibet as 'the Tibetan province of China' is adhered to; and the elaboration of 'socialism with Chinese characteristics' is taken to be a main point of departure in research programmes (National Philosophy and Social Science Planning Office 1997).

Nation-framing as academic strategy in PRC 151

In this 'Orientalist' spirit, discussions about the nature of Tibetan rule and religious texts are to be expected rather than debate about the legitimacy of Tibetan rule. Doubting Tibet's status as a part of China is out of the question, and so is arguing in favour of the socio-political features of Lama rule. If scholars do not feel free to ponder such issues, it is unlikely that they can come up with innovative ideas, research problems or theories. In other words, the tendency in nation-centrism to conform hampers practicable innovation, competition and creativity.

Present official policies stimulate patriotism (*aiguozhuyi*), national unity and competition between schools of thought. The idea behind this seemingly paradoxical policy is to stimulate creative research and innovation, provided that it remains within politically acceptable limits.[24] Academic guidelines hamper uninhibited rational thinking as they can be found all around, provided through documents, meetings, regulations and compulsory focus point research plans and a vocabulary to go with it. Political (academic) dissenters, too, find themselves adhering to guidelines, as familiarity with their vocabulary is needed to communicate with opponents. To formulate counter-arguments it is necessary to know at what occasions to quote which parts of the sacred classics, documents and texts on and by the historical great, such as Marx, Lenin, Lu Xun, Engels, Kang Youwei and Mao, and, nowadays, Confucius, Lao Zi, Zhuang Zi and the *Yi Jing*.[25] As a result, compulsory patriotism in nation-framing may resemble scholastic debate: the burden of the argument is frequently carried by quotations from authoritative texts, citations from the works and speeches of respected elders, and endless classifications of key items and their symbolism. Patriotic loyalty therefore makes scholars conform to guidelines, although they usually try to twist and apply them in favour of furthering their own ends. Discourse becomes obscure, and in the worst cases the work of individual scholars becomes scattered with clumsy applications of official vocabulary, or reiterates official guidelines stuffed with new filling.

Framing the nation in the PRC: Some features

Since the beginning of the reforms in 1978, PRC politics continued to steer academic activities. Instead of focusing on the political functions of science at the direct level of practice, the emphasis changed in favour of its broader, guiding role in the administrative politics of nation-state building. In this sense, the influence of politics on the regulation of, in particular, the social sciences increased. In building up the Chinese nation-state, the social sciences were to be expedient in maintaining social stability and in strengthening the national state administration.

Political strategies that focus solely on the nation (or other regional units of research) in the academic process of acquiring knowledge, I refer to as nation-framing. Nation-framing affects the social sciences in various ways. Its emphasis on the unit of the nation as a framework of research encourages

152 *Group-framing habits and strategies*

the neglect of the local and specific and the subordination of the universal to the national. A systemic emphasis on the national hampers the ability of researchers to check national policies so that they become dependent on convention and political motto. Nation-centric discussions consist for a major part of ideal types, such as those of East and West, generalizations (e.g. about capitalism and socialism) and national essences (e.g. about the Chinese character). The prejudices nation-centrism produces with regards to the home nation and the enemy create an atmosphere of political hostility and chauvinism.

The example of Li Shangkai's national psychology shows how description and prescription in framing the nation are easily confused. Furthermore, nation-centrism tends to privilege the views of certain interest groups over those of others, and its plans for ameliorating the relationships between social groups remain sterile. The 1991 symposium on Tibet indicates that in nation-centric research scholars tend not to imagine, to the establishment, alternative views of the nation. It discourages officials to understand ethnic and social problems from local viewpoints and to foresee political instability in border areas. They fail, for example, to seize opportunities to persuade the less radical members of their dissenting groups of their goodwill. And, finally, only the researchers that are initiated in the particular language used in politically and socially constrained discourse are capable of following the intricacies of political innuendo in debates. They are the ones capable of participating actively in the production of an, often, predictable scholastic form of academic discourse.

At the same time the influence of scientific and historical metaphors in politics, such as those of the family, the Great Wall, the Chinese dragon and China envisaged by President Jiang Zemin as a great project of systems engineering, blur the differences between social science and ideology. Such metaphors applied in academic analysis hamper efforts at defining research problems accurately, let alone solving them. This confusion of the nation with national metaphors produces an illusion of control over Chinese border areas, its unified spirit and its organization as an integral multinational state.

11 Core themes and an outlook on future research

In discussing the concept of framing the nation, in Parts I and II, I made a distinction between different kinds of criteria used by academics for delineating national identities. I described three different categories of criteria, and argued that it is not only taxonomies built around cultural and particularist markers that play a main role in nation-centric theory. Although it is commonly thought that national identity is composed of factors that emphasize national culture, I have shown that cultural, natural and globalist categories are all deployed in the course of nation-centric research. Class, 'middle-mass', modern civilization, science, liberalism and *kanjin* are all supposed to be universalistic categories but have been deployed to ascribe a particular character to nation-states at the same time. Physiological categories, such as race and the brain, turn out to add extra force to other forms of national particularism. They are usually presented as expressional forms of nature, obeying the laws of nature, and therefore regarded as 'scientific'. When used to reinforce the boundaries of the nation, isolationist forces and discrimination obtain a political free hand, especially in the case of cultural markers that take ancient tradition and collective spiritual purity as their base. Cultural markers, in general, however, leave space for negotiation between different factions, although national identity markers that are employed by establishment academic nationalists may dominate discourse. Whether criteria originate in nature, science, the economic system, human genetic codes or social organization, framers of the nation use their creativity in free academic debate to discover new theoretical boundaries between nation-states.

In Part III I addressed the practice of using nation-centric research as a strategy for acquiring knowledge in the social sciences. I argued that nation-centrism inclines to neglect the local and specific (1), to subordinate the universal to the nation (2), represent the views of certain interest groups and not others (3), and proceed from the illusion of the controllability of the nation as an 'organ' and as a 'system' (4).

1   In discussing the neglect of the local and the specific I kept in mind that 'the sum of the parts is greater than the whole': holistic generalizations

154 Group-framing habits and strategies

of facts about the nation-state should be treated with caution as incomplete and aspectual. In a nation-centric framework, research objects acquire their meaning through the mediation of the logically closed whole of the national unit. The research frame of the nation tempts researchers to ask questions that treat history as a series of photographs, based on rigid periodization, and designed to answer questions that project the unit of the nation into the past. Such approaches are one-sided. Alternatively, perspectives for observing phenomena found across national borders can generate innumerable new insights into functions, and historical relations between the parts of constellations of social facts. In this way, insight can be obtained into processes that are not totally dependent on, or even independent of, the particular state of the nation.

2   Researchers that apply universalistic principles (of systems, of individual behaviour, of neurobiology) to perceived changes in the development of nation-states may fail to discern universal patterns that explain problems in various local contexts by the same universal principles, and that may have wide consequences for the ways in which human groups are formed and behave anywhere. For instance, using the idealized experience of one nation-state in order to find solutions for region-specific problems could have hazardous consequences. One example of a view that applies universalistic ideology to the unit of the nation declares the world a hostile place in terms of Hobbesian and international systems principles, presuming the behaviour of Other units to be predicated on universalistic principles of survival in a world of competing interests of nations. At the same time, the Us-group is an exception, and, hence, 'We' is placed uniquely above so-called universal principles of selfish behaviour (though history teaches Us to struggle or perish).

Destructive influence on social science derives from debates of national uniqueness. When gaining authority in the social science community at large, it selectively hampers researchers to perceive similar problem-solving situations elsewhere. Furthermore, nation-centric comparison is predicated on the fallacious point of departure that comparative research, in the first place, is about comparing nation-states. Instead, it could be about comparing topics that belong to various research frames, chosen for their suitability to the subject concerned. In such an approach, national identity and nation-state policies would just be variables whose importance is dependent on the research question. It is easily forgotten that other forms of identity, such as identification with the local community, religion, trade, gender, ethnic group, peer group, depending on the research question, can be units of research more relevant than that of the nation-state.

3   Academic writings that emphasize 'the people' in the construction of policies on economic growth and national identity may favour certain interest groups more than others. Especially when a monopoly on communication and information systematically distorts information flows,

Core themes and future research 155

academic knowledge about politics, economy and society becomes obfuscated. Ironically, among the factors that inhibit long-term economic growth and social science research, most damaging are forms of government that attempt to restrict and manipulate communication and information flows to control its opposition. In the long run, academic organizations and economic systems built upon the exchange of favours for party patriotic loyalty produce a distorted incentive structure and an inadequate framework for understanding phenomena that fall outside the official list of problems. In the Chinese case, these are based on the policy of national restructuring, and establishing socialism with Chinese characteristics. Short-term gains from building national consensus may be weighed against related long-run price as a result of political corruption, social injustice and economic inefficiency.

4   Understanding the nation-state through organic metaphors, such as the dragon, the family or the open feedback system, creates the illusion of the controllability of its 'character', 'order' or 'functioning'. This confidence in the ability to construct a nation may derive from the fact that the metaphor can turn the nation-state into an object 'out there', amenable to the mass psychoanalysis of 'national selves' and experimentation with 'open doors'. In such metaphors, the national unit is logically isolated from the world on which its existence is premised. Saying anything about any person or phenomenon requires, first of all, drawing a circle around it: the static boundaries of the nation-state. The opening of 'national doors' are premised upon the (logically) isolated 'home' unit of the nation. Its doors are safety valves that allow communication and exchanges to be planned, regulated and stopped. Doors make possible the requirement of permission for exit and entrance; the idea of a bounded nation is a condition for the notions of national tolerance, national banning and national taboo. Analogous to territorial state borders, socio-cultural boundaries are created, marked, protected, researched and planned, fit into systems, and equipped with forefathers and a soul. Some academics control the system and others protect the motherland and tame the enemy, while again, others aim to keep the nation in good health, away from foreign contamination.

Despite the difference in jargon employed by the various kinds of mechanical, cultural and organic framers of the nation, they regard 'chance' as a danger when it concerns the foreign, exactly because the outside is crucial to the recognition of its existence. Although the foreign takes on a different shape to each of the nation-centric researchers, all aim to channel the required but dreaded flows of exchange under academic nationalist control.

Some academic problem-solvers handle the nation as if it were a test tube, subject to operations applied to it in a laboratory situation. They ascribe power to the nation-state through the forces of push and pull, provide political justification through the principle of 'action is reaction'

156 *Group-framing habits and strategies*

and attempt to control the populace through the mechanism of stimulus–response. They also use input–output analyses to activate national growth, and apply cybernetic principles of positive and negative feedback and of yin and yang to manipulate the nation as a system. The efficacy of such nation-centred research hinges entirely on whether the boundaries of the nation as a systems problem can be justified in the light of the task intellectuals have set out to fulfil.

The case-studies of CASS and Nichibunken tried to link the different levels of abstraction at which research problematic frames the nation. Academic debate is made up of people with various needs, under various pressures and with various ambitions. Furthermore, the local socio-political circumstances in which academic debates are held and the prospects of financial remuneration filter potential academic crew. At the same time academic debates are part of ever-changing but ongoing intellectual traditions. Although the nation is framed in creative research produced through concrete human interactions in an academic habitat, its creative products are both a reaction to and an inherent part of processes of knowledge creation and steering that take place on a macro-level. Research institutes are a main link at which communication takes place between academics and academic policy-makers, constitute the location at which research facilities are provided, status is conferred and regulations are laid down. Debates that frame the nation have developed in relation to, but are not determined by, processes of the emergence, shaping, reshaping and replacement of nation-states. They are developed within the framework of emerging nation-states.

The universal and particular in framing the nation

Academic research that is mobilized for the reconstruction of the nation and the identification of national culture is subject to political and ideological constraints. When the ultimate goal of academic work is presumed to be 'national self-strengthening', 'the construction of national identity', or 'comparative studies of national culture', a framework emerges that restricts intellectual inquiry by the boundaries it presumes and, at the same time, expands it by the links it constructs with the rest of the world. In the final analysis, however, the particularity of the national unit overrules universal principles that constitute the basic aim of scientific inquiry. Not even the universalistic principles of science, valued by scientistic framers of the nation, can overcome this problem, because their academic inquiry is embedded in, and co-opted by, politico-cultural strategies that use universalistic principles to justify, legitimate and prove the ('relative') uniqueness of the nation.

Nation-centric research explores national particularity by skimming the nation's hidden historical layers, dreams, atmospheres, ideals, ethics, systems and symbolical mementos in order to mark off its own intellectual fields, thereby expanding the reach of particularist principles; nation-centric research

Core themes and future research 157

cannot conduct comparative research into the universal aspects of research problems effectively as it systematically reduces society to its national dimension; nor can it distinguish between the universal and the particular without becoming blinded by the consequences of doing so for national narrative and symbol. If domestic problems are not explained away by optimistic nationalist imagery or ignored, they are thought to be inherent in the particular nature of Our nation and on the way to being solved by Our particular methods for dealing with destructive foreign influence. The reduced capacity of imagining Our problems in similar scenarios elsewhere hampers attempts at solving domestic problems by learning from Others.

One form of framing the nation employs scientistic mechanisms and metaphors and principles from biochemistry to explain world issues, and claims to know how to handle and solve them. Taking the units of civilization and the nation as the academic point of departure, metaphors in scientistic nationalism focus on explaining research issues in terms of natural laws and principles that prove Our nation is in congruence with nature more than others. Particularly xenophobic versions of framing the nation offer irrefutable arguments to explain trouble and political dissent at home. Such arguments are often based on the personalized traits of national behaviour, reaching from nasty practices such as foreign remote-control by hostile countries and brain-washing through their ideologies to dangerous effects such as contagion by the enemy's impurity and the impact of cultural supremacy. Especially the high-boundary effect of the use of the natural symbols of race, climate and cerebral function tend to debilitate cross-group communications. Methodological effects in scientistic forms of nation-centric research are just as damaging. The consistency criterion is used here in order to uphold the scientific metaphor: subject matter is chosen selectively, and evidence is stretched to keep up a correspondence between metaphor and the national units. Thus the attributes of the left cerebral hemisphere are defined so as to accommodate a selections of features believed to vary with the East–West duality. Cultural nationalists tend to be less concerned with inconsistencies, especially the ones that themselves scorn scientific rationality.

Culturalist versions of framing the nation tend to advertise the fuzziness, mysticism and narrative nature of academic theory. As the world seems to be essentially fuzzy, some academics believe this fuzziness has to be reflected in representations of it in academic theory. Representation therefore acquires precedence over explanation. Furthermore, culturalist notions in nation-centric research, such as narrative, poetry, intuition, linguistic purity and philosophical essences take priority over cognitive activities in the intellectual exploration of society. Such, otherwise possibly useful mental tools, are turned into approaches for understanding the world in Our way, stressing particularist solutions deployed as a panacea for saving the nation and the world from the results of Their or Other approaches. Culturalist nation-centric research celebrates an ascientific or irrational attitude to the nation.

158 *Group-framing habits and strategies*

It seeks to gain plausibility as an approach to define the nation in holistic and functionalist terms. The spontaneous nature, harmony and sometimes mystic character of human thought and behaviour are stressed in descriptions of the unique nation and its cultural origins.

Approaches that emphasize the universality of civilization and advocate a borderless world make the ultimate claim of civilization: universality. The evidence gathered for legitimizing a universalistic approach, however, is found in models of certain observed developments, such as modernization, free trade or collectivization. By denying the regional links and origin of these concepts, a nation-centric researcher, in his efforts to civilize the world, in between the lines communicates the message that We know best, as Our country is superior by objective and universal standards. In civilization theories salvation is found on the path of purposeless evolution, in the authorless systems of self-organization, or the statistics of self-reproductive systems (autopoeisis). In practice, however, one cannot conduct experiments on the unit of the nation-state: variables are too manifold, and controlled isolation is out of the question. Image and reality do not coincide. Even in a thought experiment, complex (open) systems presume logical isolation as they proceed from the possibility of measuring all that comes in and goes out (information flow). In framing the nation the art of measuring variables, the national unit and political pressure are closely intertwined. Even if the recipe for national self-strengthening were to be known, the inclination of nation-centric research to control information traffic would guarantee the failure of any attempt at emulation.

I believe there is a need in academic research to investigate the extent to which our thought is determined by the habitual application of the framework of the nation (including the use of the national unit as standard research entity and unit of comparison). Awareness is especially important with regards to the ways in which natural symbols influence processes of academic thinking and the creation of research hypotheses. This is also true for certain genres of, especially long-term, historical thought. In nation-centric historical research some long-term views of nations are trapped in metaphysical thinking and drawn propagandist and political writings. It is notably not just in the field of culture history that we can find nation-centric research, but also in the realm of scientistic (universalist) research. In brief, the use of natural symbols, long-term histories of civilization and the scientistic conceptualization of nation-state development I believe to be vulnerable to uncritical attempts of nation-framing.

Framing the nation and spatial and temporal order

Research engaged in framing the nation, generates a frame of mind in which the nation and its characteristics are focus points of attention. It tends to neglect issues that cannot be generalized to the unit of the nation, and overlooks problems that call for variables irrelevant to the nation as a unit

Core themes and future research 159

of comparison. The unit of the nation as the departure point of research is a major stumbling block for social science research contingent with local and concrete factors. The hunt for national particularity and the search for ways to strengthen the nation tend to condition the academic into selecting and combining a research frame and units of comparison that are legitimized by means of national tradition, nationalist politics and dogmatic definitions that seem to have no purpose but erecting ideological walls between nations and civilizations.

In analysing theoretical constructs of the nation, I made use of a distinction between temporal and spatial aspects of national constructs, corresponding roughly to theories that place emphasis on universal values and those that stress particularist values in nation-centric research. Temporality referred to a theoretical emphasis on development in time, and assumes universal applicability of principles of development and evolution. Here, a distinction has to be made between naturalist theories of evolution and environmental change, and civilizational or globalist ones that describe processes of the modernization of nations. In globalist theories, other nations in principle are able to overcome obstructions to development (the Other can become like Us by adopting Our standards), but in naturalist theories biological factors and physiological characteristics render it impossible: the Other cannot become like Us. Spatiality relates to particularist, essentialized, synchronic patterns and properties ascribed to the nation, such as ethnicity, tradition and national character. In spatial constructs of the nation, the difficulty of mingling different ethnic groups and traditions is emphasized (the Other is like Us but different). In nation-centric theories of civilization, spatial and temporal constructs of the nation appear combined, and this combination shows the extent to which cultural particularity limits the universal claims of civilization theory.

The temporal dimension of nation-centric theory is expressed in, for example, the linear direction of developmental stages, and in the cyclicality in which history repeats its own patterns. The minimal use of temporal markers in globalist theory implies the possibility of a universal dissemination of civilization under certain conditions, facilitates the visualization of territorial and cultural expansion, and gives meaning to the dogmas and mission of civilization. Time is on the side of the globalist as time in globalism is least irreversible: civilization depends on conditions that are shaped by man, so anyone may compete by following the successful path of civilization. The problem is, however, that owing to the path dependency of the success of tools and facilities such as language, health, education and financial investment, not everyone has equal access to the means of developing and advancing their ideas and inventions. Owing to established monopolies over the markets of science and technology, potential competition often lacks backing; and, in a world in which some scarce resources, such as energy and territory, are already divided, newcomers are disadvantaged.

In the case of Lamarckian evolution theories (such as that of Imanishi Kinji)

160 *Group-framing habits and strategies*

and in the case of racism, time is clearly arrowed and boundaries between groups are unbridgeable. Social evolution, Marxist theory, Christianity and other universalistic religions, development theory, systems theory and globalization theory, theories of the rise and fall of civilization and dynasties are examples of theories that construct the nation around arrowed time. Some theories are endowed with a special engine, pushing forward the nation in mechanical time, or with an organic time-clock, based on vitalist principles upheld by the 'natural', cyclical order of life. For instance, natural selection, modernization, self-organization, communication technology, military power, peace forces, science and technology, historical divinity, sophistication and bodily control and moral rule have all served as hallmarks of temporal organization, on which the nation could measure its level of civilization.

The spatial dimension of efforts to frame the nation stresses the, largely, static aspects of the cultural, environmental and biological features ascribed to the particularity of the nation. They provide the roots of national essence, the stable factor in time. Spatial factors emphasize cultural and ethnic markers that do not seem to change in the history of the nation and civilization. Examples are found in the essentialized properties of religion (e.g. Shinto), language, ethnicity, race, climate, forests, place/field (*ba*), brain structure, collective psyche and the unconscious. The relevance of making a distinction between markers employed in the temporal and spatial dimensions of nation-centric research lies in their unequal distribution over what I call naturalist, culturalist and globalist systems of classifying the nation into superior and inferior, friendly or hostile units. Scientistic theories of nationalism tend to make use of universalistic principles that are ruled by time. This especially holds true for nation-centric theories of nation-states that regard the nation as closed off and isolated, and for theories of civilization that, although they ascribe regional origins and particularity to a civilization, at the same time embrace the entire world as a potential target of civilizing efforts. Although both take as their point of departure the nation-state, the universal validity of principles used in these theories are in principle adaptable by other nation-states that recognize their value. In 'closed China', scientific Marxism was supposed to be universally applicable; in Japanese academic ideologies of civilization, Japanese systems principles and management are applicable all over the world; Eastern values, buttressed by ('Western') popular scientific theory, similarly, are of universally value and applicability. Scientistic theories therefore lend themselves favourably to theories of civilization and legitimize expansionist thinking by their universalistic pretence.

Examples from China and Japan

I have used examples of academic theory in China and Japan to illuminate the theme of framing the nation, although social science elsewhere could have served the same purpose. The examples derive from diverse fields and, in the case of social science at CASS, must be seen in the context of an effort to build a strong nation-state and to achieve fast economic development. Partly for this reason, China provides many examples of research in which the nation figures prominently. Whether this role can be justified is of course dependent on the aim of each research project. The examples from Nichibunken, on the one hand, tended to focus less on the question of future national development, regarding the world much less as an arena ruled by struggling nation-states. On the other hand, the Japanese past in framing the nation is enveloped in one-sided imperialist threat and cultural and military humiliation. In the examples, therefore, the themes of national victimization and the civilizing mission of Japan played an important role.

Most remarkable, in my view, is the similar structure of nation-framing in both countries. Examples of nation-centred research from both countries employ natural, cultural and globalist markers in group categorization and use similar techniques of distancing. Natural group categorization in framing the nation in CASS and Nichibunken is based on linking nationals genetically to some ideal community or form of life in the past. In examples from both countries the brain is used not infrequently as a metaphor for expressing taxonomies of difference between East and West.

Although cultural group categorization in both China and Japan favours a return to the past, examples from China hardly ever show an unqualified embrace of the past. This reservation toward the past can be explained partly by official policies that emphasize the need to overcome feudal practices, propagating socialism with Chinese characteristics. In other cases, corruption and bureaucracy in the Chinese Communist Party are criticized as feudal practices, as is the case with some phenomena associated with Confucianism such as sexism, empty ritual. In both countries many examples can also be found of stressing the nation as one big family. However, the possibility of 'mixing races' is far less an item in nation-centric research in China than it is in Japan. This is, I believe, partly due to the acceptance by official Chinese policy of the merits of internal diversity. Diversity in China is even propagated as a form of strength and a source of unity, and according to some party theorists, it is subject to dialectical laws.

I have illustrated globalist categories by providing examples mainly related to systems science and complexity. Ironically, in both China and Japa, these modern sciences have not infrequently been argued to have Chinese, Japanese and Eastern origins. Arguments to prove such points are taken especially from the fields of Buddhist and Taoist philosophy, amplified with references to the works of modern scientists and popular science writers. Scientific evidence for the special value of Our nation to many nation-centric researchers seems to be essential for legitimizing theories of exporting Our civilization. Just as is the case with many classical modernization theories, universal pretences in such globalist theories are ultimately based on the localized cultural or racial superiority of Our civilization. In both Japan and China such theories can be found. The examples provided in this thesis,

162 *Group-framing habits and strategies*

however, drew on Japanese examples of comparative civilization theory and Chinese examples of systems theory.

At this point, I can only account positively for instances that I have studied, that is, by reporting on examined examples that categorize groups in similar ways. Whether it is meaningful to conduct research into the differences between group categorizing in the context of the two different national polities is up to subsequent research to demonstrate. I suspect that as long as social science debate is conducted by a predominant use of the nation-frame, debates between intellectuals are bound to make use of academic nationalist forms of group construction and nation-based markers, each interest group and school using its own interpretations of national symbols and metaphors. It is of value, I believe, to trace the similarities between ways new groups are construed transregionally. In times of increasing emphasis on cultural difference between nations, the cross-national and inter-disciplinary study of the differences and similarities between research definitions of the nation is of great value to understanding academic forms of national identity production. Such studies, of course, are not limited to east Asia.

Features of nation-framing

The use of specific styles in various disciplines, institutes, organizations and the entire state education system may be telling about the effects of science policies on academic research. Nation-centred research is not just a product of one institute but is part of a politico-cultural environment and finds its impetus in general academic policies and policies of state education. Therefore contents, style and methods in academic nationalist theory produced in various educational and research institutions may show similarities on a regional basis, but at the same time, similar internal structures of nation-centric research can be found in research institutes universally.

Because the political and administrative powers of a nation influence local and transregional cultures, it is plausible that the nation-state as an explanatory unit is employed suitably in particular cases. But if generalizations about 'our nation-state' reach beyond demonstrable political and administrative functions by ascribing historical necessity, 'natural' causes or disputable cultural legitimation to its historical existence, one can compare such generalizations with other views, definitions and legitimation of the nation-state. For example, if the characteristics of political and administrative organization are systematically defined as natural attributes of national culture, the researcher can check whether this link is defendable by matching various political options of nation-state building with different conceptions of national culture; and, if forms of political and administrative organizations are defined as a necessary outcome of the history of the nation, the researcher can compare them with available political choices and circumstances of

Core themes and future research 163

decisions made about state organization at historical turning points and trace the processes that led to state formation.

In Part III I have discussed aspects of framing the nation involving the relationship between academics and their institutional environment, including the politics of research policy. I maintained that a sharp distinction between that nation-state and national culture is misleading, as the influence of the state administration pervades all aspect of the social community. The two are just different aspects of a process of historical development. Any attempt at a general definition without a concrete research problematic is bound to be a political one, also when not intended. For even the perception of the absence of the state is not an apolitical phenomenon, but serves as a topic of political debate in communitarian formulations of the nation-state. The form and extent of nation-state influence, as defined in dominant discourse, however, can be compared with competing views of state organization in both history and in the present.

A major impediment to social science research and factors inherent to framing the nation are the confused presentations of the description of facts and prescription of national behaviour. It is expressed in the political innuendo, a scholastic inability to generate fresh views and research problems, and in the failure to imagine the ways in which the Other views the nation, and leads to the loss of capacity to deal with conflict. Due to its conservative formulations, ideological grammar and vocabulary, nation-centric research tends to instil into researchers an establishment bias and encourages judgements and distortions of Other (possibly rival) national groupings.

Nation-centric research thrives when the reader can predict an argument by correlating certain political and ideological signs, such as the unreasoned use of the nation as a main frame of research and as the unit of comparative analysis, in which Our nation is set off against the Other or Them. Other signs are the (context-dependent) simplified representation of links between national friend and foe; the presence of absentees; the undefended (direct and indirect) use of rigid and (semi-) closed markers of boundary construction in characterizing a national people (brain, race, language, cultural system, *fūdo*); the use of symbolic concepts to explain the specific nature of peoples (Chinese character region, chop-stick culture, rice-civilization); the use of abstract and ambiguous notions (ancient tradition, golden age, fairy-tales, evolution, instinct, the beginning of the universe, the infinite universe, climate, god, the unconscious, mass psychology) for explaining politically charged conflicts; the unreasoned deployment of categories and variables in defining differences and similarities between units of research (e.g. the definition of the East as female and the West as male; China as female and Japan as male); the interchangeable use of categories of prescription and description in relation to defining national policies; and, specific patterns of classification that do not vary with the subject matter in question but with the politics of certain social groups and institutions.

164 *Group-framing habits and strategies*

In subsequent research an elaboration of this list and its systemization could yield insight into our conditioning by the habit of framing the nation. The results of such exploration could serve as a critical 'check' to the formulation of research projects. It could also be used for the generation of new hypotheses by studying the interaction between official versions of national history and its socio-cultural and political features, and the features and methods used in the creation of other, not necessarily localized, identities. Research into the ways in which the nation provides a frame and vocabulary as a base for the interaction of various academic schools of research and interest groups could offer further insights into the ways in which we perceive the world and each other.

Appendix I: Joint research, Nichibunken (1988–96)

The name in the first colunm is that of the leader of the joint research group; the second colunm shows the research theme; the date after the research theme is the year in which the particular team research started.

Nakanishi Susumu	Japanese literature and 'I' (*Nihonbungaku to 'watakushi'*) 1988
Hanihara Kazurō	The basic structure of Japanese culture and its natural background (*Nihon bunka no kihon kōzō to sono shizenteki haikei*) 1988
Kunō Akira	The Japanese view of the other world (*Nihonjin no takaikan*) 1988
Murai Yasuhiko	The Japanese culture of *ba* (*'Ba' no Nihon bunka*) 1988
Donald Keene	The reception and alteration of foreign art in the Edo period (*Edo jidai no geijutsu ni okeru gaikoku bunka*) 1988
Umehara Takeshi	The sociology of knowledge of Japanese research in the world (*Sekai ni okeru nihon kenkyzū no chishiki shakaigakuteki kenkyū*) 1988
Hamaguchi Eshun	The merits and demerits of the Japanese model (*Nihongata moderu no meritto to demeritto*) 1989
Murakami Yasusuke	The international comparison of market systems (*Shijō seido no kokusai hikaku*) (new) 1989
Yamaori Tetsuo	The multi-layered nature of Japanese thought (*Nihon shisō no jūsōsei*) 1989

166   *Appendix I*

Yamada Keiji

East Asian 'Chinese materia medica' and the world of natural history (*Higashi-Ajia no honsō to hakubutsugaku no sekai*) 1989

Īda Tsuneo

The dynamics of market systems: with reference to Japan (Shijōseido no dōtai) 1990

Itō Shuntarō

The Japanese view of nature (*Nihonjin no shizenkan*) (new) 1990

Hayami Akira

Historical awareness and historical consciousness: historical research of Japan (*Rekishi ninshiki to rekishi ishiki: nihon no rekishi kenkyū*) 1990

Kawai Hayao

Old tales: the study of the common base of Asia and Afrika (*Mukashibanashi, sono Ajza – Afurika ni tsūtei suru mono no kenkyū*) 1991

Itō Shuntarō

Japanese science and civilization (*Nihon no kagaku to bunmei*) 1992

Nakanishi Susumu

The imaginative power of *Japan* (*Nihon no sōzōryoku*) 1992

Hayami Akira

Population and family in the process of modernization (*Kindaika katei ni okeru jinkō to kazoku*) 1992

Kimura Hiroshi

International comparison of negotiation behaviour in various nations (*Kōshō kōdō yōshiki no kokusai hikaku*) 1992

Hamaguchi Eshun

Japanese systems in the global situation (*Sekai no naka no Nihongata shisutemu*) 1992

Haga Toru

Comparative cultural history of 'Utopia' (*'Risōkyō' no hikaku bunkashi*) 1992

Hayakawa Monta

Life and contemporary civilization (*Seimei to gendai bunmei*) 1993

Tsuji Nobuo

New approach to Japanese culture: *kazari* (Japanese ornamentation) and *kijin* (eccentrics) (*Nihon bunka no shindanmen – kazari narabi ni kijin kenkyū*) 1993

Murai Yasuhiko	Aristocracy and military families (*Kuge to buke*) 1993
Sugimoto Hidetarō	The study of *tanzaku* (*Tanzaku no kenkyū*) 1993
Yamaori Tetsuo	How have the Japanese accepted Christianity? (*Nihonjin wa kirisutokyō o dono yō ni juyō shita ka*) 1993
Umehara Takeshi	The deep layer of Japanese culture and Okinawa (*Nihon bunka no shinsō to Okinawa*) 1993
Suzuki Sadami	A comprehensive study of the *Taiyō: the dynamic study of the self-image of Japanese culture in modernity* (Sōgō zasshi no sōgōteki kenkyū no serufu-imeji no kindai ni okeru dōtai kenkyū) 1993
Omoto Kei'ichi	The Japanese and the regionality of Japanese culture (*Nihonjin oyobi Nihon bunka no chi'ikisei*) 1994
Gunji Takao	Constraint-based study of the structure of the Japanese language (*Seiyaku ni motozuku Nihongo no kōzō no kenkyū*) 1994
Yamada Keiji	Medicine and disease in history – focusing on Japan (*Rekishi no naka no yamai to igaku – nihon o chūshin ni*) 1994
Sepp Linhart	View of recreation as well as the development of historical behaviour: the Japanese view of work and spare-time and concretely showing its historical development (*Gendai Nihonjin no rōdō, asobikan oyobi kōdō no rekishiteki hattatsu*) 1995
Yasuda Yoshinori	Climate and witches – a reconsideration of animism (*Majo to kikō no bunmeishi*) 1995
Sonoda Hidehiro	The emergence of the middle class in modern Japan (*Nihon ni okeru chūsankaikyū no seiritsu katei – jinkō, kazoku, shokugyō, kaisō*) 1995
Haga Toru	Modern Japanese women – image and self-presentation (*Kindai Nihon no onnatachi – sono hyōshō to jiko hyōgen*) 1995

168 *Appendix I*

Ishida Hideomi

Religious communication in east Asia through physical techniques (*Karada gihō o tsūshitemita higashi ajia no shūkyōkōryūshi*) 1995

Īda Tsuneo

Americanism in the Japanese social sciences (*Gendai Nihon no shakai kagaku ni okeru amerikanizumu*) 1995

Ishii Shirō

Law and society in a period of transition; translated as: 'Law in changing *society*' (*Tenkanki ni okeru hō to shakai*) 1996

Inami Ritsuko

Modernism in literature: various aspects in transition (*Bungaku ni okeru kindai: tenkanki no shosō*) 1996

Tsuda Yukio

The Japanese and the English language: an interdisciplinary study of anglicized (Americanized) Japan (*Nihonjin to eigo: eigoka suru nihon no gakusaiteki kenkyū*) 1996

Kasaya Kazuhiko

Aristocracy and warriors: the comparative study of civilization (*Kuge to buke: sono hikaku bunmei kōsatsu*) 1996

Senda Minoru

The formation process of cultural areas in the east Asian Mediterranean world from the 3rd to the 7th century (*Hagashi-Ajia chichūkai sekai ni okeru bunkaken no keisei katei: 3 seiki kara 7 seiki ni kakete*) 1996

Appendix II: General research meetings, Nichibunken

Overview of the general research meetings: April 1996–March 1997

Research field	Research frame	New/ old	Research theme	Members[a]	Professor in charge	Assistant	Period	Meetings[b]
Field 1: Dynamics	Present	New	Law and society in a period of transition	12/9	Ishi'i	Morioka	Apr96–Mar99	5
	Basic	New	The Japanese and English	14/11	Tsuda	Kashioka	Apr96–Mar97	6
	Tradition	New		27/10	Inami	Suzuki/ Inoue	Apr96–Mar99	5
Field 2: Structure	Nature	Old	The rediscovery of animism	31/23	Yasuda		Apr95–Mar97	5
	People	Old	The regionality of the Japanese and Japanese culture	31/22	Omoto	Kitagawa	Apr94–Mar97	6
	Society	Old	The formation principles of Japanese style systems	27/19	Hamaguchi	Kurose	Apr95–Mar97	6
Field 3: Comparative culture	System	Old		19/12	Sonoda	Kurose	Apr95–Mar98	5
	Thought	Old	Modern Japanese women	46/28	Haga	Ochiai	Apr95–Mar97	6
	System	New	*Kuge* and *Buke*: Explorations of comparative civilization	28/21	Kasaya	Kitagawa	Apr96–Mar99	6

continued

Research field	Research frame	New/old	Research theme	Members[a]	Professor in charge	Assistant	Period	Meetings[b]
Field 4: Cultural relations	Ancient exchange Region II	Old	Disease and medicine in history	34/21	Yamada	Kuriyama	Apr94–Mar97	4
	New Exchange Region	Old	How have the Japanese received Christianity	22/14	Yamaori	Nagada	Apr93–Mar97	2
	Ancient Exchange Region I	New	East Asia – the formation process of the cultural region in the Mediterranean world: 3–7 century	31/24	Senda	Kamigaito/ Mitsuda	Apr96–Mar99	5
Field 5: Cultural information	Japanese studies and other countries I	Old	Americanism and the present Japanese social sciences	11/7	Īda	Kashioka	Apr95–Mar98	5
	Japanese studies and other countries I	Old	International comparison of forms of negotiation behaviour	29/23	Kimura	Hayakawa	July 91–Mar97	4
	Japanese studies and the Japanese	Old		34/22	Suzuki	Mitsuda	Apr93–Mar97	6
	Total			396/266				77

[a] The second number represents the members from outside.
[b] Number of meetings in the academic year of 1996/7.

Appendix III: Fields of basic research

Kiso Ryōiki Kenkyū (Fields of Basic Research)

Research theme	Representative	Contents	Planned meetings
Elements of English style (continued)	Kimura Hiroshi Kuriyama Shigehisa	Research into various elements of effective English expressions concerning English presentation and style	Once a month
Family and population history (continued)	Ochiai Emiko	Co-operative research concerning the history of the family and demography, reading of basic academic works and data management with the aid of computers	Every week
Classical literature (continued)	Senda Minoru Kasaya Kazuhiko	The interpretation of pre-modern hand-written classics, diaries, records, etc.	Twice a month
Comparative history of the body (continued)	Kuriyama Shigehisa	Discussing and reading on the history of European and American (Oubei) science and medicine concerning views of the body and bodily experience	Once a month
Comparative culture of visual materials (continued)	Shirahata Yozaburō	Comparative cultural research between Japan and the world and between regions within Japan by means of discussing 'visual materials' such as photographs, pictures, maps, prints, etc. from the view of every field of specialization	Once a month
	Hayakawa Monta Mitsuta Kazunobu		Twice a month

continued

Research theme	Representative	Contents	Planned meetings
DNA archaeology (new)	Omoto Kei'ichi	Analyse and interpret archaeological materials (plants, animals, humans) after abstracting and multiplying DNA. Discussing and exploring the issues concerning the present state of DNA archaeology	Once a month
Reading Japanese classical poetry and songs	Mitsuta Kazunobu Hayakawa Monta	Although *Waka*, *Renga* and Haiku are densely represented in literature and form an important part of Japanese culture, they are hard to understand. Thinking of a basis for adequate understanding	Twice a month
Japanese research and the management of visual information	Yamada Keiji	Researching methods of dealing with visual information as an expedient of Japanese research	Once a month
Fundamental concepts and methods of cultural theory	Suzuki Sadami	Discussing nature, ethnic groups, civilization, culture, nation, tradition, sex, etc. Fundamental concepts in cultural theory, making use of English, French, German, Japanese and Chinese dictionaries, and reading relevant classical academic books and present-day research	Twice a month

Glossary of frequently used Japanese [J] and Chinese [C] terms and persons

Aidagara [J] A central concept in the work of Watsuji Tetsurō, referring to the relationships between people.

Ainu [J] An ethnic minority in Japan, believed to be the offspring of the earliest human inhabitants of Japan.

Amae [J] Coaxing, presuming upon someone one has a special bond with.

Bushi [J] Samurai.

Chūgoku [J] China.

Eikaiwa [J] English conversation.

Fūdo [J] Milieu, climate.

Furusato [J] Old local community; home-town.

Furusato-zukuri [J] Recreating old local communities.

Giri [J] Sense of obligation and of duty.

guojia [C] State; country.

Guoxue re National studies fever.

haji [J] Shame.

Hanzu [C] The Chinese race; the Chinese nation.

Himitsu [J] Secret.

Huaxia [C] China.

Jōmon [J] A neolithic culture of settlers that settled in Japan approximately 12,000 years ago.

Kangaku [J] Chinese studies.

Kanjin [J] 'Relatum,' a term denoting the 'space between people'.

Kanjinshugi [J] The ideology of the 'relatum' (see *kanjin*).

Minzu [C] People; race; nation.

Mushi [J] Selflessness.

Nasake [J] Mercy.

Neidanxue [C] A form of training of the ordinary conscious, the purification of the subconscious, and the opening up of the original unconscious in order to find the true self.

Nichibunken [J] (*Kokusai Nihon Bunka Kenkyū Sentā*) International Research Centre for Japanese Studies. Nichibunken is a research institute founded in 1987 by the Ministry of Education, Science and Culture, and its establishment was made possible by the enthusiastic support of former

174 *Glossary*

prime minister Nakasone Yasuhiro. The centre's first director, Umehara Takeshi, defined the aim of the centre's research programmes as 'to identify the uniqueness of Japanese culture and pass this on to the rest of humanity'.

Nihonjinron (Nihonbunka-ron) [J]   Discussions on the meaning of Japanese-ness.

Ningjuli [C]   Coherent force.

Ōbei [J]   Europe and America (literally).

Oumei [C]   Europe and America (literally).

Renmin [C]   People.

Seiyō [J]   The West.

Shina [J]   China.

Shōgi [J]   Japanese chess.

Tamashi [J]   The logic of the soul.

Tōyō [J]   The East.

Tōyōshi [J]   History of the East.

Wajin [J]   The Japanese; literally 'peace people'.

Xixue re [C]   Western study fever.

Yayoi   Name used for the people and wet-rice culture of the Yayoi era (*c*. 300 BC–AD 300).

Yuinōron [J]   Brainism.

Zhongguo [C]   China.

Zhonghua [C]   China.

Zhonghua Minzu [C]   The Chinese people/race/nation.

Zhongyong [C]   The doctrine of the mean.

Notes

1 Introduction: Framing the nation in China and Japan

1 In the Confucian classics, the 'golden age' was located in the past rather than in the future. Thus state planning was achieved by reference to a past ideal projected into the future.
2 Umehara Takeshi is the founding director of The International Research Centre for Japanese Studies (Nichibunken, Kyoto).
3 See Chapter Three.

2 The power of national symbols: The might of a Chinese dragon

1 This chapter is based on an article previously published as 'The Power of National Symbols: The Credibility of a Dragon's Efficacy', *Nations and Nationalism*, May 2002.
2 The theories of Ernest Gellner and Anthony Smith indirectly support the idea of an objectively pre-existing nation. Not many scholars would support the claim that no objective differences exist between groups of people, but these authors link those differences between peoples to a static definition of the nation, which is used by nationalists to legitimate certain forms of rule. In Gellner's modernist image of the nation, nationalism creates national identity, but it does not come from nowhere: 'Nationalism is not the awakening of nations to self-consciousness; it invents nations here they do not exist – but it does need some pre-existing differentiating marks to work on, even if, as indicated, these are purely negative' (Gellner 1964: 168, *Thought and Change*, London: Weidenfeld & Nicolson, p. 168 (quoted in Smith 1991: 71). Gellner's nationalism is 'weak', therefore, precisely because there are many more 'objective' cultural differences than ethnic nationalism. Only some differences become the sites for ethnic mobilization; the others 'fail' to provide bases for the development of nationalism (Gellner 1983: Chapter 5). Anthony Smith in his *Ethnic Origins of Nations* explores the features that enables ethnic nations (ethnies) to survive. Among the most important features he found were a shared communal religion, a home land, language, and a shared view of national history (Smith 1986).
3 The dragon as national symbol has only been about since the May Fourth. Wen Yiduo was one of its foremost proponents. His theory had been accepted widely in academic circles.
4 Quoted by Hu from the 'The History of the Han Dynasty' (*Han shu – Gao Di ji*).
5 *Lixue* or neo-Confucianism increasingly took hold in social life since the eleventh century. It emerged as a response to the cosmopolitan spirit of the Tang, and as a political ideology it is often associated with cultural conservatism. Neo-

176 *Notes*

Confucianism is a generic term and covers not only Song–Ming Confucianism but also that of later dynasties, and sometimes also that of Tokugawa Japan (1644–1912) and the Korean Chosŏn Dynasty (1392–1910). For a history of gender and familial relations in China, see also Min Jiayin (1995).
6 For a general anthropological discussion of the monkey in Japanese society, see Ohnuki Tierney (1987).
7 All countries are forced by the PRC to make a choice between Taiwan or the PRC. For instance, the US broke off its diplomatic relations with Taiwan in 1978 in order to continue its diplomatic approach to the PRC.

3 The coherent force of struggle and diversity in Chinese nationalism

1 This chapter is based on an article previously published as 'The Coherent Force of Struggle and Diversity in Chinese Socialism', *Studies in Ethnicity and Nationalism* (LSE), Vol. 2, No. 1, 2002.
2 For examples of discourses on race in modern China, see Frank Dikötter (1992, 1997). Dikötter refuses to provide a ready-made definition of racism: by imposing a definition of an ideal type of 'racism,' racial discourses which do not conform to the imposed model are ignored, marginalized or trivialized (Dikötter 1997: 4). However, he does give us a clue to the use of the concept: 'they all primarily group human populations on the basis of some biological signifier, be it skin colour, body height, hair texture or head-shape' (Dikötter 1997: 5), suggesting that socially constructed races can be contrasted with socially constructed ethnicities.
3 The concept of *minzu* is usually translated as 'nation' or 'people' but in many contexts clearly has racial overtones. According to Dikötter (1992: 108–9), at a conference in 1962 it was decided to use the concept of *minzu* in a broad sense including biological, political and ethnic features of tribe, nation, state, people or ethnic minority.
4 The concept of nation in English, Russian, German and French can all mean both nation (*minzu*) and state (*guojia*), the two concepts being intimately related. In China this is not so: first, historical circumstances are different; second, the linguistic systems in relation to nation and state are different. For example, Tibetan and Mongolian make a clear distinction between the *minzu* and *guojia*. The first refers to cultural and the second to political aspects. Only recently have the two tended to be combined into the concept of *minzu*. For example, *minzu* in the concept of *Zhonghua Minzu* is first of all political, and cultural and psychological elements come only second. This *minzu* is clearly different from the *zu* in *Mengzu* (Mongol nationality), *Zangzu* (Tibetan nationality) and *Chaoxianzu* (Korean nationality). In English *guojia* can be expressed through the concepts of state, nation or country. 'State' refers to political unity; 'nation' to the historical emergence of national independence, and country stresses the territorial delineation of a state. In Chinese these concepts can only be translated as *guojia*. If we say 'the *guojia* is a dictatorial organ', we clearly mean state, not nation or country (Nari Bilige 1990).
5 '*Zhongguo jiruo suyuan lun*' (On the Source of China's Weakness), 1900 in *Yinbingshi wenji* (Fitzgerald 1995: 86).
6 Hongshan culture stretched out over the provinces of Liaoning and Qinghai.
7 The unity of plurality theory/thesis of *Zhonghua Minzu: Zhonghua Minzu duoyuan yitilun*.
8 According to the Garden of Eden hypothesis, *Homo erectus*, the precursor of *Homo sapiens*, evolved in East Africa and spread out to Asia as early as 2 million years ago (or at least prior to 1 million years ago). The subsequent migration 'Out of Africa' gave birth to *Homo erectus*, which has been called both Peking Man and Java Man. *Homo erectus* had reached Java about a million years ago, and

Notes 177

survived to about 400 thousand years ago in China. Much later – within the last 100,000 years – *Homo sapiens* emerged, also in East Africa, and replaced *Homo erectus* throughout the Old World (cf. Barnes 1999: 43).

9 Jia Lanpo and Huang Weiwen, *The Story of Peking Man: From Archaeology to Mystery*, Beijing: Foreign Language Press, 1990 (quoted in Sautman 1997: 84; also see Jia Lanpo 1989).

10 *Huaxia Sanbuzu* is a generic term for Huaxia, Xiongyi and Nanman.

11 The three cultures were the Yangshao, Dahanko and Qujialing.

12 In fact, Chinese intellectuals have historically made much use of the image of 'struggle for survival' and 'survival of the fittest' in terms that took China and other nation-states as the units that were in competition with one another (cf. Pusey 1983; Fitzgerald 1996).

13 Du Ruofu (b. 1930) is a professor in the Research Institute for Genetics at CAS; Xiao Chunjie (b. 1960) is a professor in the Department for Biology at Yunnan University.

14 In other words, genetic variation is greater internally (between north and south) that it is between the Han and minorities in north China or between the Han and minorities in south China.

4 Natural categorization

1 The Golden Age refers to natural perfection at the beginning of time, before the fall, when an 'intruder' brought corrupting influence of sophistication and civilization. (ibid.: 66).

2 According to Blacker's description, Mabuchi Kamo (1697–1769) wrote commentaries on classical works such as Genji Monogatari, the Norito or Shinto prayers, Ise Monogatari, Mamato Monogatari and Manyōshu. Stripped of Chinese accretions, he believed, they expressed lost paradise. A special concept signified the Japanese spirit: *magokoro*. It meant life according to the natural laws of heaven and earth, simple innocence and goodness, devoid of extravagance and lust. The fall from paradise came with the introduction of Chinese learning, or Confucianism.

   Motoori Norinaga (1730–1801), inspired by Mabuchi, wrote commentaries on *Genji Monogatari* (*The Tale of Genji*), poems, philology, grammar and aesthetics, attacks on Chinese philosophy and expositions of the ancient way. His greatest work is a commentary on the *Kojiki(den)* which had fallen into oblivion. Norinaga believed that the sun goddess had given the Japanese a special quality of virtue which he called *kodō*, that is, the ancient way. The way was transmitted by the line of emperors; the fall was brought on by Chinese learning, which vocabulary chopped up the spontaneous *magokoro* of Japanese notions such as righteousness and justice, correct etiquette and wisdom; and, its superiority was reflected in Japanese ancient language, which was thought to be perfect. Only the 'fifty syllables' of ancient speech were truly correct sounds.

   The Golden Age thus was monopolized by the Japanese. Inspired by Motoori, Hirata Atsutane, dealt with the exposition of *kodō*. The Japanese in the golden age were by nature perfectly virtuous, perfectly healthy (diseases had spread through Buddhism and Confucianism) and gigantic in stature. In *Kodō Tai-i*, he wrote that only Japan was created directly by Izanagi and Izanami, while other countries were leftovers and inferior (Blacker 1988: 67–75).

3 *Kokutai no hongi* (Fundamentals of Our National Polity) was designed by the Ministry of Education to set the ideological course for the Japanese people. It concerned the question of how Western influences were to be absorbed by Japan without permitting them to destroy Japanese national traditions, and how Japan could resolve the dilemma created in the West itself by the inherent contradictions

178 Notes

of individualism. *Kokutai no hongi* was based on an original manuscript by Tokyo University professor Hisamatsu Senichi, the principles were revised and finalized by a committee of scholars and bureaucrats before publication. Laden with references to Shinto mythology and classical poetry, and burdened with archaic vocabulary, according to Morris-Suzuki, *Kokutai no hongi* offers the quintessential statement of the uniqueness and superiority of the Japanese nation. When it was issued in 1937, initially 300,000 copies were sold and eventually 2,000,000. Study groups were formed to discuss its content also in schools (De Bary *et al.* 1964: 278–88; Morris-Suzuki 1998: 94–5).

4 In fact, one trend in nation-centred writing is whitewashing the nation from racial discrimination and blaming the Other of the same thing. Hanihara Kazuroo, who carried out anthropological research on the Ainu in Hokkaido, traces back the theory that says the Ainu population derives from Caucasoid populations and therefore very different from adjacent populations such as the non-Ainu Japanese to a prejudice against the Ainu. According to Hanihara, this prejudice is made exclusively by Caucasoids. The prejudice stems from a 'magic logic' underlying this theory: 'Quite unfortunately, we have to confess, large-scale magic is performed by anthropologists and related scientists in recent history, and it led the world to a serious tragedy. The director of this miserable drama was a Nazi.' 'Such investigations undertaken from sinister motives must be criticized, but we, particularly the anthropologists, have to reflect (upon) the fear of this kind of magic on our own minds.' Here, Hanihara suggests that non-Nazi anthropologists, too, can be subject to the 'magic logic'. Next, Hanihara suggests that it is mainly *Ōbei-ans* (Americans and Europeans, usually white ones, see note 32) that cause racist trouble: 'Honestly speaking, there still are a few Euro-American anthropologists who are white-supremacists. They believe that "the man of men" is the Caucasoid, or the white people.' 'Until recently, for example, they tended to draw a human phylogenetic tree with the stem attributed to the Caucasoids and the small branches to the coloured populations' (*Nichibunken Newsletter*, vol. 1, no. 1, 1988, Magic in Logic, by Hanihara Kazurō).

5 Tsunoda is an ear, nose and throat specialist. Tsunoda uses a 'tapping method' to determine which hemisphere plays the dominant role.

6 According to Yōrō, culture is the aggregate of expressions of the conscious and the unconscious. In the process of transplanting (*ishoku*) conscious expressions, e.g. knowledge, unconscious expressions, that belong to a certain people, are lost (Yōrō 1997: 6). Yōrō proceeds from the Jungian idea that the brain has been shaped and influenced by the remote experiences of mankind. The traces of such primordial experiences are most clearly expressed in art, instinctive behaviour and dreams.

7 The evolution theory of Imanishi Kinji is based on the gradual but collective change of species. Imanishi Kinji (1902–92), founder of Japanese primatology, studied troops of *Macaca fuscata*. The relevance of this discussion lies in the claim that only Japanese can individuate monkeys and that Westerners are too much separated from nature to be able to do the same. In this view, Western anthropologists do not mingle with the natives, and treat animals as mere objects of study. The Japanese closeness to nature implies a realization of evolution theory. This model of evolution is based on an original biological affinity linking all biological orders. The underlying intuitive perception or instinct (*honnō*) resembles Nishida's 'pure experience' (*junsui keiken*) inheritable by an entire species. Imanishi replaces the individual with the species as the unit of evolutionary change (as does Tanabe Hajime in his *Logic of Species*), and enables the species to control evolution by drawing on its pre-existing repertoire of possible mutations when presented by environmental challenge. All the individuals within the species, or most of them, change simultaneously and in the same way.

Notes 179

(Imanishi Kinji 1996: 27). In his *The Formation of Human Society*, the multiple individuals of a group society change collectively in a similar way at the same time. Imanishi also refers to the concept of 'horizontal relations' between members of highly evolved groups and communication between species on a regional basis (intraspecies), in contrast with lower forms of species that are constituted of disordered individuals (Imanishi Kinji 1994: Chapter One).

8 For *Kokutai no hongi*, see note 3.
9 The 'ancient stratum' of the historical conscious: *Rekishi ishiki no kōsō* (1972); also see Maruyama Masao (1990).
10 The phrase *Wakon Yōsai* denotes borrowing (learning) from the West while retaining the core of what is regarded as the native Japanese civilization. During the Heian period, the phrase used to be *Wakon Kansai*, referring to borrowing from China and retaining Japanese civilization (cf. Fogel 1994: 6–9). Without China as Other, nativism had no meaning in Japan. Now 'the West' had become its referential Other.
11 Ōbei is short for America (*bei*) and Europe (*ō*). The frequently used notion of Ōbei is a strongly generalizing, historical concept, hardly conducive to serious social science research. Ōbei usually refers to the USA and western Europe, and sometimes to 'the West'. Geography is not the most important characteristic of Ōbei. Rather, everything associated with a Japanese understanding of modernity is attributed to Ōbei. It is often imagined as aggressive, individualistic, ruled by whites, very moralistic and the inspirational source of modern music, and is especially used for contrasting Us with Them. The frequent use of contrastive generalizations such as Ōbei, implies a relative absence of confrontation with the diversity of the region so designated. The concept of Ōbei has many dimensions that are discussed daily in Japanese institutions of higher education.
12 Kawai Masao (1924–97) is a student of Imanishi Kinji, the establisher of Japanese primatology, and is a brother of Kawai Hayao (Kawai Hayao's ideas are discussed in Chapter Eight). He graduated from the Department of Biology at Kyoto University, and specialized in animal ecology. He served as professor at Japan Welfare University (*Nihon Fukushi Daigaku*), and head of the Japan Monkey Centre. His main publications are *Ningen no yūrai. kami, shimo* (*The Origin of Man*, vols I and II) (pub.: Shōgakukan), *Bōenkyō kara mita sekai* (The World Seen Through a Monkey- (teles)scope (Pun: (*bōenkyō*) means telescope. The character for *en* (far) is replaced by that for monkey) (pub.: Asahi Xinbunsha); *Senrin ga saru o unda* (The Forest Gave Birth to the Monkey) (pub.: Heibonsha).
13 Kawai bases his observations of the interaction between animals and human on the primatology of the Iminishi Kinji, whose evolution theory is based on the gradual but collective change of species. (For Imanishi, see index.)
14 Yasuda Yoshinori (1946–) graduated from Tōhoku University (Ph.D.) and since 1994 has been employed as a research fellow at Nichibunken. His specialization is environmental archaeology. Yasuda's main works are *kihō ga bunmei o kaeru* (Climate Transforms Civilizations) and *Mori to bunmei no monogatari* (The Narrative of Forest and Civilization) (Yasuda 1993: 140).
15 *Fūdo* is a concept often translated into English as 'climate'. Augustin Berque's translation of Watsuji's concept of *fūdo* into the French 'milieu' seems to be more apt, as it also includes the human environment (cf. Berque 1998). Watsuji Tetsurō was appointed assistant professor of ethics at Kyoto University in 1925, was sent to Germany in 1927, where he studied in Berlin for 2 years, and travelled extensively in Italy and Greece. Travelling was his source of inspiration for his *Climate and Culture* (Watsuji 1961: 4). It was a direct response to Heidegger's *Sein und Zeit*, which he thought placed too much emphasis on time and the individual and too little on space and the social dimension of human beings. He proposed that 'it is only when human existence is treated in terms of its concrete duality

180 *Notes*

(social and individual) that time and space are linked and that history also is first revealed in its true guise. And at the same time the connection between history and climate becomes evident'. By climate Watsuji means to include not only weather patterns of a region but the natural geographic setting of a people plus the social environment of family, community, society, lifestyle and even the technological apparatus that supports community survival and interaction. *Fūdo*, then, is the entire interconnected network of influences that together create an entire people's attitudes and that represents geographic and climatic influences on human society and human interaction with climatic necessities, together with the human transformation of geographic aspects of the environment. Climate therefore is the mutuality of nature and culture (Watsuji 1996: 5).

Together with Hisamatsu Sen'ichi, Watsuji played a significant role in the drafting of *Kokutai no hongi* (Fundamentals of Our National Polity, 1937). In it, views of the national spirit (*kotodama*) were employed for the purpose of mass mobilization and inculcating a spirit of obedience to the nation (Morris-Suzuki 1998: 115–19). Interestingly, the mysterious power of Japanese words, 'words that are not liable to be put into practice are shunned, and are not uttered' could have been directly taken from texts attributed to Lao Zi. This culture of silence involves the self-censuring of dissident consciousness.

16 The concept of rice culture plays an important role in theories of scholars who aim to improve relations between China and Japan. Emphasizing their common historical roots in an ancient rice civilization contributes to this end. The Japan–China Joint Academic Survey Group of the Yangtze Civilization (1995–8), for example, found the ruins of a city called Longma in the lower reaches of the Yangtze valley in Sichuan, going back approximately 4,500 years. The project had several aims, among which was to discover the 'fifth' ancient civilization after the civilizations of Mesopotamia, Egypt, Indus valley and Yellow River valley, and the conservation of the archaeological remains of the middle and lower reaches of the Yangtze River valley. Another aim was to start a new phase of cultural exchanges between China and Japan, after commemorating the fiftieth anniversary of the end of the Second World War. It was recently discovered, Yasuda informs us, that ancient rice civilization is 150 years older than that of the middle reaches of the Yellow River valley, which cultivated wheat. According to Yasuda, the thesis that the origin of Chinese civilization lies in the middle and lower Yangtze has begun to be accepted (Yasuda Yoshinori 1995).

17 *Nichibunken Newsletter*, no. 3, July 1989 'Passivity and Activity of Japanese Studies', Yasuda Yoshinori 1989: pp. 7–8.

18 BP (abbr.): before the present. One way to express a rebellious spirit against the West, which is intimately associated with Christianity, is by refusing to use BC and AD in expressions of time.

19 Shinto is often described as the indigenous belief of the Japanese people. Since the 1868 Meiji Restoration, it has had a substantive link with state nationalism. Early Shinto was a cult of native deities (kami), including spirits of nature, deified emperors, heroes and other mythological beings.

20 For an account of Japanese politics in relation to environmental problems, see McCormack (1996: 95).

21 The audience of Umehara and Yasuda is mainly located in Japan, even though some of Umehara's work has been translated into English and Chinese. Umehara headed the International Research Centre for Japanese Studies (Kyoto) for 8 years (see Glossary and Chapter Eight). Although the institute's stated purpose was the enhancement of international mutual understanding, not many foreigners have openly announced their support of Nichibunken's activities, although quite a few have made use of the elaborate research facilities and attractive financial and material conditions it offers. Even though in Japan Umehara draws a lot of

Notes 181

popular support and regularly appears on TV, in the newspapers and at symposia, many of his academic colleagues distance themselves from his views.

22 Umehara wrote his thesis on Heidegger (Iwasaki 1989: 36).

23 In another version of this legend left by history in cuneiform script, King Gilgamesh and his friend Enkidu defeat the guardian of the wicked forest, Chumbaba, who was appointed to protect the cedar woods by the god of the Earth, Enlil. When the two heroes killed Chumbaba, Enlil cursed them and decided to punish humankind by flooding the earth, but he later regretted it.

24 For example, 'when I play the piano then I am so involved that the piano is no longer there, nor I am. We have become one. This situation is a "pure experience": the union of subject and object' (Umehara 1993: 24). The concept of 'pure experience' Umehara borrows from Nishida Kitarō (1870–1945), also known as a great unifier of Eastern and Western thought. He studied at Tokyo University and taught at Kyoto University. Based on his critical reading of Bergson, James, Kant, Leibnitz, neo-Kantians, Husserl, Aristotle, Hegel and Marx, he attempted to criticize the concept of consciousness, put forth theories of subjectivity and knowledge, and established a new philosophical logic of *basho* (place or Platonic *chora*) in order to question the relationship between knowing and action. Some of his followers formed the Kyoto school, and the New Kyoto school (see Chapter Eight). In *A Study of Good* (1910), Nishida sketched the basics of a Japanese school of thought based on ideas eclectically borrowed from philosophies and religions of various origins. His key notion of 'pure experience' (*junsui keiken*) attempted to redefine the notion of 'no mind' and *satori* in Buddhist philosophy. To Nishida, experience meant to follow reality without any preconceptions of it, that is, in a 'natural' way, without attaching any thought or applying any value distinctions (discrimination) to the experience in itself (*jijitsu sono mama*). Naming experience, therefore, is outside the realm of pure experience, which is immediate and direct (*chokusetsu keiken*). Similar concepts can be found in Chu Xi's doctrine of man's true nature being identical to external nature; Wang Yangming's mystic concept of the unity of thought and action; the Buddhist notion of *samadhi* (transformation of the mind into the object it contemplates in meditation, as in Umehara's piano example) and, in Heidegger's doctrine of *For Augen Sein* (cf. Nishida 1997: 34–52; O'Leary 1997; for a critique, see Dale 1995).

25 For an elaboration of the concept of *aidagara* see Hamaguchi Eshun's discussion in Chapter Six.

26 Fukui Kenichi in 1981 won the Nobel Prize for his chemistry research. He served as the director of the University of Industrial Fibres at Kyoto University and as the head of the Research Institute for Basic Science. Although Fukui is an engineer and Umehara a literary man, they feel they share a similar attitude toward science and nature. Umehara considers this due to the specific atmosphere at Kyoto University. In spite of his interest in the alpha-sciences, Fukui ended up studying physics and chemistry, regarding the young discipline of quantum mechanics (1926) as the basis for practical chemistry. As Fukui had decided to concentrate on the foreign theories of quantum mechanics, he read the Bible and Plato in Greek, Descartes and Pascal in French and Kant, Hegel, Nietzsche and Heidegger in German. Although he was taught by Nishida Kitarō and Tanabe Hajime, he felt he was becoming alienated from Japan, and decided to study Japanese culture, Buddhism and history (Umehara and Fukui 1996).

27 This also means, that the king could not win because he had the wrong *fūdo* to start with: if he had not killed the snake god he would have violated his *fūdo* by not acting like an urban king, while because he did kill the snake, the fate of his *fūdo* was realized and it worsened.

28 Eighth-century Japanese sources first mentioned the Ainu: they were settled in

182 *Notes*

Hokkaido, on Sachalin and on the Kuril Islands. Until 1869, Hokkaido, which until 1869 was known as Ezochi, 'Ainu-land' was colonized by Japanese settlers and formally annexed to become part of the Japanese empire. Since ancient times, the Ainu have been described as barbarians, fulfilling a function as the 'radicalized other', allowing the Japanese to contrast themselves with the backward natives who were kept at a distance through tribal law.

The incorporation of Hokkaido into the Japanese state was largely motivated by strategic concerns on the part of the Tokugawa government, which perceived the Russian expansion in the Far East as a threat. The Ainu became subjects of the Japanese empire and its administration so that tribal law was no longer recognized. In the 1870s, most Ainu were entered on family registers and given Japanese names. Many were forced to resettle to make room for Japanese colonizers. Government policies toward the Ainu were assimilationist and segregationist at the same time. Education was aimed at civilizing the Ainu, but given their 'backwardness' it was of inferior quality and short duration. Even the Hokkaido Former Natives Protection Act of 1899 turned out to be means of assimilation as the Ainu were to be transformed into good subjects through the eradication of their language, customs and values. On the other hand, segregationist policies designated the Ainu to outlying parts of villages and towns. Only in the 1970s did the Ainu start a revival movement to reassert their 'ethnic' identity and to define their relationship to the state (cf. Siddle 1996).

29 In 1975 a Hokkaido court first questioned the legitimacy of the term 'former aborigine' as the official expression for Ainu. It was challenged as being inconsistent with equality before the law of all Japanese citizens as enshrined in Article 14 of the Constitution. The collapse of the LDP's (Liberal Democratic Party) one-party rule in 1993 encouraged Ainu hopes for official recognition as a distinct minority, that is, for the creation of a category of native-born Japanese citizens who are not of Japanese blood. The UN's declaration of 1993 as the year of aboriginal peoples was an important stimulus. Rejecting the conventional defence of Japanese racial and ethnic homogeneity, PM Ryūtarō Hashimoto declared, 'It is a fact of history that the Ainu people are aboriginal to Japan' (*Japan Times*, 13 May 1997).

30 In 1980, the Japanese government said in a report to the United Nations that no minority races exist in Japan. 'Japan has no racial minorities' remarked former Prime Minister Nakasone Yasuhirō in 1986, claiming Japan to be a 'single-race state'. He gave expression to a common belief in Japan, concerning its ethnic and cultural homogeneity. Since then this belief has been receding. In 1987 Tokyo officially recognized the Ainu as a minority group and the government has enacted a new law designed to preserve Ainu culture and guarantee their human rights.

On 8 May 1997 the Diet passed the 'Law to Promote Ainu Culture and Disseminate Knowledge of Ainu Traditions', guaranteeing human rights of the Ainu and committing the state to helping them to preserve their distinct culture. There are 24,000 people who register themselves as Ainu, but Ainu rights groups say that the actual number is more likely to be 50,000, less than 1 per cent of Japan's 124 million population. The new Ainu law replaces the 1899 Hokkaido Former Aborigine Protection Law (*Japan Times*, 13 May 1997). It contains implicit recognition of an ethnic minority, but it fails to designate the Ainu explicitly as a legal Japanese aboriginal minority; this has been affirmed in a separate non-binding resolution. The new law is thought to bolster a growing Ainu cultural revival movement in terms of support for cultural festivals and establishing a literary award for works in the Ainu language.

31 Omoto defends the argument that the Ainu have the same Asian roots as do other Japanese:

Notes 183

Firstly, it is shown by the genetic distance and cluster analyses that three ethnic groups of Japan, namely, the Wajin (Japanese), the Ainu and the Ryukyuan, are clearly distinguished from each other. Among them, particularly the Wajin has the genes supposedly introduced from the continental Northeast Asia through Korea in high frequencies. Secondly, it is demonstrated that the Ainu belongs to the Mongoloid race, rather than to the Caucasoid. Their phenotype features are explained as generalized Proto-Mongoloid characters. Thirdly, the genetic link between the Ainu and the Ryukyuan is suggested genetically, and they both are considered to be descendants of Proto-Japanese populations. Fourthly, several cases of gene frequency cline are observed, suggesting that relatively large number of immigrants came through Korean peninsula to Northeast Kyushu and then spread eastward and southward since the Yayoi period.

(Omoto 1992: 137–45)

32 The Ainu are different from the Wajin in that they are not resistant to the cold, resembling the ancient Mongoloids, but have the Jōmon people as ancestors in common with the Wajin. They started to differ culturally from one another directly after the Jōmon era. During the Yayoi period more cold-resistant people came to Japan via Korea. They especially interbred with the population in the West, notably the Kinki region. There is clear evidence of regionality in Japan. The Wajin (Japanese) of the Yayoi era interbred with the immigrants, probably from a cold region such as Siberia (skeletons in Doigahama are similar to those from Siberia). They probably came in from the Korean peninsula through northern Kyushu and before long established the Japanese kingdom. So there are two types of Japanese: the Kinki (the country around Kyoto) type and the Ainu type. Nevertheless, the differences between the two types have started to disappear since Taishō and Showa, as a result of intermarriage (Umehara and Hanihara 1982: 157–8).

33 Dancers dance Ainu dance and wear Ainu clothing and perform bear hunts, and plays that have been based on the Ainu. At the start of March 1997, the first Ainu-language newspaper was unveiled (*Japan Times*, 11 June 1997). However, after a century of assimilation and intermarriage with Japanese, there are few Ainu who are master of their language. Actually, linguists and other scholars are the main subscribers to the quarterly publication (*Japan Times*, 13 May 1997).

5 Culturalist categorization

1 Allegedly, the persistence of the Jōmon view in Japanese culture is indicated by the survival of the concept of the mirror image. According to Umehara, the Ainu were thought to believe that the nether world is the mirror image of this world, and even now the Japanese dress the dead with the right side of the kimono over the left, and break rice-bowls at funerals (what is imperfect here, is perfect over there). The belief that everyone after death survives and becomes a *kami* also survived. Everyone becomes a *hotoke*, a spirit dwelling in a realm much like ours. At the New Year and Bon festivals, the soul returns to visit and joins the festivities. The custom of sending off the souls of living creatures that human beings are obliged to kill at funerals survives today in special 'memorial rites' for, for example, the *unagi kuyō* (service for eels) and the *fugu kuyō* (service for blowfish). Even sewing needles and worn-out dolls are sent off. The principle of rebirth is essential to the creation myths in the *Kojiki* (AD 712) and *Nihonshoki* (AD 720) (Japan's first books, containing mythological texts and records of imperial reigns used as a historical legitimization of the imperial regime (cf. John Brownlee 1991)). The heart of these myths is the retreat of the sun goddess Amaterasu

184 *Notes*

Omikami, the imperial progenetrix, into the celestial rock cave and her subsequent re-emergence. This episode relates to the ceremony known as the *Daijōsai*, in which the spirit of Amaterasu is 'reborn' in the person of the new monarch. The idea of rebirth is also manifest in the ritual rebuilding of Ise Shrine, which is dedicated to Amaterasu, once every 20 years.

Umehara argues that much of Shinto can be found back in the Jōdo Shinshū (Pure Land sect) as the typical Japanese religion. The Jōdo Shinshū in Japan has the most temples and followers, and Shinran remains the most popular religious leader. Thereby he insists that it is not just a Chinese import like early Jōdo, but an original Japanese creation. The Pure Land came increasingly to resemble the prototypical indigenous view of the nether world: the Japanese embraced those aspects that they found congenial, rejected the rest, and ultimately fashioned the import into something very much their own. Thus, Shinran founded a unique form of Jōdo in which the soul circulates forever between this world and the other, and it was probably Pure Land priests who initially incorporated into Buddhism the funeral ceremonies that originally belonged to the indigenous religion (Umehara Takeshi 1998: 79–82).

2 Note that, diverting from the usual 'We Japanese', Umehara here adopts a quasi-scientific mode using 'They' when referring to the Japanese.

3 Umehara elaborates on one of the panels of the seventh century Tamamushi Shrine in Hōryūji temple.

4 Hanaoka Seishū (1760–1835) experimented with narcotics on himself, his wife who became blind as a result and on his mother (cf. Ariyoshi Sawako 1978).

5 Ye points out that Needham expressed the different modes of thought in East and West as 'China harmonizes the two aspects of rational cognition and romantic spirit', and 'the European spirit is schizophrenic' (Needham quoted in Ye Qiaojian 1995: 75).

6 Holography (*quanxilun*) spread in China first in the field of biology. In 1973, Zhang Yiqing presented the holographic theory of the distribution of acupuncture points over the human body. In 1981, another theory on the holographic structure of plants and animals was developed. In 1984, Wang Cunzhen and Yan Chunyou created the theory of universal holography, and in 1991, the 'cultural holographic theory' by Yan Chunyou and Yan Chunbao was published (Yu Weizhao and Zhang Aibing 1992: 160–2). Wang Cunzhen and Yan Chunyou's 'The Holographic Unity of the Universe' (1988) engendered a heated discussion in academic circles on whether the universe really equals all information or not (cf Shi Qiliang 1991: 73–84). Theories of holography often refer to the *Zhou Yi*, and emphasize that the logic of thought in the *Zhou Yi* is very different from Western thought: it is ambiguous, dynamic and synthetic. Zhang Qicheng, for example, argues that *Zhou Yi* numerology constitutes the origin and is representative of the Chinese (*Zhonghua*) mode of thought, determining the behaviour forms particular to *Zhonghua Minzu*. The two characters '*zhou*' and '*yi*' can be interpreted as 'cycle' (*zhouhuan*) and 'change' (*bianhua*). Thus, it can be regarded as a treatise on the cyclical laws of change of all things in the universe. The *Zhou Yi* is also a whole and its sixty-four hectogrammes form the layers of a holographic system. Yin and yang show that man and nature are harmonious opposites (Zhang Qicheng 1996: 65–73).

7 Hu tests his Korean students on their views of the West. One of his students told me he was taken on as his view of the West included the concepts of rationalist, individualist, antagonistic (interview with his student, October 1997).

8 The concept of *Zhonghua Minzu* is translated as both Chinese race and Chinese nation. In Chinese there is no one word in referring to 'nation', as distinct from 'state' (*guo*). Alternatives include 'people' (*renmin*) and 'race' (*minzu*), and its derivative 'Han race' (*Hanzu*) and 'Chinese race' (*Zhonghua Minzu*).

Notes 185

9 The May Fourth refers to a student movement in opposition to the terms of the Treaty of Versailles held on that date in 1919. At the same time the concept is used to include other opposition movements, such as those against outmoded Confucian practices and ideas, those in favour of alternative political models such as those associated with 'democracy and science,' and the movement for the adoption of the use of vernacular Chinese in literature.

10 *Neidanxue*, according to Hu, in fact, is the systems engineering of an intensive kind of training of the ordinary conscious (*chang yishi*), the purification of the subconscious (*qian yishi*) and an opening up of the original unconscious (*yuan yishi*) in order to find the true self. *Neidanxue* has rich contents in the fields of modern philosophy, cerebralogy and psycho-biology. Only research by scientists into the field has been lacking; people have not yet clearly acknowledged its value to the truth (Hu Fuchen 1993: 22).

11 Chapter 42 of *Lao Zi* (Gu Zhengkun 1995: 188–9):
The Tao begets the One; (*dao sheng yi*)
The One consists of the Two in opposition (yin and yang); (*yi sheng er*)
The Two begets the Three; (*er sheng san*)
The Three begets all things of the world; (*san sheng wanwu*).

12 *Qi* here is the basic initial substance connecting everything organically, roughly the same as 'field' (*chang*) in modern physics: the united essence of matter, energy and information. It is the basic substance constructing all things under heaven, and the vehicle for the mutual effect of all things under heaven (Hu Fuchen 1995: 76).

13 The Great Void (*tai yi zhengqi*) is not really empty but, as does a vacuum, contains particles, although they are relatively few.

14 Qian Xuesen is regarded as one of China's most famous scientific and ideological leaders, celebrated as the introducer of cybernetic theory into China, and in the 1990s still quoted as a great senior authority of scientific wisdom and political correctness.

15 Tsuda Yukio teaches at Nagoya University, and is responsible for the Department of English. He specializes in international communications. In the capacity of visiting lecturer at Nichibunken, he organized a research group entitled 'The Japanese and the English Language' (*Nihonjin to eigo*).

16 Film production: *Fengkuang de yingyu* (Crazy English) producer Chen Ziqiu; director: Zhang Yuan, Beijing: in association with Ocean Film Co., Ltd, Beijing Film and Video Library.

17 Cf. Tsuda 1996 (*Asahi Shinbun*, 27 December 1996).

18 Ibid.

19 For an explanation of Ōbei, see Chapter Four, note 11.

20 The so-called Sapir–Whorf hypothesis by Edward Sapir and Benjamin Lee Whorf says that a speaker's native language sets up a series of categories which act as a kind of grid through which he perceives the world, and which constrains the way in which he categorizes and conceptualizes different phenomena (Trudgill 1980: 24–5). Therefore, a language can affect, or determine, the way in which the speakers of a certain language society perceive the world.

21 Nakanishi Terumasa (Editorial, *Kyoto Shimbun*, 25 April 1997), a Kyoto University professor in international relations, argues against the idea of Edo Japan having being closed off, and criticizes Engelbert Kemper, who in his diary contributed to this image. In fact, Nakanishi argues, Japan had ordinary diplomatic international relations with Korea. It also communicated with the Ryukyu, China and Southeast Asia. Despite the ban on naval trade, Japan had a large commercial regional network over a wide area. The Meiji political strategy of 'Opening Up', the slogans 'enrich the nation and strengthen the military' (*fukkoku kyōhei*), and 'retreat from Asia, enter Europe' (*datsuya nyu-ou*) were meant to

186 Notes

bring into disrepute conservative policies by depicting the Edo period as 'closed'. Nakanishi argues that blaming the Tokugawa for closing up was a strategy for those who wanted to attack the Edo government during the Bakumatsu, thereby twisting history.

22 Kishida Shū (1996) advises against compulsory English in schools. This advice is based on his theory of the schizophrenic personality of the Japanese: the inner self dislikes English culture associated with it, while the outer self presents itself as if it does like it. During the war and of late, the inner self has become stronger: English and internationalization are approached more negatively. The English boom, according to Kishida, is a symptom of the outer self. The Japanese struggle with learning English, because their inner selves rebel against being compelled to learn it. Apart from leading to an inferiority complex, compulsory English is not necessary, as people have a natural ability to learn language when they need to. Kishida explains that the Japanese split personality always expresses one of its extremes: Japanese superiority or the 'outside', while the inferiority complex is suppressed (in the Freudian sense). The flood of Katakana English (Katakana is a script designed for writing down loan words) is another example. According to Kishida, it has the effect of a girl wearing a mini-skirt and lipstick: it causes the boys to flee. It is neither English nor Japanese, and just severs the split personality even further. Kishida draws a parallel between learning English and learning Chinese Kanji (written characters). Kanji and Chinese culture were also adapted and indigenized. But direct communication with the Chinese was eschewed. At the time, China formed the 'outer self' which became partly internalized (Kishida Shū, *Eikaiwa to iu byōki* (The English Conversation Disease), *Daikōkai*, 1991 no. 11).

23 Pearl Harbour, the Jiaoyu (Senkaku) Islands, the emperor system, the national anthem (*Kimigayo*) and the Yasukuni Shrine are some of such symbols. Ultra-nationalists believe that Pearl Harbour was an honourable reaction to US policies on Asia; that Chinese estimates that as many as 300,000 Chinese were slaughtered in the city of Nanjing are grossly exaggerated; and that Japanese soldiers never forced foreign women into sexual slavery. They assert Japanese sovereignty over the Senkaku Islands. They believe that a society of equals united under a divine emperor breeds fairness and harmonious relations among people, that schoolchildren should sing a national anthem that honours the emperor and that the nation should be proud of a flag that flew over its troops in World War II. They are motivated by their belief that they must take up arms to fight to restore Japan's dignity. They believe the country's dignity has been eroded further by Japan's apologies for its part in the war, and by scandals caused by dishonest politicians and businessmen. The hard-liner nationalists are inspired by the Emperor system that ruled Japan from the Meiji Era to the end of World War II. That is why the Yasukuni Shrine, a symbol of wartime nationalism, is so important to them. In April 1997, 150 MPs went to pray for the war dead at the controversial Yasukuni Shrine, where Japan's notorious Class A war criminals are also enshrined.

24 See, for example, Murakami Yasusuke's history of Japan in terms of the '*ie*' (family, household) (Murakami 1984: 281–363).

6 Global categorization

1 PHP is an abbreviation of Peace and Happiness through Prosperity. PHP is an institute established by Matsushita Konosuke and allied with the transnational Matsushita Co. Its activities vary from organizing workshops and symposia, financing projects and publishing periodicals and books. The institute's mission is to create a peaceful international society by pooling the insights of many

Notes 187

scientists and harmonizing people's will. In such society, people can grow spiritually and materially (cited in a PHP pamphlet: the late Matsushita Konosuke 1995).

2 Ohmae Kenichi is managing director of McKinsey & Company, an international firm, in Japan. Ohmae is a leading thinker on business and frequently writes for the Wall Street Journal and the Harvard Business Review. He is the author of *The Mind of the Strategist, Triad Power: The Coming Shape of Global Competition* and *Beyond National Borders: Reflections on Japan and the World* and *The Borderless World*.

3 Ohmae Kenichi *The Borderless World* (1990), London: Harper Collins Publishers (Ohmae 1990: 63). Ohmae provides the example of Matsushita's donation of an entire broadcasting station to a local government abroad so as to improve the quality of receiving colour television. It was good business (Ohmae 1990: 90). In fact, this practice is quite common in strategies of goodwill creation. Ohmae does not mention Matsushita's nickname: *Mane shita* ('copied').

4 Stages 1 to 4 are: (1) arm's length export activity of essentially domestic companies, which move into new markets overseas by linking up with local dealers and distributors; (2) the company takes over these activities on its own; (3) the domestic-based company begins to carry out its own manufacturing, marketing and sales in key foreign markets; (4) the company moves to a full *insider* position in these markets, supported by a complete business system including R&D and engineering (Ohmae 1990: 91).

5 For an explanation of Ōbei, see Chapter Four, note 11.

6 Hamaguchi tells us the following about the pitfalls of naïve internationalization: Formerly, internationalization meant subordinating regions to common international juridical rules. Lately in Japan, however, internationalization has come to mean abandoning the constraints of the system in order to open up to the outside and cast off Japan's 'island mentality', suppressing the will of the nation in order to co-operate with other countries. This new meaning should rather be called 'globalization' and we should consider whether it is right to adopt so-called international Ōbei standards in order to comply with Ōbei's political and economic requirements. 'Internationalization' requires Japan to accept foreigners unconditionally, even though Japan never has been a multinational country or tied up in eternal international struggles.

Hamaguchi does not think that one-sided Ōbei demands or denunciations are a suitable solution to the problem. Around the issue of the universality of international standards many other issues revolve: the present mutual respect or cultural relativism on the international scene is in danger of being replaced by the come-back of Ōbei-centrism. Here, Hamaguchi claims to quote the critic of theories of Japaneseness (*nihonjin-ron*), Aoki Tamotsu, in stating that some hysterical Ōbei-ans even consider cultural relativism to be reverse discrimination directed against Ōbei, as an attempt at restoration (*fukenshugi*) (of their rights); Japan-bashing as a result of trade friction even reaches the cultural sphere and everyday life. It is said that Japan lacks a spirit of 'fair play'. This notion is based on ideological universalism. But according to the Japanese, the trade imbalance is merely a necessary outcome of their export of superior products. As for the idea of 'fairness', it is a matter of cultural disagreement (Hamaguchi 1988: 10–12).

7 Alfred Kuhn's concepts of 'acting system' Hamaguchi equates with civilization and his concept of 'patterned system' as culture, meaning that culture constitutes the design and the model (values, code) that check the structure of the system of living (Hamaguchi 1996b: 52). He regards the unique conceptual life-system of societies, ethos, nationality (ethnicity) and the *emic* that preserve the characteristics inherent to a society as a patterned system that has the function of

188 Notes

software (ibid.: 53). The hardware consists of the actual elements of the life-system and the structure and operation of organizations and communication media, in other words, artefacts.

8 Hamaguchi is the representative of the Research Project Team for Japanese Systems of the Masuda Foundation for International Communication and Education. Its research reports are published by Sekotac (Sekotac 1992: 2–4).

9 Umesao Tadao regards civilization as a system, system of living or equipment, while culture refers to the value system formed by the social mind. Itō Shuntarō regards the relation between civilization and culture as that between an outer shell and a kernel. The outer shell consists of a system, organization and equipment, while the kernel constitutes ethos, conceptual forms and a value system, and is the producer of civilization. Kumon Shumpei regards civilization in biological terms as a phenotype which is designed by what Dawkins calls *memes*, or psycho-ethical tendencies, functioning as a cultural mould for civilization.

10 A change in a feature that characterizes a system. Phase here refers to the fusion and integration of systems such as culture (a system of values; design) and civilization (social system; equipment) as co-ordinates of modes of life systems.

11 Hamaguchi refers to Koestler's concept of holon. According to Hamaguchi, Koestler regards man and man-made systems as open hierarchical systems. He calls the sub-systems 'holons': a real entity that 'looking inward' sees itself as a self-contained unique whole, looking outward, as a dependent part. The self-assertive tendency of holons is a dynamic expression of their wholeness and the integrative tendency is a dynamic expression of their partness. A holon is a system that (1) subordinates its components as an autonomous whole, (2) subordinates as a part to the control from higher levels, and (3) co-ordinates with its local environment. Koestler calls such hierarchy a holarchy (Hamaguchi 1985). It is important to note, however, that Koestler himself does not speak of society in terms of hierarchical *systems*. He uses the concept of holon to understand organizations from complementary points of view.

12 Hamaguchi's individual actor can be compared with an atom and his contextual to a molecule, as part of a larger system. The social relationships between these atoms can be described as composed of a segment of a line – direct connections between independent points, and the social contexts (*aidagara*) as relationships are defined in terms of the relations between lines, each containing local points (Hamaguchi 1985: 307). For individuals, it is a necessary condition for interaction to be simultaneous and equal. An exchange of equal value is obviously the *sine qua non* of social relations (instrumental transaction). Alfred Kuhn calls such transactions 'value-based interactions' (Hamaguchi 1985: 309). In this positive-sum-gain, each party endeavours to maximize its own benefits and is indifferent to its partner's position: the selfish and indifferent attitude is dominant in the transaction model (Hamaguchi 1985: 310).

13 When two people have a preference for each other's product, first, they proceed from profit maximization and cost-minimization and, second, are not interested in their partner's position, although they do co-operate. Because such strategic negotiation entails a risk, they use contracts. Such relations are rational and instrumental, based on individual autonomy, which, in turn, is based on Ōbei value. Loss results in frustration and may lead to aggression (frustration–aggression hypothesis) (Hamaguchi 1996a: 103–5).

14 In the case of *aidagara*, the exchange of mutual favours can be regarded as *on*. When *on* is not repaid, *giri* begins to work (a moral enforcement on reciprocating a service). Because the exchange concerns contextuals, the strategic manipulation of relations is categorically rejected. Also, relationships that are not considered useful at a given time are not discarded, since one must always, at least potentially, have someone with whom co-operation is possible (Hamaguchi 1985: 311). The

Notes 189

latter argument, however, seems to clash with the categorical rejection of the strategic manipulation of relations.

15 A description of the stage that a periodic motion of variables has reached, usually by comparison with another such motion of the same frequency.

16 To the Japanese, 'person' (*ningen*) cannot, according to Hamaguchi, be conceived of except in relation to 'other persons' (Hamaguchi 1991: 62–3). In English, one needs two words to describe this meaning: 'interpersonal relations' (Hamaguchi 1991: 64). In Japanese, *ningen kankei* (person relation) is superfluous, whereas in the West, the words 'individual' and 'people' are strictly separated. In China (*ren*) and Japan, according to Hamaguchi, this is not the case (Hamaguchi 1991: 65). Because the word *ningen* includes the relationship between people, it is clear that the Japanese (and Eastern people, in general) knew about 'human relations' for a long time, before they imported the term. The Chinese, for example, have the words *haoren* (sociable person) and *huairen* (unsociable person) which express the relationship between people (Hamaguchi 1996a: 94–5). In the West, the concept of 'human relations' is based on cold logic, while in the East *ningen* is based on need, feeling and attitude.

Hamaguchi does not mention that *haoren* (sociable person) is just one meaning (the others are 'good person' and 'healthy person'). The sociable *haoren* in the *Han-Ying Cidian* (1986: 270) is defined as 'a person who tries to get along with everyone (often at the expense of principle)'.

17 In self-organizing systems changes in the structure of the system are produced by the system itself.

18 Following Husserl, Luhmann defines *Sinn* (meaning) as the horizon of possibilities that is present virtually in every one of its actualization. As the difference between the possible and the actual, meaning itself is a category 'without difference', which designates the medium through which social systems process world complexity (Knodt 1995: xxiii).

19 Suzuki Ryōji introduced the term autonomously distributed hierarchical system (*kaisōgata jiritsu bunsan shisutemu*), which refers to a system that makes decisions in a distributed (non-centralized) way (Sekotac/Masuda Foundation 1992: 19–20).

20 Sakamoto Kenzo, a member of the Sekotac Team, introduced the term internal goal-setting of Japanese systems (*naizai mokuhyōshugi*). In contrast to Western systems, in which transcendental goals are set externally (i.e. by mediation of God), the Japanese systems set their goals internally: the system has its own maintenance as its goal. In this sense, it might be considered a biological system as such. Japanese goals are 'gradually fermented (matured) within themselves' (Sekotac 1992: 93).

21 The problem of double contingency occurs in a state of potential paralysis that results from a situation in which two black boxes make their own behaviour contingent upon the behaviour of the other. The 'pure circle of self-referential determination, lacking any further elaboration, leaves action indeterminate, makes it indeterminable' (Luhmann 1995: 103). Parsons tried to solve the problem by referring to a prior social consensus concerning cultural norms and rules of conduct.

22 Hamaguchi does not doubt that the historical fate of the era in which the 'hard' principle of the supremacy of the individuum, that is, individual behaviour based on rational choice and self-consistency, is over. Individualism may have stimulated modernization and democracy, but when modernization was established, the principle of the individuum became a disturbing element in the system. If society is not seen as a dynamic, complex system based on a rich flow of information, self-organization will not be achieved, but will become rigid and will probably destroy itself. Japanese work organizations, in contrast, are based on the formative

190 *Notes*

principle of the 'relatum', in which the relationship between self and others forms its existential basis. A social system therefore should be based on the 'soft' relatum. A condition for such a society is 'mutual trust' rather than 'contract'. Since Japan is a high-trust society, Hamaguchi believes that the 'relatum' and the concept of '*aidagara*' that underpins the trust in the system makes Japan a suitable model for globalization (Hamaguchi 1996a: iv–v).

23 'Trust and distrust appear only in the domain of double contingency; they should not be confused with a general optimism or pessimism about life. Trust must be given contingently, that is, freely. It cannot be demanded or normatively prescribed. Trust has its social functional value as trust only if it sees the possibility of distrust – and rejects it: it rests on negating its opposite. One begins with small risks and builds on confirmations, trust has the *circular*, self-presupposing and confirming character that belongs to all structures emerging from double contingency.' It makes the formation of systems possible and in return acquires strength from them for increase, riskier reproduction (Luhmann 1995: 127–8).

24 In this spirit, Eva Knodt remarks that 'the distinction between action (purposive behaviour of human subjects) and events (random behaviour of objects) becomes relevant only at the level where the autopoiesis of communication requires self-observation, and the system faces the problem that communication – which in itself consists of nothing but a series of "subjectless" selections – cannot be observed as such' (Knodt 1995: xxx).

25 Interestingly, the book does not tell us which members of the Project Team wrote which chapters; only the introduction has the name of the representative of the Project Team, Hamaguchi Eshun, under it. Does this mean that the 'writing subject' may be discarded entirely?

26 According to Luhmann, in provoking 'undecidable decisions', the problem of double contingency fulfils a catalytic function in the emergence of a constantly changing social order whose instability is the only source of its own stability (Knodt 1995: xxviii–ix).

27 Yoshida Kazuo 1997: recording symposium by Hamaguchi Eshun's research group: 24–25 January, 1997 'The holonic structure of Japanese social systems' (*Horon kōzō no nihongata shakai shisutemu*) (Yoshida 1998).

28 At present Von Neumann's serial processing forms the main current in computer architecture, but in the next era parallel processing modelled on the brain will be the centre of attention.

29 A hologram receives and reflects light in different directions which together form one image.

7 Grouping

1 For example, 'The Wind and Thunder Combat Team' of the August First Middle School was accused of propagating the 'bloodline theory', which asserts the inheritability of a revolutionary mentality, claiming that the only guarantee against revisionism is revolutionary dedication. When Peking High School wanted to introduce self-reform in order to counter the propagation of this theory, the Propaganda Department protested: 'Selling their own rotten, private, disgraceful goods under the signboard of "criticizing the reactionary bloodline theory" absolutely cannot work' (Commentator of the Propaganda Department in Greenblatt 1969: 48).

2 For example, in the late 1980s, the democratic reformer Liu Binyan was a sincere socialist as well, and the liberal reformer Wu Jiaxiang believed that establishing an authoritarian regime was imperative (Goldman 1994: 276).

3 In Chinese academic circles of the mid-1980s, the concepts of humanism, alienation and democracy were heavily laden with symbolical meaning. And it is

Notes 191

this symbolic logic which makes discussions around these topics so predictable: as humanism and democracy are believed to originate in the capitalist West, even though the concepts sound positive and have important historical connotations, they could be of no use to Chinese authorities convinced of China's socialist superiority unless they were redefined as socialist or Chinese. For example, 'democracy' replaced 'proletarian' in the 'people's proletarian dictatorship, so that it became 'people's democratic dictatorship'; and democracy became the 'people's democracy', unconvincingly adding 'people' to something that is already defined as 'people's rule' (democracy = *minzhu*). Similarly, 'humanism' could not be tolerated as it was identified with the bourgeois phase of history and individual rights, but 'humanitarianism', or 'socialist humanism' did not carry the symbolically problematic load of bourgeois origin. Similarly, alienation could only exist under capitalism. Interestingly, in the argument of propaganda chief Hu Qiaomu and former head of CASS, alienation spilled over from the materialistic determinism into the cultural realm of contagion: people, according to Hu, had to be explained by means of the society they live in. They have duties and contributions to make to society. Although materialist determinism still formed the ultimate explanation of alienation, the phenomenon of alienation was to be considered in the light of society. This also explained why it was possible for spiritual pollution, which is an expression of alienation, to contaminate a pure society such as that of socialist China.

4 A word used to express the meaning of country in both Chinese (*guojia*) and Japanese (*kokka*) includes the character for family. Of course such linguistic expression is no evidence of nationalism. I only point out that the association between 'country' and 'family' is not an unfamiliar one.

5 It should be noted, that in both China, but particularly in Japan, We is used in daily conversation as meaning 'We from . . . company' or an other acknowledged group one identifies with. This kind of We (*wareware*) can be mobilized as a powerful authority in discussions to exert pressure on to the Other.

6 Especially the Other of the capitalist West has been the subject of debate (Fabian 1983), and denotes an unequal relationship of power between the Self and the Other.

7 For example, Chinese newspapers were silent about the Nobel Prize for Literature won by the since 1989 Chinese dissident and, now, French national Gao Xingjian on 12 February 2000.

8 The Falungong is a religious movement under the leadership of Li Hongzhi. It wants to exercise its rights to conduct public meetings and spread Li Hongzhi's insights based on a mixture of meditational techniques, science, Taoism and Buddhism. Li's wisdom has been written down in his *Zhuan Falun*, which can be viewed or downloaded from *www.falundafa.org*. The followers of Li Hongzhi, and Li himself, believe in the (scientifically proved) existence of a multifold of dimensions that determine our lives completely. For example, if you have done something wicked, and you have a nasty fall, then this is no coincidence, but a consequence of your former deed (Li Hongzhi 1999: 17).

9 For example, the socialistically hued Confucian scholar, Fang Keli, in a speech in Japan's Nichibunken emphasized the Asian concepts the two nations have in common *vis-à-vis* the West, and only touched upon past disagreements between the two countries. At home he emphasizes the ways in which Confucianism can be a support for the formal policy of socialism with Chinese characteristics, making a point of displaying his socialist loyalties (Fang Keli 1994, 1996).

10 'This means: take the ideas of the masses (scattered and unsystematic ideas) and concentrate them (through study turn them into concentrated and systematic ideas), then go to the masses and propagate and explain these ideas until the masses embrace them as their own, hold fast to them and translate them into

192 Notes

action, and test the correctness of these ideas in such action. Then once again concentrate ideas from the masses and once again go to the masses so that the ideas are preserved and carried through. And so on, over and over again in an endless spiral, with the ideas becoming more correct, more vital and richer each time. Such is the Marxist theory of knowledge' (Mao Tze-tung (Mao Zedong) 1967: 119).

11 The research interests of Nichibunken's Kasaya Kazuhiko, a specialist in Japanese history and palaeography, lie in Samurai society in Edo Japan.

12 Yamamoto Tsunetomo (1716) wrote the *Hagakure*. The popularization of the term *bushidō* (Way of the warrior), owes much to the Christian scholar and moral educator Nitobe Inazō (1862–1900). Although he noted that *bushidō* was an unformulated teaching, he listed seven virtues of *bushidō*, which have been quoted by authors ever since: justice, courage, benevolence, politeness, veracity, honour and loyalty. After 1868 these virtues, according to Nitobe, had been inherited and adopted by the Japanese populace as a whole. He argued that *bushidō* had become 'Japan's animating spirit' even before it was formulated into a code – that it was the moral force motivating Japan's behaviour. His work became influential internationally, and was popularized during a period of rising nationalism. *Bushidō* was part of a rediscovery of the past by Japanese scholars and popular writers, who had for some time rejected tradition in favour of Western ideas and institutions. The nationalist philosopher Inoue Tetsujirō compiled a collection of works on *bushidō* (*bushidō sōsho*) in order to develop Japan's national defence by inculcating a *bushidō* spirit. Japanese of all persuasions came to see *bushidō* as embodying traditional Japanese values. Other scholars took Nitobe a step further: Nakariya Kaiten wrote of *bushidō* as the religion of Japan, while Takagi Takeshi compared it with European chivalry. Nitobe's fellow Christian, the famous journalist Uchimura Kanzō, went so far as to call *bushidō* Japan's 'finest product' and to suggest grafting Christianity on to *bushidō*. In the 1930s, young military officers read Nitobe and studied the *Hagakure* to inculcate bravery and to imbue themselves with a sense of loyalty to the emperor, who embodied the nation. Save for the glorification of the *Hagakure* text in post-war Japan by such self-professed nationalists as Mishima Yukio, the way of the warrior has been largely discredited (cf. Huffman 1998).

13 This *bushidō* was a narrow stream of thought that sought to recapture and idealize the sacrificial form of loyal service to a lord, a way of life that threatened to disappear under the changed social conditions in which the samurai actually functioned. Freedom in *bushidō* lies in the transcendence of life and death, or the point at which one can tread a correct path of conviction without worrying about the opinions of the lord or the people around.

14 Kasaya in *Asahi Shimbun*, 1 September 1996; Kasaya 1993a, 1993b.

15 Dumont states there is only one law in the social sciences, which is 'Parsons Law': 'each social subsystem is governed in the first place by the system to which it belongs' (Dumont 1980: 245).

16 Nakane Chie asserts that the emotional element in vertical relations in society goes beyond that of horizontal relations because it is not an equivalent exchange. Protection is repaid with dependence and affection with loyalty, and it facilitates the control of actions of individuals (Nakane 1973: 67). It also binds the leadership, which might sometimes appear despotic, but whose authority is checked and controlled at a great many points. The sympathy of leader for subordinates is a kind of 'paternalism' (*onjōshugi*). Leaders do not force their ideas on their subordinates, instead, the latter spontaneously lay their ideas before him and have them adopted (Nakane 1973: 68).

17 Prime Minister Miki Takeo, who came to power in December 1974, gathered around himself some liberal intellectuals led by Murakami Yasusuke of Tokyo

Notes   193

University. This group generated a new ideological definition of Japan as a 'middle-mass society' that was egalitarian and free of conflict. The role of the government was to ensure full employment and economic security to meet the requirements of desirable life cycles (*shōgai sekkei*, or life-cycle planning). A concerned government and self-reliant individuals together would ensure a higher degree of social welfare and equity (*kōsei*). However, this ideological wishful thinking was soon clouded by controversy over the 'middle mass' hypothesis (Taira Koji 1993: 181–2). Murakami Yasusuke argues that Japan is not a class society owing to the homogeneity in Japanese society: in companies there is no status barrier between white- and blue-collar workers, unions are company based, and an administrative élite that plays a crucial political role is absent. There is only a new middle mass, which is either for or against the system (industrial society); they either have universalistic values or indigenous ones, but they are apolitical and tend to vote for the stronger party (Murakami Yasusuke 1982).

18 Fabian describes how two approaches deny coevalness: the cultural relativist approach circumvents the question of coevalness; the taxonomic approach pre-empts that question (Fabian 1983: 38).

19 Evolutionary time naturalized time and separated it from events meaningful to mankind unlike the Christian unilinear concept, which indicated a chronology of events crucial to mankind. The new concept of time linked geology, biology and mankind together into one (tabular) frame. The operation of evolutionary laws in the history of mankind was shown by rehistoricizing Darwin's new concept of time and by spatializing it.

20 Umehara Takeshi, founding director of Nichibunken, advocates the revival of the ancient Jōmon spirit of the forest zealously. To this end, Umehara advocates research into the change of the environment, not just by means of the reliable data of science, but also by means of social science research, as social science is linked with human fate. Moreover, he wants social science to take part in saving the world from science. Umehara finds it useful to consider Japanese culture in terms of the interplay between the Ainu hunting and gathering culture of the Jōmon era (*c.* 10,000–300 BC) and the wet-rice culture of Yayoi era (*c.* 300BC–Ca. AD 300). Hitherto mainstream nationalists asserted Japanese culture is unitary and based above all on agriculture. Umehara, however, thinks that the unchanging elements of Japanese culture – religion and mores – still bear the imprint of Jōmon times, whereas those elements most subject to change – technology and political organization – are largely Yayoi in character (for more on Umehara's views, see Umehara Takeshi 1993: 10–16).

8   Framing the nation in the short history of the International Research Centre for Japanese Studies (Nichibunken, 1987–)

1 Other concepts denoting the special relations between Japanese people are *aidagara* (Watsuji Tetsurō 1996) Japanese networks (Kumon Shumpei 1982); vertical society (Nakane Chie 1973); collective unconscious (Kawai Hayao 1997), *haragei* (art of silence, literally 'stomach art') (Matsumoto Michihirō 1989), Japanese systems (Sekotac/Matsuda Foundation 1992).

2 Additionally, in the *nihonbunka-ron* the concept of Japanese nation (*nihon minzoku*) is often used to refer both to the idea of Japanese nation-state (*nihon kokka*) and Japanese national identity.

3 Since April 1992, Nichibunken also houses the Department of Japanese Studies, which is one of the three departments of the School of Cultural Studies (the others are the Department of Regional Studies and the Department of Comparative Studies located at the National Museum of Ethnology – Senri Expo Park, Osaka). The purpose of the department is stated as 'to promote integrated studies in

194 *Notes*

doctoral education on the culture, civilisation, society and environment of Japan, from an international and interdisciplinary perspective'. It aims to incorporate research from the humanities, social sciences and natural sciences. The School of Cultural Studies belongs to the Graduate University for Advanced Studies. Both Ida Tsuneo (1995/6) and Hamaguchi Eshun (1996/7) served as head of Japanese Studies, some of whose work is discussed below.

4 According to current quark theory, mesons are unstable elementary particles with a short life span, and consist of quark and anti-quark pairs. Japan's famous Nobel Prize winner, Yukawa Hideki, explained the stability of the nucleus (1935) by suggesting that the exchange forces that hold protons, neutrons and electrons in the nucleus involve short-lived particles, called mesons. They jump from proton to neutron, and back again. Despite what is suggested by the following, there is no full agreement among scientists yet about the exchange forces associated with the cohesion of nucleons within nuclei.

Yukawa's childhood in Kyoto is often referred to as of major influence on his intellectual development. Itō Shuntarō, another ex-professor of Nichibunken and friend of Umehara, puts it as follows:

Let's see why meson-theory (*chūgenshiron*) was produced by Yukawa and not by a European scientist. Heisenberg also tackled nuclear force, but he soon withdrew. Yukawa, however, was determined and found the following: by means of the exchange of mesons between particles in the atomic nucleus, neutrons become protons and protons become neutrons, so that nuclear force emerges. In European thought the idea of a fundamentally changing reality, e.g. that of elementary particles, presents a problem. That is why Heisenberg never understood it. To Yukawa, who had mastered the Eastern idea of transience (associated with the transmigration of souls, or *samsara* (*rinen*)), change wasn't strange at all.

Heisenberg, too, had created a local quantum theory based on electric force. But it is based merely on the exchange of photons by electrons and protons: nothing actually changes. Nuclear force was quite different. Even though Yukawa owes a lot to Heisenberg, what could not be overcome by European tradition could be surpassed by Eastern tradition. In this way, Yukawa's new meson-theory had not just solved nuclear power but had exploited a new genre of elementary particle theory. To create a new genre is something great.

(Itō Shuntarō 1996)

5 Alfred Rosenberg (1893–1946) was a German politician and the main ideologue of German national socialism. In *Der Mythus des 20 Jahrhunderts* (1930) he tried to provide a scientific justification for anti-Semitism.

6 Kawai continues triumphantly: 'I am not hinting at anything, but it was a real success. Therefore the number of people who wish to come to Nichibunken has increased tremendously.'

7 Umehara finds it useful to consider Japanese culture in terms of the interplay between the Ainu hunting and gathering culture of the Jōmon era (*c.* 10,000–*c.* 300 BC) and the wet-rice culture of Yayoi era (*c.*300 BC–*c.* AD 300). Hitherto mainstream nationalists asserted Japanese culture is unitary and based above all on agriculture. Umehara, however, thinks that the unchanging elements of Japanese culture – religion and mores – still bear the imprint of Jōmon times, whereas those elements most subject to change – technology and political organization – are largely Yayoi in character.

8 Kawai Hayao (1928–) was professor of psychology at Kyoto University. He retired as professor at Nichibunken on 31 March 1994. Kawai is the former director of Nichibunken (1995–2001). His specialization is clinical psychology.

Notes   195

He was a student at the Jung Institute in Switzerland. He is a Jungian analyst. Kawai is especially known for his book *Bosei shakai Nippon no byōri* (The Pathology of Japan as a Maternal Society) (1976). He is also a popular 'infotainment' personality in Japanese television, radio and the press. He also serves as head of the Japan Liars Club.

9 Kawai's Jungian influence is very clear in the notion of unconscious, which is quite different from that of Freud. The unconscious mind does not only contain the results of repression (the Freudian concept of subconscious) but also aspects of mental life which have been neglected in the course of development. More importantly, the personal unconscious in the Freudian sense is only a fraction of the total collective or racial unconscious, which lies below the personal unconscious. It contains the collective beliefs and myths of the race to which the individuals belong. An even deeper layer of unconscious is common to all humanity and primates (Brown 1972: 45).

10 In his *The Japanese Psyche: Major Motifs in the Fairy Tales of Japan*, Kawai as he decodes Japanese legends describes the basic motivation in the Japanese psyche as 'the beauty of rancour' (*urami*), which is fundamentally feminine. *Urami* draws on *aware* (softly disappearing sorrow), 'which a Japanese (man?) would feel for the female figure who disappears in silence' (Kawai 1988: 22). At the psychological level, Japanese daughters live in incest with their fathers, and continue to do so if the female's consciousness does not enter a condition of her acceptance of a man other than the father. The majority of Japanese nowadays probably still live in this state (Kawai 1988: 56).

> Such a wonderful feminine image can be found only in Japanese fairy tales, so it must epitomise the consciousness of Japanese, regardless of sex. Realising that fairy tales always compensate for a culture's formal attitude and that they thus predict the future, this image might be seen as the future orientation of the Japanese mind. If we notice further that the Western modern ego is moribund, this heroine could be presented as a meaningful symbol not only for Japanese, but also for all the people in the world.
>
> (Kawai 1988: 181)

11 In Freud's view, the unconscious is largely equated with the suppression from the conscious, as a result of conflicts between *libido* and *Überich*, and which causes disturbed behaviour in our daily intentions ('*Fehlleistungen*', 'Freudian slip') (Barz 1981: 71). According to Jung, however, the consciousness of ego stems from the collective unconscious (ibid.: 75). Jung regards the unconscious not just as a place for the disposal of repression, but also as the source of the conscious and the creative and destructive human spirit.

12 It is probably not coincidental that Kawai is attracted to Jung's theory, which shows strong resemblance with yin–yang theories. To Jung (1875–1961), the psyche is a primary feature of human beings. It is a self-regulating, dynamic system, the energy (libido) of which fluctuates between two polar opposites: progression, which satisfies the needs of the conscious and actively adapts to the environment, and regression, which satisfies the needs of the unconscious, that is, it responds to internal urges. Referring to Heraclitus' concept of eternal processes of continual change, Jung regards both poles essential as the two tides flowing into one another (Fordham 1966: 16–19).

13 *Tamashi* values imagination. Its straightforward experience is the dream. Its important characteristic is that the actor subject is not ego, but *tamashi*. The source of imaginative power works on the mystic quality of *tamashi*.

14 Kawai refers to the hierarchical structure of ego, the subconscious and the unconscious.

196 Notes

15 Kawai in *Monogatari to ningen no kagaku* (Narrative and the Science of Man) (1993), relates how stories connect to the unconscious of a people, and how narrative contributes to the stable identity of a people.
16 Kawai Hayao 1997 (recording): symposium organised by Nichibunken: 'Japan's Narrative, The World's Narrative' (*nihon no katarimono, sekai no katarimono*, 16 March 1997).
17 For an explanation of Ōbei, see Chapter Four, note 11.
18 Appointments have to be sanctioned by the Ministry of Education.
19 Nichibunken professor Sonoda Hidehirō in his *gyaku ketsujoron* proposed an alternative to theories of Japanese uniqueness, proceeding from the universality of Japanese phenomena instead: 'if another culture could be found which has much culture in common with Japan, then we would transgress the *nihonbunka-ron*. For example, Hamaguchi's *kanjinshugi* could be used to analyse other Asian societies.' The theory proposes a thought experiment for observing foreign countries through Japanese concepts, forming an heuristic tool for exploring other countries and a conceptual framework for rediscovering Japan:

1 It proposes that Japanese behaviour and systems are characterized by 'purpose-rationality'(in the Weberian sense);
2 Things existing in Japan all possess universality and are supposed to exist abroad as well;
3 As such, foreign countries can be studied by means of the framework with which Japan is interpreted;
4 If Japanese phenomena cannot be found abroad, we must consider the circumstances, which lead foreign countries to such lack;
5 We must reconsider the presuppositions of the universality and purpose rationality of Japanese phenomena (Sonoda 1991: 16–18).

9 Nation-centred political strategies in academic thought: Examples from China and Japan

1 See, for example, the mass-psychology of Li Shuyi, 'Wenhua wuyizhi' (Cultural Unconscious), *Zhexue Yanjiu* (Philosophy Research), February 1988, 54–9.
2 For example, *Chinese Sociology and Anthropology* 1, Summer 1969, ed. S.L. Greenblatt.
3 See, for instance, Hao Shiyuan (1993, 1996); Ma Dazheng (1995, 1997); Zhao Yuntian (1993).
4 CASS Yearbook Editorial Committee (1993–9); Bureau for Spreading Education of the CCP Central Committee Propaganda Department 1994.
5 An example of this genre *of furusato-zukuri* is the work of Kawakita Jirō, a professo emeritus of Tokyo University of Technology and participant in the International Symposium Southeast Asia (ISSEA): Global Area Studies for the twenty-first Century (Kyoto, Japan, October 18–22, 1996). Kawakita explained his KJ-method of consulting the locals in order to rethink the meaning of 'home-town', the meaning of 'tradition' and the meaning of 'creation'. In his 'bottom-up' approach 200 'spontaneous opinions' were summarized by persons listening to one another, 'making possible the integration of individual perspectives'. Kawakita believes the nature of this method is especially Chinese, Japanese and Buddhist. He makes use of 'abduction' instead of pre-Christian forms of 'deduction' and Cartesian 'induction' (Kawakita Jirō 1997). This approach ignores the fact that it is the researcher who initiates the research and evaluates it, ignores the kind of political impetus for asking specific kinds of questions and does not point out the role of its outcome in national politics, while the politico-economic implications of the research results are out of the reach of the 'village people'.
6 The frequently used notion of Ōbei, short for America and Europe, is a strongly

Notes 197

generalizing, historical concept. Ōbei usually refers to the US and western Europe, and sometimes to 'the West'. Geography is not the most important characteristic of Ōbei. Rather, everything associated with a Japanese understanding of modernity is attributed to Ōbei. It is often associated with aggression, individualism, rule by whites, extreme moralism and the inspirational source of modern music. But most of all, it is used as a foil to delineate the national self. Its frequent use as a foil implies a lack of confrontation with the diversity of the region so designated. The many dimensions of the concept are part and parcel of every day discussed in institutions of higher education.

7 For an example of this genre, see Doi Takeo (1990).

8 Japanese circumstances, before the country's economic take-off in the late 1950s, are frequently ignored. They include open international markets, the American defence umbrella, the American occupation and installation of democratic institutions and little competition from other countries in the same favourable position (cf. Hein 1993). Economies that rely on duplicative growth and borrowed technology and have no free-thinking entrepreneurial class imbued with a sense of inventiveness are bound to be shaken out. In 1996 this problem emerged in the electronics industry. Also, these economies can expect price competition from other developing economies that are poised to enter the 'catching-up' phase of economic development.

9 See, for instance, Pusey (1983); Harrell (1992).

10 Realism usually has three main assumptions. First, it regards the nation-state as the prime actor in international relations. Second, in the absence of central world authority it assumes a state of anarchy between nation-states, and third, it treats international politics essentially as power politics. Neo-realism has refined these classical assumptions by taking the international system to be a structure that shapes state behaviour. Realism in a Chinese academic context is conditioned by what is felt as 'hundred years of suffering and humiliations under the international domination of Western powers and Japan'. They view the growing transnational network through a state-centric prism, only focusing on how China could take advantage of these new 'eternal environments' to protect and maximize its national interests (Yong Deng 1998: 310–12).

11 In the Nanjing period (1927–37), underlying the continuation of a great diversity of activities such as translation, conducting social surveys, community studies and the research of historical sociology and macro-sociology a broad ideological division among intellectuals between a Marxist current of remoulding society and a pragmatic, liberal tradition of gradual reform widened (cf. Wong Siu-lun 1979; Y.C. Wang 1938). Historical sociology received impetus from this controversy, especially after the 1927 massacre of communists by the Nationalist government, as some Marxist theoreticians believed that a correct revolutionary theory of society could guide the search for the correct future revolution (Kwok 1965: 163–4). Functionalism in this period tended to regard culture as an instrument for change, albeit gradual change. Despite its stress on concepts of process, adjustment and change, it tended to neglect historical data on the evolving of social institutions in a broader context, which was regarded as a shortcoming, sharply criticized by Marxists.

12 Peaceful evolution is an ideological concept, used in politics to reflect the view that society changes gradually and by means of competition such as is thought to be prevalent in the West. Evolutionary change is contrasted with revolutionary change, in which the proletariat is the subject of history. This latter view requires the subject of history to 'struggle' against its enemies.

13 Wu Guoguang, a speech writer in the late 1980s to Premier Zhao Ziyang and a chief editor in the Editorial Department of the *People's Daily*, argues that the Chinese communist regime operates through directives from the oligarchic

198 *Notes*

top leadership, that have their main form of expression in political documents. Wu calls this 'rule by document'. Such documents give the regime ideological legitimacy, and a successfully completed document enjoys both symbolic and administrative authority. The drafting of such a document makes up a central part of the political process and consists of several stages. First, ideas are formed to formulate the central issues and an agenda is set. Next, leaders are appointed to select the drafters of the planned document. For a political document, a special drafting group may be set up, for which drafters are selected and borrowed from several political institutions and academic research organs (Wu Guoguang 1995: 23–38). The prescribed and proscribed formulations in academic writing, and the documentocracy that regulates the organization of research disciplines, their purpose, scope and application, all built around the national quest of socialism with Chinese characteristics greatly limits the thinkable and publishable in academic circles over a whole range of social science disciplines (cf. CASS Yearbook Editorial Committee; Schoenhals 1992, 1993).

14 For a detailed critique of the planned nature of success and its meaning, see Hein (1993).

15 Ren Jiyu (1916–) is a well-known historian of philosophy, specializing in Buddhist studies. In 1987, Ren became head of the Beijing Library, and concurrently held posts as professor at Beijing University and the CASS Graduate school. His other functions include tutor of Ph.D. students, honorary professor at CASS, Institute of Religion, head of the Chinese Association of the History of Philosophy, and head of the Chinese Society for Atheist Studies (Hu Fuchen 1988: 47–56). Ren's work 'Zhonghua Great Classics' (*Zhonghua Da Cangjing*) is a classic and his four-volume work on the history of Chinese philosophy was used in all universities in the 1960s. After the Cultural Revolution he edited other volumes on the history of the development of Chinese philosophy (Fang Keli and Wang Qishui 1995: 588–92).

16 To Professor Fang, the director of the Graduate School of the CASS, and main editor of *CASS Yanjiusheng Xuebao*, the communication and mingling between China and the West are the most important characteristic of Chinese twentieth century philosophy. The main stream of Chinese twentieth-century philosophy is Marxist philosophy: it carries the responsibility of scientifically summarizing historical experience and the hopes of the future. Fang's list of the main events of the twentieth century in China consists of the May Fourth movement, old nationalism and new nationalism, the establishment of the Republic and the survival of Chinese socialism after the disintegration of the SU (Fang Keli 1994: 2).

10 Nation-framing as an academic strategy in the PRC

1 International co-operation presumed necessary to the implementation of the policies of reforms and opening up made it also imperative to communicate with former enemies on their terms. Before the 1980s and 1990s there was a complete absence of the concept of 'interdependence' in Chinese writings (Yong 1998: 317).

2 For example, Li Shenzhi, former vice-president of CASS (1988–90) and president of the China American Study Association (*Zhong-Meiguo Xuehui Huizhang*) does not like using the concepts of East and West. Li argues that the differences within Asia are as big as those between China and the West. There is no sense in putting them in a unit of 'the East'. Li criticizes those who do and then say that the East is superior to the West, announce the century of the East and the convergence of East and West. According to Li, the concept of 'West' is a remnant of the Cold War. Since Russia has become a Western country, Li argues, there seems to be no sense in contrasting East and West. Moreover, the Czech Republic, Poland and Hungary have all joined NATO.

Notes 199

Li argues that imperialists have tried to split up East and West, even composing poetry claiming 'East is East/West is West/Never the twain shall meet'. It was based on a world which had London as its centre. According to Li, the Chinese who still retain such views of East and West do this under the banner of patriotism. Central Asia (including Xinjiang) used to be the western heavenly kingdom of Buddhism (*xitian foguo*). Now this area has become Islamic and its inhabitants do not acknowledge that their ancestors were pious Buddhists. Since the end of the Cold War many peoples have moved around the world. People of all kinds of religious backgrounds have moved to 'Christian' Europe. And America, according to Li, although it is a nation based on racism, has no cultural problems (although it has religious ones). Cultural pluralism has already become a part of modern society (Li Shenzhi 1998: 53).

3   See, for instance, the research projects reported on in the CASS yearbooks (*Zhongguo Shehui Kexueyuan Nianjian Bianji Weiyuanhui* 1993–9).

4   On the Sino-African Conference of 9–12 October 2000, President Jiang Zemin asked forty-four African countries to stand up against Western hegemony, and to help China build a new world order. He also said China would release the poorest countries from a 1.2 milliard dollar debt and that Chinese investment into Africa and aid would be stepped up (*Volkskrant*, 12 October 2000).

5   For Chinese scholars and officials alike, national interests are the embodiment of the nation. 'National rights (*guoquan*) are more important than are human rights and the latter should not be allowed to undermine the former' (cf. Deng's speech at a national working conference, 25 December 1980, 'Implement the Policy of Readjustment to Ensure Stability and Unity' in Deng Xiaoping (1984)). In contrast with the loud-mouthed pursuit of socialist national interest during the Cultural Revolution, many Chinese scholars now insist that national interests have an objective existence and should be studied by scientific methods (Yong 1998: 313–14).

6   For an example see the guidelines for social science research in the *Subject Compass of the 1998 State Plan for Philosophy and the Social Sciences*, National Philosophy and Social Science Planning Office (December 1997).

7   The famous dissident astrophysicist Fang Lizhi and his research group at Hefei University discussed the following issues with their students as official policies toward science that had caused much confusion. The list aptly illustrates the nature of debates that have muddled up issues of science and politics ever since the reforms:

1   the material world does not at all always have two aspects (*liangdianlun*) (the doctrine that everything has two aspects);
2   infinite can be finite, vice versa;
3   the indestructibility of matter is not applicable everywhere;
4   existential being without time;
5   nothing gives birth to being and the prime mover;
6   essence of the universe;
7   whether subjectivity and objectivity are separable in quantum phenomena;
8   the basis of free will;
9   the scientific 'spirit is not dead';
10 the least understandable about the universe is that it is understandable.

Fang argues, that physicists are interested in these philosophical issues, but do not welcome a quasi-scientific philosophy that claims 'universal truth'. Physicists have the experience that it takes a generation for incorrect things to disappear and one generation for correct things to become acknowledged (Fang Lizhi 1986).

8   The 'unity of opposites' was an adage used during the Cultural Revolution in

200 *Notes*

political propaganda. Countless debates were held to stress the necessary distinction between 'one divides into two' (*yi fenwei er*) and 'two combined into one' (*he er er yi*). The former stood for struggle and revolution and was 'proved' by science, while the latter phrase was staked against it and labelled 'out-and-out' bourgeois metaphysics and idealism. In 1980, however, it became possible to describe 'two combine into one' as the 'temporary coexistence of opposites in a period of quantitative change'. Nevertheless, both were thought to be indispensable, as the struggle between opposites (struggle from within) was necessary to generate qualitative change (revolution), while unity implied change as a result of external intervention, which could only lead to (objectionable) compromise, adjustment and quantitative change (evolution). These two dimensions of change (evolution and revolution) were applied to the national unit of socialist China. In the 1980s, they were replaced by other polarities, such as the concepts of negative and positive feedback from systems theory. Applied to the unit of China, they depicted China as a giant project of systems engineering. During this time the concepts of revolution and evolution were still associated with capitalism and socialism but, gradually, increasingly culturalist definitions of East and West received attention from the broader academic public. The latter initially served in support of discussions on liberalism, democracy and neo-authoritarianism, but were soon also redefined in socialist culturalist terms. In the 1990s their combination created a research setting in which the compromise of dualistic extremes was encouraged, the limits of which the prescriptions and proscriptions of academic leaders defined.

9 Stalin in 'Marxism and the National Question' wrote that a nation has an historically formed common language, common territory, common economic life and it is expressed in the common psychological elements of a culture's stable community.

10 The Four Modernizations were announced on 26 February 1978, at the first session of the Fifth National People's Congress. They concern the modernization of agriculture, industry, national defence and science and technology.

11 Oumei, as does its equivalent in Japanese, Ōbei, is an abbreviation which refers to Europe and America. In China, however, the concept is not used as intensively as it is in Japan.

12 Similarly, the study of mass psychology and mass psychoanalysis has attracted attention from nation-framers. They seem to share structural characteristics. Li Shuyi's article on the cultural unconscious (in the renowned philosophical journal *Zhexue Yanjiu*) does not distinguish between description and prescription. Neither is it clear why Li is interested in changing the unconscious of the masses, and what masses he is referring to: the Chinese masses or the human masses? Li argues for complementing Freud's analysis of the unconscious of the individual with that of the culture of the masses as it has great practical meaning for the study of decision-making. Because social behaviour is influenced by the instinctual and cultural unconscious this new study can reveal the principles of unconscious mass behaviour. The task of this study is to explain the necessity and possibility of cultivating the psyche of the masses. The observed positive and negative elements in the cultural unconscious shows the need for purifying and cultivating the unconscious psyche (Li Shuyi 1988: 57–9). One wonders what kind of mass manipulator Li envisages for cultivating the cream and discarding the dregs of the cultural unconscious.

13 See also the speech by Jiang Zemin on patriotism and the mission of China's (my country's) intellectuals (3 May 1990) at a public lecture of the capital youth remembrance of the May Fourth (*shoudu qingnian jinian wu-si baogaohui*) (Jiang Zemin 1994). Also, see the CASS Yearbooks (CASSYB) (Zhongguo Shehui Kexueyuan Nianjian Bianweihui 1993–2000).

Notes   201

14 CASS Yearbook criticizes academics who take their critical works elsewhere, abroad or to provincial capitals. In this particular instances, the dissident Li Zehou is criticized for publicizing his 'Farewell to the Revolution' in Hong Kong (CASS Yearbook 1998: 24).
15 For this reason critical and independent research has emerged outside official academic organizations (Mok 1998; Goldman 1998; Lin Min and Galikowski 1999).
16 Pro-Tibet independence groups waged a campaign against the loan in the weeks leading up to the vote, stating that the project would further China's goal of weakening Tibetan identity in the area. According to the President of the Tibetan Youth Congress (TYC), Tseten Norbu, who campaigned against the loan application of China with the World Bank, China's failure meant a triumph for Tibetans and people around the world. The TYC campaigned against the loan application. The World Bank's handling of the loan 'sets a historic precedent for future international action against Chinese colonization in Tibet', said Tseten Norbu, who also believes that it is 'too early to celebrate', since Beijing plans to continue the project without the World Bank funding (Sue Bruell, Wu Yiyi in www.CND.org: 07/09/00). As the United States and Germany registered the only votes against the project, the bank made a temporary decision to withhold all funds until a more detailed independent review can be completed.
17 The 1981 symposium on 'The History of Chinese Minority Relations' (*Zhongguo minzu guanxi shi*) is quoted in Meng Xianfan (1991).
18 A survey of the symposium on 'The History and Current Situation of Tibet' organized by *Zhongguo Shehui Kexue Zazhi* and *Zhongguo Zangxue Zazhi*, 17–19 March 1991.
19 According to a 1995 sample census, the Han constitute 91 per cent of the entire population, the Han occupy 36 per cent of Chinese territory (Benewick and Donald 1999: 20).
20 Weng Dujian is a famous scholar of national minorities. In the 1960s, he was one of the organizational leaders and academic theoreticians (together with Jian Bozan, Lu Zhenyu and Bai Shouyi) of national minority relations. In 1983, Weng became the head of the CASS Research Centre for the History of Border Regions. In 1988, he edited 'An Outline of the History of Chinese Ethnic Relations' (*Zhongguo Minzu Guanxi Shi Gangyao*), which was based on the sixth five year plan academic focus point from 1983. It became a standard textbook in the Institute of Nationality Studies.
21 Lu Xiaofei in Renmin Ribao (*The People's Daily*) argues that foreigners purposely mix up the territorial and ethnic signification for Tibet. Since the Yuan dynasty, Lu argues, Tibet has been an administrative region. The Tibetan region included areas in Sichuan, Qinghai, Yunnan and Gansu, as Tibetans resided there. The Yuan divided the Tibetan area into three administrative regions, and later on the three regions of Tibetan dialects were formed. Some foreigners Lu accuses of calling both Tibet (*Xizang*) and the Tibetan (autonomous) region (*Zangqu*) Tibet. Lu does not seem to realize that not all foreigners are taught or want know what is politically correct (Lu Xiaofei 1992b). Similarly, a foreign sinologist, Professor van Praag, was criticized by Wang Furen, as 'he in his "*Xizang de Diwei*" (the status of Tibet) purposely twists history, and plays with concepts'.

> He treats the concepts of *Zhongguoren* (Chinese) and *Hanren* (Han-Chinese) as if they are the same, and makes a distinction between *Zhongguoren* (Chinese) and Tibetans and Mongolians, trying to prove that China is a *guojia* (country; state) established by the Han, thus cheating many people abroad who do not understand Chinese history.
>
> (Lu Xiaofei 1992b)

202 *Notes*

22 The Central Plains is another term for what used to be there before China came about. As the concept of China is irrelevant to the discussion outside of its limited historical context, academics are forced to revert to a replacement.
23 The Panchen Lama is appointed by the government in Peking.
24 For which purpose basic guidelines are drawn. They dominate the formulation of project plans and research policies in general.
25 The *Zhou Yi* comprises the *Yi Jing* and the *Yi Zhuan*. The *Yi Jing* is a book of divination, based on a system of eight (and later sixty-four) symbols which are supposed to reflect the universe. Divination is based on a configuration of the signs: in it one can see the movement of man. Therefore this system presupposes the agreement of the 'way of man' with that of the 'way of the Universe'. The *Yi Zhuan* is a philosophical elaboration of the *Yi Jing*. It has preserved its system of symbols and the premise of the conflation of the 'way of man' with the 'way of nature', but has lost its religious character. The *Yi Zhuan*'s basic spirit remains pre-Qin Confucianism, but it absorbed the Taoist influence of the 'way of the universe': it is a result of a cultural confluence of Confucian and Taoist thought (Wang Zhiyue 1993).

References

Al-Faruqi (1988) 'Islamization of Knowledge. Problems, Principles and Prospective', in *Islam: Sources and Purpose of Knowledge*, Herndon: IIIT.

Anderson, Benedict (1995) *Imagined Communities*, New York and London: Verso.

Ariyoshi Sawako (1978) *Hanaoka Seishū no tsuma*, trans. Paul Wijsman (1994) *De Vrouw van de Dokter* (The Doctor's Wife), Amsterdam: De Geus.

Barnes, Gina L. (1999) *The Rise of Civilization in East Asia: The Archaeology of China, Korea and Japan*, London: Thames & Hudson.

Barz, Helmut (1981) *Jung en zijn psychotherapie* (Jung and his Psychotherapy), Amsterdam: Rainbow Pocketboeken, Uitgeverij Maarten Muntinga BV.

Benewick, Robert and Donald, Stephanie (1999) *The State of China Atlas*, London: Penguin Books.

Berque, Augustin (1998) 'The Question of Space: From Heidegger to Watsuji', in Joy Hendry (ed.) *Interpreting Japanese Society: Anthropological Approaches*, London: Routledge.

Bian Chongdao and Suzuki Tadashi (eds) (1987) *Riben jindai shi da zhexuejia*, Shanghai: Shanghai Renmin Chubanshe.

Blacker, Carmen (1988) 'Two Shinto Myths: the Golden Age and the Chosen People', in Sue Heny and Jean-Pierre Lehmann (eds) *Themes and Theories in Modern Japanese History. Essays in Memory of Richard Storry*, London and Atlantic Highlands, NJ: The Athlone Press.

Brown, J.A.C (1972) *Freud and the Post-Freudians*, Harmondsworth, Middlesex: Penguin Books.

Brownlee, John (1991) *Political Thought in Japanese Historical Writing: From Kojiki (712) to Tokushi Yoron (1712)*, Waterloo, Ontario: Wilfrid Laurier University Press.

Brugger, Bill and Kelly, David (1990) *Chinese Marxism in the Post-Mao Era*, Stanford, CA: Stanford University Press.

Bureau for Spreading Education of the CCP Central Committee Propaganda Department (*Zhonggong Zhongyang Xuanchuanbu Jiaoyuju*) (1994) *Aiguozhuyi jiaoyu shishe gangyao duben* (An Outline of the Implementation of Patriotic Education), Beijing: Xuexi Chubanshe, No. 314.

Capra, Fritjof (1983) *The Turning Point: Science, Society and the Rising Culture*, London: Fontana Paperback.

CASS Yearbook Editorial Committee (Zhongguo Shehui Kexueyuan Nianjian Bianji Weiyuanhui) (1992–2000) *Zhongguo Shehui Kexueyuan Nianjian* (Yearbook of the Chinese Academy of Social Sciences (1993–2000)), Beijing: Zhongguo Shehui Kexue Chubanshe.

204 References

Chen Liankai (1992) 'Zhonghua Minzu jie' (Interpreting Zhonghua Minzu), Zhongnan Minzu Xueyuan Xuebao, 5: 39–46.

China Handbook Editorial Committee (1983) Education and Science, Beijing: Foreign Language Press.

Dale, Peter N. (1993) 'Nichibunken and Japan's international cultural policy', Die Internationalisierung Japans im Spannungsfeld zwischen Ökonomischer und socialer Dynamik, Werner Pascha, Wolfgang Seifert, Meinfried Striegnitz (Hrsg.), pp. 115–32.

—— (1995) The Myth of Japanese Uniqueness, London and New York: Routledge.

De Bary, W. T., Tsunoda, Ryusaku and Keene, D. (1964) Sources of Japanese Tradition, vol. II, New York and London: Columbia University Press.

Deng Xiaoping (Teng Hsiao-ping) (1984) Selected Works of Deng Xiaoping (1975–1982), Beijing: Foreign Language Press.

Dikötter, Frank (1992) The Discourse of Race in Modern China, London: C. Hurst & Co.

—— (ed.) (1997) The Construction of Racial Identities in China and Japan: Historical and Contemporary Perspectives, London: C. Hurst & Co.

Dittmer, Lowell and Kim, Samuel S. (1993) China's Quest for National Identity, Ithaca and London: Cornell University Press.

Doi Takeo (1990) The Anatomy of Dependence, Tokyo and New York: Kōdansha International.

Douglas, Mary (1973) Natural Symbols: Explorations in Cosmology, London: Penguin Books.

—— (1987) How Institutions Think, Syracuse: Syracuse University Press.

Du Ruofu and Xiao Chunjie (1997) 'Cong yichuanxue tantao Zhonghua Minzu de yuan yu liu' (The Origin and Development of the Chinese Nation from a Genetic Perspective), Zhongguo Shehui Kexue, 4: 139–49.

Dumont, Louis (1980) Homo Hierarchicus: The Caste System and its Implication, Chicago and London: University of Chicago Press.

Fabian, Johannes (1983) Time and the Other: How Anthropology Makes its Objects, New York and London: Columbia University Press.

Fan Hao (1992) 'Dong-Xifang wenhua "ziwo" xingtai de bijiao' (Comparing the Form of 'Self' in Eastern and Western Culture), Jiangsu Shehui Kexue, 2: 108–12.

Fang Keli (1994) 'Ershi-shiji zhongyao zhexue de hongguan shenshi' (A Macro Examination of Twentieth Century Chinese Philosophy), based on a speech of 12 August 1993, given at the Eighth International Symposium of Chinese Philosophy, CASS Yanjiushengyuan Xuebao, 4.

—— (1996) 'Xiandai xinruxue fazhen de luoji yu quxiang' (The Logic and Direction of the Contemporary Development of neo-Confucianism), CASS Yanjiushengyuan Xuebao, 5: 42–50.

Fang Keli and Wang Qishui (main eds) (1995) Ershi shiji Zhongguo zhexue (Chinese Philosophy of the Twentieth Century) (2 vols), Beijing: Huaxia Chubanshi.

Fang Lizhi (1986) 'Zhexue he wuli' (Philosophy and Physics), Ziran Bianzhengfa Yanjiu, 5: 28–9.

Fitzgerald, John (1995) 'The Nationless State: The Search for a Nation in Modern Chinese nationalism', The Australian Journal of Chinese Affairs, 33.

—— (1996) Awakening China. Politics, Culture, and Class in the Nationalist Revolution, Stanford, CA: Stanford University Press.

Fogel, Joshua A. (1994) 'Nationalism, the Rise of the Vernacular, and the

References 205

Conceptualization of Modernization in East Asian Comparative Perspective', *Indiana East Asian Working Paper Series on Language and Politics in Modern China*, Paper 3, January 1994, pp. 1–12, Bloomington, IN: East Asian Studies Centre Indiana University.

Fordham, Frieda (1966) *An Introduction to Jung's Psychology*, London, New York: Pelican Books.

Fukuyama, Francis (1992) *The End of History and the Last Man*, New York: The Free Press.

Gellner, Ernest (1983) *Nations and Nationalism*, Oxford: Blackwell.

Goldman, Merle (1994) *Sowing the Seeds of Democracy in China*, Cambridge, MA and London: Harvard University Press.

—— (1998) 'Politically-Engaged Intellectuals in the 1990s', *China Quarterly*, 154: 700–11.

Greenblatt, S.L. (ed.) (1969) *Chinese Sociology and Anthropology*, 1 (4) (Summer).

Gu Zhengkun (trans.) (1995) *Laozi: The Book of Tao and Teh*, Peking: Peking University Press.

Hall, Ivan (1998) *Cartels of the Mind: Japan's Intellectual Closed Shop*, New York and London: W.E. Norton & Co.

Hamaguchi Eshun (1985) 'A Contextual Model of the Japanese: Toward Methodological Innovation in Japan Studies', *Journal of Japanese Studies*, 11(2): 320–1.

—— (1986) '*Nihon bunmei no kihonteki seikaku. "Bunka" no bunmeika moshikuwa "bunmei" no bunkaka o megutte*', in The Japan Society for the Comparative Study of Civilizations (ed.), *Hikaku Bunmei 2*.

—— (1988) '*Bunmei hendo ni okeru bunka to no iiso dotai*', in The Japan Society for the Comparative Study of Civilizations (ed.), *Hikaku Bunmei*, April: 10–12.

—— (1991) '*"Nihon-rashisa" no Saihakken*', Tokyo: Kodanshagaku Kobunku.

—— (1995) 'A new paradigm for Japanese studies: Methodological relatum-ism', in Frellesvig, Bjarke and Morimoto Hermanse, Christian (eds) *Florilegium Japonicum. Studies Presented to Olof G. Lidin on the Occasion of His 70th Birthday*, Copenhagen: Akademisk Forlag.

—— (1996a) *Nihongata shinrai shakai no fukken. Gurobaruka suru kanjinshugi*, Tokyo: Tōyō Keizai Shinhosha.

—— (1996b) '*Kachi tenkan no jidai. "Koyo" kara "shinyō"e*', *Hikaku Bunmei* 12.

Hamrin, Carol Lee and Zhao Suisheng (eds) (1995) *Decision-Making in Deng's China*, New York: M.E. Sharpe.

Hanihara Kazurō (1991) 'Dual Structure Model for the Population History of the Japanese', *Japan Review*, 2: 1–33.

Hao Shiyuan (1993) '*Jindai minzu guanxi he Zhonghua Renmin Gongheguo de jianli*' (Modern Ethnic Relations and the Establishment of the PRC), in Weng Dujian (ed.) *Zhongguo minzu shi gangyao* (An Outline of Chinese Ethnic History), Beijing: Zhongguo Shehui Kexue Chubanshe.

—— (1996) *Zhongguo de minzu yu minzu wenti. Lun zhongguo gongchandang jiejue minzu wenti de lilun yu shijian* (The Chinese Nationalities and Nationality Issues. Discussing the Theory and Practice of the CPC's Solutions for Nationality Issues), Nanning: Jiangxi Renmin Chubanshe.

Harootunian, H.D. (1988) *Things Seen and Unseen: Discourse and Ideology in Tokugawa Nativism*, Chicago and London: University of Chicago Press.

206   References

Harrell, Paula (1992) *Sowing the Seeds of Change: Chinese Students, Japanese Teachers, 1895–1905*, Stanford, CA: Stanford University Press.

He Xingliang (1990) '*Zhongguo tuteng wenhua gaishu*' (Summing Up Chinese Totem Culture), *Yunnan Shehui Kexue*, 2: 33–9.

Heberer, Thomas (1989) *China and Its National Minorities, Autonomy or Assimilation?*, Armonk, NY: M.E. Sharpe.

Hein, Laura E. (1993) 'Growth Versus Success: Japan's Economic Policy in Historical Perspective', in A. Gordon (ed.) *Postwar Japan as History*, Berkeley, Los Angeles, Oxford: University of California Press.

Herzfield, Michael (1992) *The Social Production of Indifference, Exploring the Symbolic Roots of Western Bureaucracy*, Chicago and London: University of Chicago Press.

Hu Fuchen (1987) '*Tanlong-shuofeng*' (Discourse of the Dragon and the Phoenix), *CASS Yanjiushengyuan Xuebao*, 4: 71–7.

—— (1988) '*Qingli fengjian wenhua: rang rujiao zaori xiaowang – Ren Jiyu jiaoshou dawenlu*' (Check Up on Feudalistic Cultural Legacy to Accelerate the Dying Out of Confucianism. Questions and Answers by Prof. Ren Jiyu), *CASS Yanjiushengyuan Xuebao*, 5: 47–56.

—— (1993) '*Daojiao yixue he neidanxue de rentiguan tansuo*' (Probe into Taoist Medicine and the Neidanxue View of the Human Body), *Shijie Zongjiao Yanjiu*, 4: 87–99.

—— (1995) '*Daojia wenhua tansuo*' (A Probe of the Taoist Culture), *Zhexue Yanjiu*, 7: 74–80.

—— (1997) '*Dajiao neidanxue de xichuan he kexue jieze*' (The Spread of Taoist Neidanxue to the West and Scientific Interpretation), *Shanghai Daojiao*, 3: 8–10.

Huffman, James L. (1998) *Modern Japan. An Encyclopedia of History, Culture and Nationalism*, New York and London: Garland Publishing.

Huntington, Samual P. (1993) 'The Clash of Civilisations', *Foreign Affairs*, 72, Summer 1993.

Ikegami, Eiko (1997) *The Taming of the Samurai: Honorific Individualism and the Making of Modern Japan*, Cambridge, MA and London: Harvard University Press.

Imanishi Kinji (1994) *Ningenshakai no keisei* (The Formation of Human Society), Tokyo: NHK Books.

—— (1996) *Shinka to wa nanika* (What is Evolution?), Tokyo: Kōdansha Gakujutsu Bunko.

Ivy, Marilyn (1995) *Discourses of the Vanishing: Modernity, Phantasm, Japan*, Chicago and London: University of Chicago Press.

Iwasaki Chikatsugu (1989) *Nihon bunkaron to shinsō bunseki* (Theory on Japanese Culture and Depth Analysis), Tokyo: Shin Nihon Shuppansha.

Jackson, Steven F. (1996) 'Lessons from a Neighbour: China's Japan-Watching Community', in Christopher Howe (ed.) *China and Japan. History, Trends, and Prospects*, Oxford: Clarendon Press.

Jia Lanpo (1989) 'On Problems of the Beijing-Man Site: A Critique of New interpretations', *Current Anthropology*, 30(2): 201–5.

Jiang Qian (1993) '*Dong-xifang minzu siwei fangshi de chabie: danao liangban qiu jineng de feiduichenxing yu dong-xifang siwei chayi de bijiao*' (The Difference Between the Ways of Thinking of Eastern and Western Nations: A Comparison

References 207

between Asymmetric Functions of the Two Hemispheres of the Brain and Differences in Eastern and Western Thought), *Ziran-Bianzhengfa Yanjiu*, 3.

Jiang Zemin (1994) *'Aiguozhuyi he Woguo zhishifenzi de shiming'* (Patriotism and the Mission of China's (My Country's) Intellectuals) (speech made on 3 May 1990, at a Public Lecture of the Capital Youth Remembrance of the May Fourth Movement). In Bureau for Spreading Education of the CCP Central Committee Propaganda Department (zhonggong zhongyang xuanchuanbu jiaoyuju) *An Outline of the Implementation of Patriotic Education* (readers edition) (aiguozhuyi jiaoyu shishe gangyao duben), Document No. 312, Beijing: Xuexi Chubanshe.

Jin Binggao (1992) *'Guanyu Zhonghua Minzu de yanjiu'* (Research on the *Zhonghua Minzu*), *Zhongyang Minzuxueyuan Xuebao*, 5: 43–9.

Johnston, Reginald F. (1985) *Twilight in the Forbidden City*, Oxford: Oxford University Press.

Kasaya Kazuhiko (1993a) *Kinse Buke-shakai no seiji-kōzō* (The Political Structure of Samurai Society in Tokugawa Japan), Tokyo: Yoshikawa Kobunkan.

—— (1993b) *Samurai no shisō: Nihon soshiki – tsuyosa no kōzō* (The Thought of the Samurai: Japanese Organizations – the Structure of its Strength), Tokyo: Nihon Keizai Shimbunsha.

Kawai Hayao (1986a) *Shūkyō to kagaku no setten* (The Similarities Between Religion and Science), Tokyo: Iwanami Shoten.

—— (1986b) 'Violence in the Home: Conflict between Two Principles – Maternal and Paternal', in T.S. Lebra and W.P. Lebra (eds) *Japanese Culture and Behaviour*, Honolulu: University of Hawaii Press.

—— (1988) *The Japanese Psyche: Major Motifs in the Fairy Tales of Japan*, Dallas: Spring Publications.

—— (1993) *Monogatari to ningen no kagaku* (Narrative and the Science of Man), Tokyo: Iwanami Shoten.

—— (1997a) *Mu'ishiki no kōzō* (The Structure of the Unconscious), Tokyo: Chūō Kōron Shinsho, No. 481.

—— (1997b) *Mu'ishiki no hakken: bukkyōto wa 'senjyūsh'* (The Exploration of the Unconscious: Followers of Buddhism are Aborigines), *Kyoto Shimbun*, 15 January.

Kawai Masao (1993) *'Tōsai no dōbutsukan'* (The View of Animals in East and West), in Itō Shuntarō and Yasuda Yoshinori (eds) (1993) *Sōgen no shisō – mori no tetsugaku* (Thought of the Steppe and Philosophy of the Forest), Tokyo: Kōdansha.

Kawakita Jirō (1997) 'New Horizon of Area Studies: From Personal Experiences', Proceedings of the International Symposium Southeast Asia (ISSEA): Global Area *Studies for the 21st Century*, Kyoto: Centre for Southeast Asian Studies, Kyoto University (18–22 October 1996).

Kishida Shū (1991) *'Eikaiwa to iu byōki'* (The English Conversation Disease), *Daikōkai*, 11.

Knodt, Eva M. (1995) 'Foreword', in Niklas Luhmann, *Social Systems*, Stanford, CA: Stanford University Press, pp. xxviii–ix.

Koestler, Arthur (1989) *The Ghost in the Machine* (originally published 1961), London: Arkana, Penguin Books.

Kumon Shumpei (1982) 'Japan as a Network Society', *The Political Economy of Japan. Vol. 3: Cultural and Social Dynamics*, Kumon Shumpei and Henry Kosovsky (eds), Stanford, CA: Stanford University Press, pp. 5–29.

208 References

Li Hongzhi (1999) *Falun fofa* (The Wheel of the Law (of Transmigration) and Buddhist *dharma*), Xining: Qinghai Renmin Chubanshe.

Li Shangkai (1991) '*Lun minzu xinli zhi yanjiu*' (On the Research of National Psychology), *Xinjiang Shifan Daxue Xuebao* (*Zhexue Shehui Kexueban*), 1: 27–33.

Li Shaolian (1990) '*Shilun Huaxia sanbuzu zai Zhongguo wenming shi zhong de zuoyong*' (Discussing the Influence of the Three Tribes of Huaxia on the History of Chinese Civilization), *Zhongzhou Xuekan*, 3: 106–10.

Li Shenzhi (1998) '*Dong-Xifang wenhua zhi wojian*' (The Self-Image of Eastern and Western Culture), *Tianjin Shehui Kexue*, 1: 52–5.

Li Shuyi (1988) '*Wenhua wuyizhi*' (Cultural Unconscious), *Zhexue Yanjiu*, 2: 54–9.

Lin Ganquan (1998) '*Shiji zhi jiao de Zhongguo lishixue yu women de yanjiu gongzuo*' (Chinese Study of History at the Turn of the Century and Our Research Work), CASS General Office of the Science Research Bureau (ed.) *Xin shiqi shehui kexue de huigu yu qianzhan* (Looking Back onto the New Era of Social Science and Looking Ahead), Beijing: Shehui Kexue Wenxian Chubanshe.

Lin, Min and Maria Galikowski (1999) *The Search for Modernity. Chinese Intellectuals and Cultural Discourse in the Post-Mao Era*, New York: St Martin's Press.

Lingle, Christopher (1997) *The Rise and Decline of the Asian Century: False Starts on the Path to the Global Millennium*, Hong Kong: Asia 2000 Limited.

Liu Changlin (1990) *Zhongguo Xitong Siwei* (Chinese Systems Thought), Beijing: Zhongguo Shehui Kexue Chubanshe, pp. 578–81.

Lu Xiaofei (1992a) '*Xizang wenti chun shu woguo neizheng; guojia zhuquan bu rong taren ganshe*' (The Tibet Issues Purely Belongs to My Country's Home Affairs; National Sovereignty Is Not To Be Interfered With By Others), *Renmin Ribao*, 22 February.

—— (1992b) '"*Xizang renkou wenti*" *zhenxiangi*' (The Truth About the "Tibetan Population Issue"), *Renmin Ribao*, 2 March 1992.

Luhmann, Niklas (1995) *Social Systems*, Stanford: Stanford University Press.

Ma Dazheng (1995) '*Lüelun dangdai Zhongguo bianjiang de wending yu fazhan*' (Short Discussion of the Stability and Development of Chinese Border Areas), Xing Yulin (ed.) *Zhongguo bianjiang shi de yanjiu tongbao* (Research Report of History of Chinese Borderland Areas), Urumqi: Xinjiang Renmin Chubanshe.

Ma Dazheng (1997) *Ershi-shiji de Zhongguo bianjiang yanjiu: yi men fazhan zhong de bianyuan-xueke de yanjin licheng* (Twentieth Century Research into Chinese Borderland Areas: The Evolutionary Historical Process of a Developing Borderline Subject), Harbin: Heilongjiang Jiaoyu Chubanshe.

McCormack, Gavan (1995) *The Emptiness of Japanese Affluence*, Armonk, NY and London: M.E. Sharpe.

Manabe Kazufumi (1994) '*Gaikoku ni okeru Nihongo*' (Japanese According to Foreign Countries), *Nihongogaku*, 13: 35–44.

—— (1996) '*Kaigai masumedia kōkoku ni okeru nihon kenkyū no tenbō*' (The Prospects of Japanese Language Research According to Overseas' Mass-Media Advertising), *Nikkei Hōkoku Kenkyūsho Hō*, Aug/Sept: 6–11.

Mannheim, Karl (1991) *Ideology and Utopia: An Introduction to the Sociology of Knowledge* (originally published 1921), Oxford: Routledge.

Maruyama Masao (1972) '*Rekishi ishiki no "kosō"*' (The "Ancient Stratum" of Historical Consciousness), in *Nihon no shisō 6 rekishi shisōshu* (Japanese Thought 6, Compendium of Historical Thought), Tokyo: Chikuma Shobō.

References 209

—— (1990) '*Genkei.kosō.shitsuyō teion: Nihon shisōshi hōhōron ni tsuite no watashi no ayumi*' (Prototype, Archetype, and Basso Obstinato: My Course on the Methodology of the History of Japanese Thought) in Takeda Sayako *et al.* (eds) *Nihon bunka no kakureta katachi* (The Hidden Forms of Japanese Culture), Tokyo: Iwanami Shoten.

Matsumoto Michihirō (1989) *The Unspoken Way. Haragei: Silence in Japanese Business and Society*, Tokyo and New York: Kōdansha International.

Masamura Toshiyuki (1996) *Himitsu to Haji* (Secret and Shame), Tokyo: Keisō Shubō.

Meng Xianfan (1991) ' "*Xizang: lishi yu xianzhuang*" *xueshu taolunhui zongshu*' (A General Survey of the Symposium on 'The History and Current Situation of Tibet') (organized by Zhongguo Shehui Kexue Zazhi and Zhongguo Zangxue Zazhi, held on March 17), *Zhongguo Shehui Kexue*, 4: 170.

Min Jiayin (ed.) (1995) *The Chalice and the Blade in Chinese Culture*, Beijing: China Social Sciences Publishing House.

Miller, H. Lyman (1996) *Science and Dissent in Post-Mao China: The Politics of Knowledge*, Seattle and London: University of Washington Press.

Minear, Richard H. (1980) 'Orientalism and the Study of Japan', *Journal of Asian Studies*, (39)3: 507–16.

Miyazaki Masakatsu (1992) '*Nihon to chūgoku ni okeru seiyō bunmei no juyō to 'seiyō'- 'tōyō' gainen no hensen*' (The Acceptance of Western Civilization and the Transformation of the Concepts of 'Occident' and 'Orient' in Japan and China), *Hikaku Bunmei* (Comparative Civilizations 8), Tokyo: Dōsui Shobō.

Mok Ka-ho (1998) *Intellectuals and the State in Post-Mao China*, New York: St Martin's Press.

Morris-Suzuki, Tessa (1998) *Re-Inventing Japan. Time, Space, Nation*, Armonk, NY and London: M.E. Sharpe.

Mu Hongli (1997) '*Zhonghua beifang gulao wenming zhi yaolan*' (The Cradle of the Ancient Civilization of the North of Zhonghua), *Shehui Kexue Jikan*, 2: 88–92.

Munro, D.J. (1971) 'The Malleability of Man in Chinese Marxism', *China Quarterly* Oct/Dec 1971: 609–40.

Murakami Yasusuke (1982) 'The Age of New Middle Mass Politics: The Case of Japan', *Journal of Japanese Studies*, 8(1): 29–72.

—— (1984) '*Ie* Society as a Pattern of Civilization', *Journal of Japanese Studies*, (10) 2: 281–363.

Nakane Chie (1973) *Japanese* Society, Harmondsworth, Middlesex: Penguin Books.

Nakasone Yasuhirō and Umehara Takeshi (1996) *Seiji to tetsugaku. Nakasone Yasuhirō Umehara Takeshi* (Politics and Philosophy. Nakasone Yasuhirō – Umehara Takeshi), Tokyo: PHP.

Nari Bilige (1990) '*Minzu yu minzu gainian bianzheng*' (Identify and Correct the Nation and the Concept of Nation), *Minzu Yanjiu*, 5: 11–17, 38.

National Philosophy and Social Science Planning Office (*Quanguo Zhexue Shehui Kexue Guihua Bangongshi*) (1997) '*Guojia Zhexue Shehui Kexue Yanjiu Guihua 1998 Nian Keti Zhinan*' (Subject Compass of the 1998 State Plan for Philosophy and the Social Sciences), Beijing.

Nishida Kitarō (1997) *Intuition and Reflection in Self-Consciousness* (Or.: '*jikaku ni okeru no chokkan to hansei*' [1941], trans. with an introduction, by Valdo H. Viglielmo with Takeuchi Toshinori and Joseph S. O'Leary), Albany, NY: State University of New York Press.

210 References

Ohmae Kenichi (1990) *The Borderless World*, London: Harper Collins Publishers.

Ohnuki Tierney, Emiko (1987) *The Monkey as Mirror: Symbolic Transformation in Japanese History and Ritual*, Princeton: Princeton University Press.

O'Leary, Joseph S. (1997) 'Foreword', in Nishida Kitarō *Intuition and Reflection in Self-Consciousness*, Albany, NY: State University of New York Press.

Omoto Kei'ichi (1992) 'Some Aspects of the Genetic Composition of the Japanese', *Japanese as a Member of the Asian and Pacific Populations*, Kyoto: International Research Centre of Japanese Studies, pp. 137–45.

—— (1996) '*Chō ni miserare, shinka o kenkyū*' (Fascinated by Butterflies, Researching Evolution), *Asahi Shimbun*, July 7, 1996.

Pang Yuanzheng (1986) '*Jiejue Fuza Xitong Wenti de Xiandai Kexue Fangfa*' (The Modern Scientific Method of Solving Fuzzy System Problems), in Zhongyang Renmin Guangbo Diantai Lilunbu (ed.) *Xiandai Siwei Yu Gaige* (Contemporary Thought and Reform), Beijing: Zhongyang Guangbo Dianshi Chubanshe, pp. 76–108.

Pusey, J.R. (1983) *China and Charles Darwin*, Cambridge, MA: Harvard University Press, East Asian Monographs, No. 100.

Pyle, Kenneth B. (1988) 'Japan, the World, and the Twentieth Century', in T. Inoguchi and D.I. Okimoto (eds) *The Political Economy of Japan II, The Changing International Context*, Stanford, CA: Stanford University Press.

Pye, Lucian W. (1996) 'How China's Nationalism Was Shanghaied', in Jonathan Unger (ed.) *Chinese Nationalism*, Armonk, NY, London: M.E. Sharpe, pp. 86–112.

Robertson, Jennifer (1994) *Native and Newcomer: Making and Re-making a Japanese City*, Berkeley, Los Angeles, and London: California University Press.

Rose, Caroline (2000) '"Patriotism is not Taboo": Nationalism in China and Japan and implications for Sino-Japanese Relations', *Japan Forum*, 12: 169–81.

Saeki Keishi (1998) '"*Ajia-teki kachi*" *wa sonzai suru ka*' (Do "Asian Values" Exist?) in Aoki Tamotsu and Saeki Keishi (eds), "*Ajia-teki kachi*" *to wa nani ka* (What are Asian Values?), Tokyo: TBS Britannica, pp. 21–42.

Sautman, Barry (1997) 'Myths of Descent, Racial Nationalism and Ethnic Minorities in the People's Republic of China', in Frank Dikötter (ed.) *The Construction of Racial Identities in China and Japan: Historical and Contemporary Perspectives*, London: C. Hurst & Co., pp. 75–95.

Schoenhals, Peter (1992) *Doing Things with Words in Chinese Politics: Five Studies*, Berkeley: Institute of East Asian Studies University of California, Centre For Chinese Studies.

Schoenhals, Michael (1993) *Talk About a Revolution: Red Guards, Government Cadres, and the Language of Political Discourse*, Indiana East Asian Working Paper Series on Language and Politics in Modern China Paper 1, Bloomington, Indiana: East Asian Studies Centre Indiana University.

Sekotac/Masuda Foundation (1992) *Nihongata shisutemu – jinrui bunmei no hitotsu gata* (Translated as: Japanese Systems. An Alternative Civilization?), Yokohama: Sekotac Joint-Stock Company.

Shi Qiliang (1991) '*Yuzhou tongyi yu xinxi ma? Yu Wang Cunzhen, Yan Chunyou tongzhi shangque*' (Does the Universe Unify Information? In discussion with comrades Wang Cunzhen and Yan Chunyou), *Zhongguo Shehui Kexue*, 2: 73–84.

Siddle, Richard (1996) *Race, Resistance and the Ainu of Japan*, London and New York: Routledge.

References 211

Sleeboom, Margaret (2001) *Academic Nationalism with Socialist Characteristics: The Institutional Role of CASS in the Formation of the Chinese Nation-State*, Ph.D. Dissertation (II), University of Amsterdam: Amsterdam.

Smith, Anthony D. (1986) *Ethnic Origins of Nations*, Oxford: Basil Blackwell.

—— (1991) *National Identity*, London: Penguin Books.

Sonoda Hidehiro (1991) '*Gyaku ketsujo riron*' (Reversed Absence/Lack Theory), *Kyōiku Shakaigaku Kenkyū, Dai 49 Shū.*

Strijbos, Sytse (1988) *Het Technische Wereldbeeld. Een wijsgerig onderzoek van het systeemdenken* (The Technological Worldview. A Philosophical Investigation of Systems-Thought), Amsterdam: Buijten & Schipperheyn.

Su Kaihua (1994a) '*Tuteng chongbai yu long chongbai zhi bijiao yanjiu*' (A Comparative Research of Dragon and Totem Worship), *Jianghai Xuekan*, 3: 115–20.

—— (1994b) '*Lüelun Zhongguo long wenhua de zhenzheng benyuan*' (A Brief Discussion of the True Origin of Chinese Dragon Culture), *Nanjing Shehui Kexue*, 4: 1–3.

Su Shaozhi (1994) 'Chinese Communist Ideology and Media Control', in Lee Chin-chuan (ed.), *China's Media, Media's China*, Boulder, San Francisco, Oxford: Westview Press, pp. 75–88.

—— (1995) 'The Structure of the CASS and Two Decisions to Abolish Its Marxism–Leninism–Mao Zedong Thought Institute', in Carol Lee Hamrin and Zhao Suisheng (eds) *Decision-Making in Deng's China*, New York: M.E. Sharpe, pp. 111–17.

Suzuki, Daisetz T. (1991) *Zen and Japanese Culture*, Rutland, VT, Tokyo: Tuttle Books.

Taira Koji (1993) 'Dialectics of Economic Growth, National Power, and Distributive Struggles', in Andrew Gordon (ed.) *Postwar Japan as History*, Berkeley, CA: University of California Press, pp. 167–86.

Tan Xuechun (1994) '"*zuo,you,dong, xi*": *zunbei yizhi jiqi wenhua yunhan*' ('Left, Right / East, West:' Awareness of Superiors and Inferiors and Their Cultural Implications), *Shehui Kexue Zhanxian*, 5: 259–66.

Tanabe Hajime (1969) 'The Logic of the Species As Dialectics' (translation of Chapter One of the 'Logic of Species' *Shu no ronri no benshōhō* (1946) by David Dilworth and Taira Satō) *Monumenta Nipponica* 24 (3–4): 273–88.

Tanaka, Stefan (1993) *Japan's Orient*, Berkeley, CA: University of California Press.

Trudgill, Peter (1980) *Sociolinguistics: An Introduction*, Harmondsworth, Middlesex: Penguin Books.

Tsuda Yukio (1996) *Shinryaku suru Nihongo. Hangeki suru Nihongo: utsukushii bunka o dōmamoru ka* (The Invasion of English. The Counter-Attack of Japanese: How to Protect a Beautiful Culture), Tokyo: PHP.

Tsunoda Tadanobu (1985) *The Japanese Brain. Uniqueness and Universality*, Tokyo: Taishukan Publishing Company.

Umehara Takeshi (1989a) 'The Japanese View of the Hereafter', *Japan Echo*, XVI, 3.

—— (1989b) 'A Buddhist Approach to Organ Transplants', *Japan Echo* Vol XVI, 4: 79–82.

—— (1993) '*Mori no bunmei to sōgen no bunmei*' (The Civilization of the Forests and the Civilization of the Steppe) in Itō Shuntarō and Yasuda Yoshinori (eds) *Sōgen no shisō – mori no tetsugaku* (Thought of the Steppes and Philosophy of the Forest), Tokyo: Kōdansha.

212 References

Umehara Takeshi and Fukui Kenichi (1996) *Tetsugaku no sōzō: 21seiki no atarashî ningenkan o motomete* (The Creation of Philosophy: In Search of a New View of Humanity of the 21st Century), Tokyo: PHP.

Umehara Takeshi and Hanihara Kazurō (1982) *Ainu wa gen-Nihonjin ka* (Are the Ainu the Original Japanese?), Tokyo: Shōgakukan Sōsensho.

Umehara Takeshi and Inamori Kazuo (1995) *Tetsugaku e no kaiki: Atarashii seishin o motomete* (Return to Philosophy: In Search of a New Spirit), Tokyo, Kyoto: PHP Research Centre.

Wakabayashi, Bob Tadashi (1986) *Anti-Foreignism and Western Learning in Early Modern Japan*, Cambridge, MA and London: Harvard University Press.

Wang Y.C. (1938) 'The Development of Modern Social Science in China', *Pacific Affairs*, 5: 345–62.

Wang Zhiyyue (1993) *Ru-Dao sixiang wenhua de heliu: cong "Yi Jing" dao "Yi Zhuan"* (The Cultural Confluence of Confucian and Taoist Ideas: From *Yi Jing* to *Yi Zhuan*), *CASS Yanjiushengyuan Xuebao*, 3: 63–7.

Watsuji Tetsurō (1961) *Climate and Culture. A philosophical study* (trans. by Geoffrey Bownas, Ministry of Education), Japan: The Hokuseido Press.

Watsuji Tetsurō (1996) *Watsuji Tetsurō's Rinrigaku. Ethics in Japan* (trans. Yamamoto Seisaku and Robert E. Carter), New York: State University of New York Press.

Wei Hongsen (1985) '*Xitonglun de Jiben Sixiang, Fazhan, Qushi Jiqi Yiyi*' (Systems Theory: Basic Ideas, Development Directions and Its Meaning), Wang Yingluo and Huang Linchu (eds) *Xitong Sixiang Yu Wo Guo Keji Fazhan Zhanlue Yanjiu* (Systems Thinking and Research on My Country's S&T Development Strategy), Xian: Xian Jiaotong Daxue Chubanshe, pp. 189–201.

Weng Dujian (ed.) (1991) *Zhongguo minzu shi gangyao* (An Outline of Chinese Ethnic History), Beijing: Zhongguo Shehui Kexue Chubanshe.

Williams, David (1996) *Japan and The Enemies of Open Political Science*, London and New York: Routledge.

Wolferen, Karel van (1989) *The Enigma of Japanese Power: People and Politics in a Stateless Nation*, London: Macmillan.

Wong Siu-lun (1979) *Sociology and Socialism in Contemporary China*, London, Boston, Henley: Routledge & Kegan Paul.

Wu Guoguang (1995) 'Documentary Politics: Hypotheses, Process, and Case Studies', in Carol Lee Hamrin and Zhao Suisheng (eds) *Decision-making in Deng's China*, New York: M.E. Sharpe, pp. 23–38.

Yamamoto Tsunetomo (2000) *Hagakure: The Book of the Samurai*, trans. William Scott Wilson, Tokyo, New York, London: Kodansha International.

Yang Xiulu (1990) '*Long yu long wenhua xinshuo*' (The Dragon and a New Thesis on Dragon Culture), *Zhongguo Renmin Daxue Xuebao*, 2: 81–90.

Yasuda Yoshinori (1989) 'Passivity and Activity of Japanese Studies', *Nichibunken Newsletter*, No. 3, July.

—— (1993) *Tōyō to seiyō no fūdo no kigen* (The Origin of the *Fūdo* of East and West), in Itō Shuntarō and Yasuda Yoshinori (eds) *Sōgen no shisō – mori no tetsugaku* (Thought of the Steppe and Philosophy of the Forest), Tokyo: Kōdansha, pp. 140–84.

Yasuda Yoshinori (1995) 'The Yangtze River Valley Civilization Research Project', *Nichibunken Newsletter*, No. 22, November 1995.

Ye Qiaojian (1995) '*Renshi moshi de zuo – you liangfenfa jiqi waitui zhong de ruogan*

References 213

wuqu' (The Division of Labour between Left and Right Brain and Some Misunderstandings in the Inferences from it), *Zhexue Yanjiu*, 8: 71–6, 12.

Yong Deng (1998) 'The Chinese Conception of National Interests in International Relations', *China Quarterly*, Spring: 308–29.

Yōrō Takeshi (1989) *Yuinōron* (Brain-ism), Tokyo: Aoitosha.

—— (1997) *'Bunkaron to wa nanika'* (What is cultural theory), in Kawai Hayao and Yōrō Takeshi (eds) *Kawai Hayao, Yōrō Takeshi: taiken to shite no ibunka* (Kawai Hayao and Yōrō Takeshi: Alien Culture As Experience), Gendai Nihon Bunkaron No. 7, Tokyo: Iwanami Shoten, pp. 1–12.

—— and Morioka Masahiro (1995) *Seimei kagaku mirai* (The Future of the Science of Vitalism), Tokushima Shi: Just System.

Yoshida Kazuo (1998) *'Kyoto daigaku keizaigaku kenkyūka, horon kōzō no nihongata shakai shisutemum'*, in Hamaguchi Eshun (ed.) *Nihon shakai to wa nani ka: 'fukuzatsukei' no shiten kara*, Tokyo: NHK books.

Yoshino Kosaku (1995) *Cultural Nationalism in Contemporary Japan: A Sociological Enquiry*, London and New York: Routledge.

Yu Weizhao and Zhang Aibing (1992) *'Kaoguxue xin lijie lungang'* (A Theoretical Outline of Archaeology), *Zhongguo Shehui Kexue*, 6: 147–66.

Zhang Qicheng (1996) *'Yixue xiangshu siwei yu Zhonghua wenhua zouxiang'* (The Thinking Mode of the Divinatory Diagram and Number in the Study of *Zhou Yi* and the Orientation of the Chinese Culture), *Zhexue Yanjiu*, 3: 65–73.

Zhao Yuntian (1993) *Zhongguo bianjiang minzu guanli jigou yangeshi* (The Evolution of Management Organs of Chinese Borderland Nationalities), Beijing: Zhongguo Shehui Kexue Chubanshe.

Index

Note: References in **bold** are to the Glossary.

abduction 196 n5
absentees 99–100
aidagara (relationship) 53, 82, 84, 86, 87, **173**, 188–9 n14
Ainu 11, 54, 55–6, **173**, 178 n4, 181–3 nn28–33, 183 n1
Al-Faruqi 7
amae (coaxing) 130, 131, **173**
Amaterasu 183–4 n1
America *see* Ōbei; Oumei
ancestor worship 24, 25
Anderson, Benedict 20
animals 21, 27, 48, 178 n7
Aoki Tamotsu 187 n6
autopoiesis 85–9

Berque, Augustin 179 n15
Blacker, Carmen 41, 42
brain: brainism (*yuinoron*) 43–7, **174**; Japanese *vs.* European 42–3; left–right brains 63–4; neural network 89–90
Buddhism 61–2, 113, 120, 139, 199 n2
bushi (samurai) 103, 130, **173**
bushidō 103, 192 nn12–13

Capra, Fritjof 63, 67
CASS *see* Chinese Academy of Social Sciences
change 105, 132, 197 nn11–12, 200 n8
Chen Liankai 32, 33, 127
China: Cultural Revolution 98, 136, 150, 190 n1, 199 n5, 199–200 n8; culture 66, 136–7; Four Modernizations 147, 200 n10; humanism and democracy 190–1 n3; international relations 132, 145, 197

n10; mass-line 102–3, 191–2 n10; matriarchal tradition 66; national psychology 147; nation-framing 4, 10, 160–2; as nation-state 28, 176 n7; *neidanxue* 67, **173**, 185 n10; Oumei (Europe and America) 147, **174**, 200 n11; overseas Chinese 135; patriarchal tradition 66; philosophy 25, 139–40, 143, 198 nn15–16; Qinghai 148, 210 n16; 'rule by document' 197–8 n13; social change 132, 197 nn11–12; social relations 189 n16; Tibet 148–51, 201 n16, 201 n18, 201 n21; unity of opposites 147, 199–200 n8; and the West 6–7; *see also* Chinese Academy of Social Sciences; Chinese dragon; Chinese nationalism; nation-framing as academic strategy (China)
Chinese Academy of Social Sciences 127, 142, 144, 148, 156, 161, 201 n14, 201 n20
Chinese dragon: and childbirth 24; as clan ancestor 24–5; Confucianism 25, 27; as embryo 23–4, 27; fire 26; and imperial system 25; interpretations 20–1; and national unification 26–7; as oceanic giant python 22–3, 27; and phoenix 25; totem dragon 21–2, 23–4, 27, 175 n3
Chinese nationalism: coherent force (*ningjuli*) 11, 34–7, **174**; concepts 31–3, 127, 176 nn3–4; consanguinity 34–5; *guojia* (country) **173**, 176 n4, 201 n21; *Hanzu* 32,

Index 215

173; Huaxia tribes 32, 34, 173, 177 n10; *minzu* (people) 32, **173**, 176 nn3–4; origins 32–5; *renmin* (people) 32, **174**; research policies 127; 'struggle' 35, 177 n12, 200 n8; *Zhongguo* 32, 149, **174**; *Zhonghua* 31, 32–3, 35, **174**; *Zhonghua Minguo* 32; *Zhonghua Minzu* 31–4, 147, 149, 150, **174**, 176 n4, 184 n8, 201 n19

chosen people 41–3

Christianity 50–1

Chūgoku **173**

civil society 5

civilization 50–1, 52–3, 80–2, 84, 85, 105, 187 n7, 187 n9

climate 49–50, 51, 53, 179–80 n15

Confucianism 25–6, 27, 66, 139, 151, 175–6 n5, 191 n9, 202 n25

'Crazy English' 68

cultural categorization 11–13, 14*t*, 59–60, 72–4, 157–8; betrayal and linguistic supremacy 68–71; politics and 60; Taoist universality 65–8; universality of primitive forest culture 60–3; yin–yang (East and West) 63–5, 184 n5, 198–9 n2

cultural nationalism 75–7

culture 84, 102, 187–8 n7, 188 n9; Chinese 66, 136–7; Japanese 46–7, 80–2, 108–9, 112, 113

Dale, Peter N. 8, 110

Darwin, Charles 44

democracy 190–1 n3

Deng Xiaoping 134, 199 n5

Dikötter, Frank 176 nn2–3

Douglas, Mary 19–20

Du Ruofu 35, 177 n13

Dumont, Louis 192n15

economy 78, 113, 197 n8

Eikaiwa **173**

Europe *see* Ōbei; Oumei

evolution: agriculture 50, 53; 'becoming' 45; China 33–4, 180 n16; Darwinism 44; Garden of Eden hypothesis 176–7 n8; Japanese theory 44–5, 178–9 n7; Stone Age culture 49–50; time 105, 193 n19

Fabian, Johannes 104, 193 n18

fairy tales 118, 195 n10

Falungong 100, 191 n8

family symbolism 20, 25, 99–100, 137, 149–50, 191 n4

Fan Hao 135

Fang Keli 139, 191 n9, 198 n16

Fang Lizhi 199 n7

Freud, Sigmund 118, 195 n9, 195 n11

fūdo (climate) 49–50, 53–4, **173**, 179–80 n15, 181 n27

Fukui Kenichi 53, 181 n26

Fukuyama, Francis 9, 84

furusato **173**

furusato-zukuri 128–9, **173**, 196 n5

Gao Xingjian 191 n7

Gellner, Ernest 175 n2

Gilgamesh 52, 181 n23

giri (obligation) 130, 131, **173**

globalist categorization 13–14, 14*t*, 159; *aidagara* 53, 82, 84, 86, 87, **173**, 188–9 n14; autopoiesis 85–9; borderless values 77–80; *kanjinshugi* 82–3, 84, 86, 87, 88, **173**; key persons and national systems strategies 85–9; nationalism 75–7; rigid analogous and adaptive parallel processors 89–90; scientism and unit of the nation 90–4; scientist arguments and Japanese uniqueness 80–2; social systems 80, 82–6, 89–93, 188 nn9–13, 189–90 n16–22

globalization 46, 79, 187 n4, 187 n6

Golden Age 41, 177 n1

Gorbachev, Mikhail 28

Gramsci, Antonio 5

grouping 106–7; absence of stratification 104; absentees 99–100; in academic debate 97–8; classifications 3–4, 10, 14, 14*t*, 31, 97; family metaphors 20, 25, 99–100, 137, 149–50, 191 n4; framing differences 101, 101*t*; hierarchy 102–4, 192 nn15–16; horizontal polarization 101–2; temporal project of Us and Them/the Other 104–6; transnational group formation 109; trends 9–10; Us and the Other 5–6, 7–9, 43–7, 99, 100, 101–2, 104–6, 191 n5; *see also* cultural categorization; globalist categorization; natural classification

Gunji Takao 167

guojia (country) **173**, 176 n4, 201 n21

guoxue re **173**

216 *Index*

Habermas, Jürgen 86
Haga Toru 166, 167, 169
haji (shame) 130, 131, **173**
Hall, Ivan 8
Hamaguchi Eshun 75, 80–7, 88, 91,
    92, 122, 125, 165, 166, 169, 187–8
    nn6–8, 188–9 nn11–14, 189 n16,
    189–90 n22, 190 n25, 194 n3, 196
    n19
Hanaoka Seishū 62, 184 n4
Hanihara Kazurō 54–6, 57, 114, 165,
    178 n4
Hanzu 32, **173**
Hayakawa Monta 166, 171, 172
Hayami Akira 166
He Lin 139
He Xingliang 21–2, 27
Heidegger, Martin 52, 179 n15
Herzfield, Michael 19
hierarchy 102–4, 192 nn15–16
himitsu (secrecy) 130, 131, **173**
Hirata Atsutane 41, 177 n2
Hisamatsu Senichi 178 n3
holarchy 188 n11
holography 90, 184 n6, 190 n29
holon 82, 188 n11
horizontal polarization 101–2
Hu Fuchen 24–6, 27, 65–8, 72–3,
    136–7
Hu Qiaomu 191 n3
Hu Sheng 148
Hu Yaobang 29
Huaxia tribes 32, 34, **173**, 177 n10
humanism 190–1 n3
Huntington, Samuel P. 9

Īda Tsuneo 75, 77–8, 166, 168, 170,
    194 n3
identity creation 97–8
Imanishi Kinji 44–5, 48, 110, 111, 112,
    178–9 n7
Inami Ritsuko 123, 168, 169
Inamori Kazuo 114
Inoue Tetsujirō 192 n12
Institute for Peace, Happiness and
    Prosperity (PHP) 78, 186–7 n1
international relations 112–13, 123,
    132, 143, 145, 197 n10, 198 n1
International Research Centre for
    Japanese Studies *see* Nichibunken
internationalization 81, 187 n6
Ishida Hideomi 168
Ishii Shirō 168, 169
Itō Shuntarō 81, 166, 188 n9, 194 n4

Iwasaki Chikatsugu 112

Japan: *aidagara* (relationship) 53, 82,
    84, 86, 87, **173**, 188–9 n14; Ainu
    11, 54, 55–6, **173**, 178 n4,
    181–3 nn28–33, 183 n1; *amae*
    (coaxing) 130, 131, **173**; body 45–6,
    47; brain–culture–language 42–3,
    49; *bushi* 103, 130, **173**; *bushidō*
    103, 192 nn12–13; Chinese Kanji
    186 n22; chosen people 41–3;
    culture 46–7, 80–2, 108–9, 112,
    113; economy 78, 113, 197 n8;
    English language teaching 68, 69,
    70, 186 n22; evolution theory 44–5,
    178–9 n7; foreign threats 7; form
    (*kata*) 46–7; *fūdo* (climate) 49–50,
    53–4, **173**, 179–80 n15, 181 n27;
    furusato-zukuri 128–9, **173**, 196 n5;
    giri (obligation) 130, 131, **173**;
    government 78–9; *haji* (shame) 130,
    131, **173**; *himitsu* (secrecy) 130,
    131, **173**; inferiority complex 70–1,
    186 n22; Jōdo Shinshū (Pure Land
    sect) 184 n1; Jōmon 50, 51, 54, 55,
    56, 61, **173**, 183 n1, 193 n20, 194
    n7; *kanjin* (relatum) 91, 108, 122,
    173; *kanjinshugi* 82–3, 84, 86, 87,
    88, **173**; Katakana English 186 n22;
    key persons and national systems
    strategies 85–9; Kinki people 55–6,
    183 n32; *Kokutai no hongi* 42, 45,
    177–8 n3; Kyoto school 110–11;
    local communities 128–9; as middle-
    mass society 104, 193 n17; mirror
    image 183 n1; monkeys 27, 48, 178
    n7; *mushi* (selflessness) 130–1, **173**;
    nasake (mercy) 130–1, **173**; national
    superiority 78; nation-framing 4, 10,
    160–2; *nihonbunka-ron* 108–9, 122,
    124, **174**; *nihonjin-ron* 8, 54, 76,
    80–2, 129–30, **174**; Ōbei (Europe
    and America) 48, **174**, 179 n11,
    196–7 n6; population history 54–5,
    183 n31; rebirth 61, 183–4 n1;
    Ryukyuan people 56, 183 n31;
    self-victimizing discourse 8; *shōgi*
    123–4, **174**; social systems 82–3, 84,
    89–91, 92–3, 103, 189 n16; *tamashi*
    (logic of the soul) 119, **174**, 195
    n13; Wajin 55, **174**, 183 n31;
    wakon yōsai 46, 179 n10; and the
    West 6, 7; and World War II 186
    n23; Yayoi 54, 55, **174**; *yuinōron*

(brainism) 43–7, **174**; *see also*
Nichibunken
Japanese Systems 86–7, 122, 190 n25
Jia Lanpo 34
Jiang Qian 64
Jiang Zemin 148, 152, 199 n4, 200 n13
Jin Binggao 32
Jōmon 50, 51, 54, 55, 56, 61, **173**,
   183 n1, 193 n20, 194 n7
Jung, Carl 118, 119, 195 nn11–12

kangaku **173**
kanjin (relatum) 91, 108, 122, **173**
kanjinshugi 82–3, 84, 86, 87, 88, **173**
Kasaya Kazuhiko 103, 123, 168, 169,
   171, 192 n11
Kawai Hayao 48, 98, 108, 110, 114,
   115, 116–20, 166, 194 n6, 194–5
   nn8–10, 195 n12, 195 n14, 196 n15
Kawai Masao 47–9, 57, 179 nn12–13
Kawakita Jirō 196 n5
Keene, Donald 165
Kenichi Ohmae 75
Kimura Hiroshi 123, 166, 170, 171
Kinki people 55–6, 183 n32
Kishida Shū 70, 186 n22
Knodt, Eva M. 87, 190 n24
Koestler, Arthur 82, 89, 188 n11
Kokutai no hongi 42, 45, 177–8 n3
Kōsaka Masaaki 111
Kōyama Iwao 111
Kuhn, Alfred 187 n7, 188 n12
Kumon Shumpei 81, 188 n9
Kunō Akira 165
Kuriyama Shigehisa 171
Kurose Hitomi 124
Kuwahara Takeo 110, 111
Kyoto Shinbun 115, 116, 120

language: Ainu 183 n33; Chinese
   characters 64, 186 n22; 'Crazy
   English' 68; English in Japan 68, 69,
   70, 186 n22; Japanese 42–3, 49;
   Katakana English 186 n22; linguistic
   supremacy 68–71; research 133; as
   unification 20
Lao Zi 66, 67, 151, 185 n11
Li Hongzhi 100, 191 n8
Li Shangkai 147–8, 152
Li Shaolian 11, 34–5, 127
Li Shenzhi 198–9 n2
Li Shuyi 200 n12
Li Yang 68, 73
Li Zehou 201 n14
Liang Qichao 32

Lin Ganquan 134
Linhart, Sepp 167
Liu Binyan 190 n2
Liu Changlin 12, 63
lixue (neo-Confucianism) 25–6,
   175–6 n5
Lu Xiaofei 201 n21
Luhmann, Niklas 83–4, 85, 87–9, 189
   n18, 189 n21, 190 n23, 190 n26

Mabuchi Kamo 41, 177 n2
Mao Zedong 151, 191–2 n10
Maruyama Masao 45
Marxism 25–6, 66, 67, 151, 198 n16
Masamura Toshiyuki 129–31
Masuda Foundation 81, 86–7, 188 n8
Matsushita Konosuke 78, 186 n1,
   187 n3
May Fourth 185 n9
Miki Takeo 192–3 n17
minzu (people) 32, **173**, 176 nn3–4
Mishima Yukio 46, 192n12
Mitsuta Kazunobu 123–4, 171, 172
Mitterand, François 112–13
Morris-Suzuki, Tessa 178 n3
Motoori Norinaga 41, 177 n2
Mu Hongli 33–4
multiculturality 102, 137, 149, 150,
   199 n2
Murai Yasuhiko 165, 167
Murakami Yasusuke 104, 114, 165,
   192–3 n17
mushi (selflessness) 130–1, **173**
mutual phase dynamics 81

Nakamura Yūjirō 119
Nakane Chie 192n16
Nakanishi Susumu 165, 166
Nakanishi Terumasa 185–6 n21
Nakariya Kaiten 192 n12
Nakasone Yasuhiro 29, 108, 110,
   111–15
nasake (mercy) 130–1, **173**
'nation' 32, 176 n4, 200 n9
national identity 9–10, 18–19, 97–8,
   135
national symbols 17; animals 21, 27;
   dissidents and 29; Japanese macaque
   27; nationhood 17–18; phoenix 20,
   25; politics of national identity
   marking 18–19; scale of symbolic
   power 19–20; as triggers of
   associated sentiments 27–8; *see also*
   Chinese dragon

218 *Index*

nationalism 175 n2; cultural
nationalism 75–7; group
classifications 31; political
nationalism 76–7; and racism 76, 77
nation-framing 3, 162–4; bias 4–5;
China and Japan 4, 10, 160–2;
institutionalized 108–10, 163;
Orientalist categories 5–7; as
political strategy 140–1; spatial and
temporal order 158–60; 'Them' and
'the Other' 7–9; universal and
particular 156–8
nation-framing as academic strategy
(China) 142, 151–2; appraising
national policies 144–6, 199 n5;
failure of imagination 148–50;
national prescription and
conservatism 147–8; political
predictability 150–1; social science
and state building 142–4; *see also*
political strategies
nation-states 17–18; dissidents 28–9;
legitimacy 28–9; 'significant others'
28; strategic planning 126; as unit of
research 77, 109–10, 126–7, 143–4
natural classification 11, 14*t*, 41, 56–8,
157, 159; animism renaissance 50,
51–2; chosen peoples 41–3;
civilization of deforestation 50–1,
52–3; climate 49–50, 51, 53,
179–80 n15; codified brains 42–3;
forest civilization 51; instinctive
distancing 47–9; natural group
markers 30–1; reappropriation of
the past 54–6; Us cultural brains and
Them civilized brains 43–7; Western
Cartesian thought 52–4
neidanxue 67, **173**, 185 n10
neo-Confucianism 25–6, 175–6 n5
neural network model 89–90
Nichibunken 156, 161, **173–4**, 193–4
n3; archetypal analogies and
national unconscious 116–20; basic
research 121–2, 171–2; criticisms of
111; foundation 110, 111–15;
general research meetings 121,
169–70; joint research 121, 165–8;
knowledge production: structural
aspects 120–2; reputation 114,
115–16, 120, 124; research aim
110–11, 121; symbolic knowledge:
shōgi 122–4; unit of the nation
124–5
nihonbunka-ron 108–9, 122, 124, **174**

nihonjin-ron 8, 54, 76, 80–2, 129–30,
174
ningjuli (coherent force) 11, 34–7, **174**
Nishida Kitarō 53, 110, 111, 112, 181
n24
Nishitani Keiji 111
Nitobe Inazō 192 n12

Ōbei (Europe and America) 48, **174**,
179 n11, 196–7 n6
Ochiai Emiko 171
Oe Kenzaburo 116
Ohmae Kenichi 13, 78–80, 187 nn2–3
Omoto Kei'ichi 55, 56, 57, 123–4, 167,
169, 172, 182–3 n31
Orientalism 5–8
'Other' *see* Us and Them/the Other
Oumei (Europe and America) 147, **174**,
200 n11

Panchen Lama 150, 202 n23
Parsons, Talcott 88, 189 n21
People's Daily 197–8 n13
phase conversion 81
phoenix 20, 25
PHP *see* Institute for Peace, Happiness
and Prosperity
political nationalism 76–7
political society 5
political strategies 126–7; habitual
nation-framing 140–1; nation and
interest groups 133–4, 140, 154–5;
'national organism' and 'system'
control 134–40, 155–6; neglect of
local and specific 127–31, 140,
153–4; subordination of universal to
national 131–3, 140, 154; *see also*
nation-framing; nation-framing as
academic strategy (China)
PRC *see* China
psychological metaphors 138, 200 n12
Pyle, Kenneth B. 78

qi 67, 185 n12
Qian Xuesen 67, 185 n14

racism and racist thinking 4–5, 30–1,
42, 76, 77, 176 n2, 178 n4, 181–2
nn28–30, 199 n2
Reagan, Ronald 113
reincarnation 61, 183–4 n1
Ren Jiyu 136–8, 198 n15
renmin (people) 32, **174**
'reversed Orientalism' 7, 8

Index   219

rice civilization 50, 51, 53, 180 n16
Robertson, Jennifer 128
Rose, Caroline 76
Ryukyuan people 56, 183 n31
Ryūtarō Hashimoto 182 n29

Said, Edward 5–6
Sakamoto Kenzo 189 n20
Sapir–Whorf hypothesis 70, 185 n20
Sautman, Barry 21
science and technology 26, 53, 68, 92, 119, 120, 199 n7
scientific metaphors 90–4, 138, 147, 157
Seiyō **174**
Sekotac/Masuda Foundation 81, 86–7, 188 n8
self 135; *see also mushi* (selflessness)
self-sacrifice 61–2
Senda Minoru 168, 170, 171
Shina **174**
Shinran 184 n1
Shinto 51, 180 n19, 184 n1
Shirahata Yozaburo 171
shōgi (Japanese chess) 123–4, **174**
Sinn (meaning) 84, 85–6, 189 n18
Smith, Anthony D. 175 n2
social sciences 110, 143, 146, 151
social systems 80, 82–6, 89–93, 103, 188 nn9–13, 189–90 n16–22
Song Yue 150
Sonoda Hidehirō 167, 169, 196 n19
Stalin, Joseph 147, 200 n9
story 119–20, 196 n15
Strijbos, Sytse 86
Su Kaihua 23, 27
Sugimoto Hidetarō 167
Sun Yat-sen 32
Suzuki Ryōji 189 n19
Suzuki Sadami 167, 170, 172
symbolism: family 20, 25, 99–100, 137, 149–50, 191 n4; psychological 138, 200 n12; scientific 90–4, 138, 147, 157; *see also* brain; national symbols

Tagaki Takeshi 192 n12
tamashi (logic of the soul) 119, **174**, 195 n13
Tanabe Hajime 111, 112, 178 n7
Taoism 65–8, 139, 202 n25
Thatcher, Margaret 112–13
'They' *see* Us and Them/the Other
Tibet 148–51, 201 n16, 201 n18, 201 n21

time 44, 104–6, 159–60, 179–80 n15, 180 n18, 193 n19
totemism 21, 23–4
Tōyō **174**
Tōyōshi **174**
trade 79, 80–1, 135–6, 187 n4, 187 n6
trust 83–4, 85, 88, 190 n23
Tsetan Norbu 201 n16
Tsuda Yukio 68–71, 72, 73, 168, 169, 185 n15
Tsuji Nobuo 166
Tsunoda Tadanobu 42–3, 48, 49, 57

Uchii Shōzō 115
Uchimura Kanzō 192 n12
Ueyama Shumpei 111, 114
Umehara Takeshi 11, 52–4, 55–6, 57, 61–3, 72, 98, 108, 110, 111–16, 120–1, 165, 167, 180–1 n21, 184 n1, 193 n20, 194 n7
Umesao Tadao 80, 81, 111, 188 n9
unconscious 116–17, 118–19, 120, 195 n9–11, 200 n12
unity of opposites 147, 199–200 n8
Us and Them/the Other 5–6, 7–9, 43–7, 99, 100, 101–2, 104–6, 191 n5

Van Praag, Professor 201 n21
Van Wolferen, Karel 8

Wajin 55, **174**, 183 n31
Wang Cunzhen 184 n6
Wang Furen 149, 201 n21
Watsuji Tetsurō 50, 53, 112, 179–80 n15
'We' *see* Us and Them/the Other
Wen Yiduo 22, 23, 24
Weng Dujian 149, 201 n20
Williams, David 8–9
World Bank 148, 210 n16
Wu Guoguang 197–8 n13
Wu Jiaxiang 190 n2

Xiao Chunjie 35, 177 n13
Xixue re **174**

Yamada Keiji 166, 167, 170, 172
Yamaguchi Masao 124
Yamamoto Tsunetomo 192 n12
Yamaori Tetsuo 114, 165, 167, 170
Yan Chunbao 184 n6
Yan Chunyou 184 n6
Yang Xiulu 22–3, 27
Yangtze civilization 180 n16

220 *Index*

Yao Zhaolin 149–50
Yasuda Yoshinori 49–52, 57, 167, 169,
  179 n14, 180 n16
Yayoi 54, 55, **174**
Ye Qiaojian 63–5, 72
Yi Jing 151, 202 n25
Yi Zhuan 202 n25
yin and yang 63–5, 67
Yomiuri Shinbun 116
Yong Deng 197 n10
Yōrō Takeshi 43–7, 57, 178 n6
Yoshida Kazuo 75, 89–90
Yoshino Kosaku 76
yuinōron (brainism) 43–7, **174**

Yukawa Hideki 67, 114, 194 n4

Zhang Qicheng 184 n6
Zhang Yiqing 184 n6
Zhao Ziyang 197 n13
Zhongguo (China) 32, 149, **174**
Zhonghua (China) 31, 32–3, 35, **174**
Zhonghua Minguo 32
Zhonghua Minzu (Chinese people)
  31–4, 147, 149, 150, **174**, 176 n4,
  184 n8, 201 n19
Zhongyong **174**
Zhou Yi 184 n6, 202 n25
Zu Qiyuan 149

CPSIA information can be obtained
at www.ICGtesting.com
Printed in the USA
JSHW011319201219
3107JS00002B/21